Robert Musil, Master of the Hovering Life

Robert Musil

Master of the Hovering Life

A Study of the Major Fiction

Frederick G. Peters

1978
Columbia University Press
New York

The Andrew W. Mellon Foundation, through a special grant, has assisted the Press in publishing this volume.

Library of Congress Cataloging in Publication Data

Peters, Frederick G
   Robert Musil, master of the hovering life.

   Bibliography: p.
   Includes index.
   1. Musil, Robert, 1880-1942—Criticism and
interpretation. I. Title.
PT2625.U8Z845   833'.9'12   78-5158
ISBN 0-231-04476-3

Columbia University Press
New York—Guildford, Surrey

For Diana and David

Acknowledgments

THIS BOOK REPRESENTS the culmination of many years of work with the texts of Robert Musil. I would like to thank a number of colleagues for their help and encouragement along the way. My interest in Musil's works was first stimulated in a seminar on the modern German novel given many years ago at Columbia College by Professor Walter H. Sokel, now Commonwealth Professor of German at the University of Virginia. I am also deeply indebted to him for having inspired my earlier work on Franz Kafka and thus supporting my interest in psychoanalytic approaches to literature in general. My thanks also to J. M. S. Pasley, Magdalen College, Oxford University, whose emphasis upon the close reading of texts remained an ever present admonition in my analysis of Musil's work; to Ronald D. Gray, Emmanuel College, Cambridge University, who encouraged me to take a personal and moral stand toward works of literature; and to J. P. Stern, St. John's College, Cambridge University, now Professor of German at University College, the University of London, who in supervising my dissertation on Musil strengthened my interest in the philosophical background of literary study. His enormous knowledge of and enthusiasm for the works of Nietzsche provided invaluable inspiration in the writing of my dissertation. I am also grateful to Barnard College for a research travel grant and to the Mellon Foundation for its grant to Columbia University Press for the purpose of encouraging the publication of books in the humanities by younger scholars. Finally, I would like to express my deepest debt of gratitude to my wife, Dr. Diana Stone Peters, whose constant labors and devotion to this project over the years made this book possible.

Barnard College
Columbia University
June 1977   FREDERICK G. PETERS

Contents

Robert Musil, Master of the Hovering Life

I

The Writer in Search of Utopia

HOW BLEAK, HOW utterly different were Robert Musil's final years from those of Thomas Mann and Hermann Broch, the two other exiled German writers to whose work Musil's fiction has been most frequently compared both in intention and form. For all three writers were the creators of monumental novels intended to capture the intellectual, social, and political complexities of an age tottering on the edge of doom. Musil's *The Man without Qualities*, Mann's *The Magic Mountain*, and Broch's *The Sleepwalkers* were, in fact, consciously designed by their authors as philosophical and intellectual *tours de force* in the form of the novel, since nothing less than an encyclopedic novel seemed adequate to the task of diagnosing and describing the manifold causes that led to the collapse of Germanic culture, a culture as old as it was intellectually and artistically distinguished. Moreover, these novelists did not seek to present only the decline of a great culture existing at the geographical heart of Europe. They also attempted to analyze the widespread degeneration of the values that had once formed the foundation of Western man's concept of civilization in general.

As a result of World War I, Austro-German culture underwent a profound transformation. The subsequent age of irrationality was widely welcomed as a means of rejuvenating a moribund civilization. But it was precisely in opposition to this anti-intellectual tendency in German life and letters that Musil, Mann, and Broch directed much of their artistic energies. Their novels are informed by a sense of urgency and passionate concern made all the more poignant by the fact that the very culture these writers were in the process of describing finally cast them out in the 1930s. But whereas Mann's and Broch's final years spent in the United States were marked with recognition and artistic fulfillment, Musil's fate was one of ever-increasing weariness, poverty, and resentment.

A Life of Unfulfilled Hopes

Shortly before the entrance of Hitler's armies into Vienna in 1938, Musil and his Jewish wife left Austria forever and took up residence first in Zurich and then in Geneva. The financial support that he had been receiving from the Musil Society of Vienna was thereby cut off. Instead of devoting himself to his fiction, Musil now found himself compelled to spend enormous amounts of time writing appeals for money, thanking those people who had responded, and searching for yet further financial resources. The money he received was never sufficient to provide any sense of security, and the small sums that did arrive came only haphazardly and often only at the last desperate moment. Musil not only felt himself reduced to playing the role of beggar but was for a time also burdened by the fear that his visa to remain in Switzerland might not be renewed. In addition, he had lost his publisher in Germany, the Jewish firm of Rowohlt, and thus all future royalties from his works. His books were banned in Germany and Austria, and he was unable to gain the interest of any Swiss publisher. Musil's endless financial worries, the emotional upheaval caused by his flight from Vienna, and deteriorating health severely hampered work on his magnum opus, *The Man without Qualities*.

Throughout the years of his Swiss exile (1938-1942), Musil felt abandoned and forgotten. His unhappy state in Switzerland seemed only to mock his earlier high hopes. In 1930 in Vienna, at the age of fifty, he had been able to look forward to the publication of the first volume of *The Man without Qualities*. When the book did appear it was warmly received by the critics. International recognition and even greater artistic success seemed inevitable. The approach of Musil's sixtieth birthday, ten years later in exile in 1940, served only to make all the more poignant the total absence of public response. By now it had also become clear to Musil that the completion of the novel was as yet only a distant prospect. A small group of Musil's friends in Switzerland decided to bolster his spirits by organizing a large public reading at which he was to present selections from *The Man without Qualities*. They hoped that this occasion would facilitate Musil's discovery by the Swiss

public. But only fifteen people attended the reading, and none of these were men of influence in the cultural life of the country. When Musil died in 1942, only eight people attended his funeral. His death went almost unnoticed by the press.

Hermann Broch once wrote of himself and Musil that neither of them had a real biography; they merely lived and wrote and that was all. Their inner biographies, however, reveal the existence of a similar battle, one that they both fought for many years and resolved only comparatively late in life. It was only against the greatest internal resistance that Broch and Musil were able to liberate themselves from the traditional professional pursuits of their respective parents in order to become nothing but writers. Broch left his family's textile mills in 1928 and Musil his post (albeit involuntarily) at the War Office in 1922. Both Broch and Musil had to reach the age of 42, then, before they were finally able to commit themselves irrevocably to the precarious prospect of being professional writers. For Musil, it had been a particularly long and difficult road from the point of his birth into a prosperous Austrian family to that of an independent artist without means engaged in writing one of the longest novels in literary history.

Robert Musil was born on November 6, 1880, in Klagenfurt, Austria, into a family whose members were noted for their professional successes in the army, the civil service, and various branches of technology. His father Alfred, who was an engineer at a machine factory when Robert was born, eventually came to occupy the Chair of Mechanical Engineering at the Technical University of Brünn. He was ennobled in the final year of his retirement. The Musils gave the appearance of being a well-established upper-middle-class family with a solid background of public and academic service. But behind the bourgeois façade there existed a situation with which young Robert could not deal and which had a profoundly adverse effect upon his psychological development. If Musil's father seemed too rationalistic and pedantic in spirit, too withdrawn and emotionally inhibited, his mother Hermine possessed an extravagantly temperamental nature and was given to violent emotional outbursts and sudden hysterical collapses. Alfred Musil had always been unable to comprehend and cope with his wife's

personality. Apparently, he simply retreated. Seven years after their marriage, she became deeply attached to a teacher, Heinrich Reiter, who moved in with the Musils the year Robert was born and became a permanent member of the family for the next forty years.

It was in the midst of this strange relationship that Robert grew up as an only child. (His one sister had died ten months before he was born.)   Both his parents were aloof and cool toward him and each lived an independent life.   There must have existed a great deal of confusion in Robert's mind concerning the role of each of the two men toward Hermine, which in turn must have produced corresponding confusion in his own relationship to his mother. Who was the husband? Who the father? (When Hermine died, it was Heinrich Reiter and not her husband who remained at her deathbed.) If Alfred and Hermine were difficult parents, Musil was no doubt a difficult child. He spent much of his young life in silent brooding, staring out of the window, being extremely stubborn and withdrawn. In the third grade he had to be sent home for half a year in order to recuperate from a nervous breakdown. Finally, as the extraneous and disturbing element in an apparently well-functioning domestic triangle, Robert was sent away from home as soon as it became socially feasible.

Musil's father decided that young Robert was to pursue a career in the army. In 1892, at the age of twelve, Musil was enrolled in his first military academy at Eisenstadt, where he remained for two years. In 1894 he attended the senior military academy at Mährisch-Weisskirchen in Moravia (now Czechoslovakia). The latter institution was the same one at which several years earlier the young Rainer Maria Rilke had suffered torments of humiliation at the hands of the other students. For the highly sensitive Rilke, this episode marked the beginning (as he once stated) of his own radical introversion, which subsequently led to recurring periods of acute and prolonged depression. The experience at the military academy remained a bitter memory that Rilke was simply never able to eradicate, for although Rilke had always intended to exorcise the horrors of these years by eventually writing about them, he was never able to do so. Musil, however, drew

upon the experience of these three years at Weisskirchen for the creation of the major characters and setting of his first novel, *Young Törless*. In spite of his nervous sensibility, Musil managed to remain at the top of his class scholastically. And what was even more important at such a paramilitary institution, he was able to hold his own in fist fights with his fellow students. In 1897, he proceeded to the Technical Military Academy of Vienna, but shortly after arriving he decided to give up the idea of becoming an army officer in order to study civil engineering.

If Musil at the age of seventeen rejected an army career, his new plan brought him not only directly into his father's profession but into his father's university as well. Musil attended the Technical University of Brünn from 1898 to 1901 and took his diploma in engineering at the conclusion of his studies. After serving the one year of his obligatory military service, he spent twelve months at a post in the engineering laboratories of the Technical College in Stuttgart. It was out of a sense of extreme boredom, Musil admitted, that he began to work on his first novel, *Young Törless*, while living in Stuttgart. He also published several papers on engineering subjects and patented an improved design for the chromatometer. In this first decade of the twentieth century, the professional lives of Musil and Broch were amazingly parallel. Broch, also still pursuing his father's business interests, qualified in 1906 as a textile engineer and obtained patents for milling processes. As Musil decided in 1903 (at age 23) to give up his father's career of engineering in order to study philosophy, psychology, and mathematics at the University of Berlin, so Broch, the textile engineer, enrolled at the University of Vienna in 1910 in order to study these same subjects.

Musil remained for five years at the University of Berlin and in 1908 submitted his dissertation on the epistemology of the physicist and philosopher Ernst Mach. He also used the freedom of these years to read widely and concentrated particularly on the works of Nietzsche, Emerson, and Dostoyevsky. Musil seriously considered the possibility of becoming an academic philosopher and university professor. But since he had gained a certain amount of recognition as a writer with the publication of *Young Törless* in

1906, he decided against a university career. In 1911 he published two short stories entitled "The Perfecting of a Love" and "The Temptation of Quiet Veronica", which were collected under the title *Unions*. In this year he also married Martha Marcovaldi, who was to serve as his selfless secretary and faithful companion throughout his life, sparing none of her own energies in order to protect Musil in every way possible from expending his energies upon the trivialities of everyday living.

On the occasion of Musil's marriage, his father thought that it was about time for Robert to become financially independent. He secured a job for his son as a librarian at the Technical University of Vienna. Although Musil's working day lasted only from ten in the morning until two in the afternoon, he soon began to loathe this position because it seriously interfered with his writing. In 1913, he decided to return to Berlin in order to become an editor of the *Neue Rundschau*. During the 1914 - 1918 war, he was an officer in the Austrian army, and from 1918 to 1922 he held various semi-military posts, first as a liason press officer with the Austrian Foreign Ministry and then as a scientific advisor to the War Office. In the early 1920s, he wrote two plays: *The Visionaries*, which closed after one performance, and *Vinzenz and the Girl Friend of Important Men*, which ran for one month in Berlin and briefly in Prague and Vienna. In 1922, Musil lost his job at the Ministry due to cutbacks in government expenditures. This traumatic event ended a period of almost twelve years of steady employment that had begun with his marriage in 1911.

After 1922 and until his death in 1942, Musil lived as a free-lance writer of essays, literary criticism, and articles for literary journals and newspapers. His three short stories "Grigia," "The Lady from Portugal," and "Tonka" were published in 1924 under the collective title *Three Women*. Musil, liberated from a regular job, was now free to devote himself totally to his second and last novel, *The Man without Qualities*. But the financial uncertainties of this period, combined with the enormous intellectual and emotional strain that accompanied Musil's work on the first volume of this two-volume novel, made the years from 1924 to 1930 extremely difficult ones. Musil suffered a nervous breakdown in 1929,

the year before Volume One of *The Man without Qualities* was published. After 1932, he was partially supported by the Musil Society of Berlin. After he returned to Austria, he received further support from the Musil Society of Vienna between 1934 and 1938.

It was not without feelings of envy and resentment that Musil regarded the lives of his two rivals, Broch and Mann, especially during but also before the early years of their exile. Musil's comparison of himself with Broch (1886-1951) began as early as 1930, when he read Broch's "Exposé" of *The Sleepwalkers* and remarked that Broch's intentions were in part very similar to his own in *The Man without Qualities.*[1] In fact, the similarities seemed so striking that he found it necessary in 1933 to deny that he had plagiarized Broch's work.[2] In a letter written in 1941 Musil noted, apparently with some surprise, the total absence on Broch's part of a feeling of "sibling rivalry" toward him.[3] The fact that Musil expressed his relationship to Broch in terms of "sibling rivalry" reflects an obvious projection of his own feelings toward his more successful colleague.

In these years, his "competitor"[4] (as Musil termed Broch) had managed to find a sponsor to bring him to America; in addition, he continually received grants from such prestigious American organizations as the Guggenheim, the Rockefeller, and the Bollingen Foundations. (Musil's applications were always rejected.) Broch had also secured the dedicated services of an excellent translator and was befriended by such important and influential people as Thomas Mann, Albert Einstein, and Hannah Arendt. An American publisher was eagerly awaiting Broch's next work. He was given a lectureship at Yale University, and was for a time "Poet in Residence" there. Musil's own obscurity, when compared to the growing recognition of his "rival," must have added to his sense of resentment toward the world at large. It must be added, however, that in reality Broch's situation in his American exile was not much better than Musil's life in Switzerland. Broch may have received occasional grants, but (quite unknown to Musil) they never represented more than temporary relief from chronic poverty.

Musil's relationship to Thomas Mann (1875-1955) was perhaps even more ambivalent. In Musil's opinion, Mann was an

overrated writer, a "literary tycoon," and one of the three archphilistines of the age (together with Galsworthy and Undset).[5] Mann did not have to seek foundation grants; he was in the position of being asked to write recommendations for other writers who were applying. Indeed, in 1938 he wrote such a letter on behalf of Musil, who was applying for a grant from the P.E.N. Club of London. Although Musil's application was rejected as usual, he declared that he was particularly touched by Mann's letter and admitted that in the past he had probably often been unjust to him.[6] But Musil was apparently never able to forgive (what he considered to be) Mann's lukewarm description of *The Man without Qualities* as merely "one of the most significant prose works in recent decades."[7]

Musil's generally negative responses in his letters and diaries to the work of Broch and Mann reveal his all too human side. Nevertheless, his vanity, his vulnerability, and his sense of injured justice seem quite understandable and justified: it was against the background of Broch's and Mann's ever-growing worldwide recognition that he was forced to regard his own continuing obscurity and desperate financial circumstances. The artistic stature of Broch and Mann suffices to explain their fate and critical acclaim during their lifetimes. But the works of any number of mediocre writers, already forgotten today, were widely read and supported by those very institutions and foundations that constantly rejected Musil's appeals for aid. Therefore, even if one takes into account the adverse effect that exile must have had upon Musil's work as well as the fact that his unexpected death left *The Man without Qualities* only half finished, the explanation for Musil's obscurity is to be sought and found in a consideration of Musil as a writer rather than of Musil as the victim of World War II and an untimely death. An attempt to account for the absence of recognition leads directly to a consideration of Musil's fiction. For his destiny as a writer condemned to be unknown during his lifetime rests in the very nature of his work—in his intentions, in his subject matter, and in his style. And it is here also that the reasons can be found for his ever-growing audience today.

Musil had his own explanation for his lack of popularity. Late

in his life he admitted that his attitude and his work tended toward the severe and that, therefore, his readers had only gradually come to him rather than he to them. Concerning his attitude toward the world, as revealed in an undated aphorism, Musil confessed to "autism, negativity, and fanaticism," to being a person who was seldom "warm."[8] His general feeling of contrariness and repugnance toward life he attributed partially to his "untimeliness" and partially to his own idiosyncratic nature. He was not surprised, therefore, that many a reader's first response to his work was one of loathing and repulsion. Musil felt that if readers were slow in coming to his work, it was probably because they sensed his own attitude of complete self-absorption as well as a negativity toward everything generally accepted as worthwhile.

Given such reasoning, it is not surprising that he held Mann's popularity in contempt while feeling proud of the small and elite group of readers of his own work. Musil considered that Mann was too tolerant a human being, too much in tune with his times as a writer ever to be able to achieve true unpopularity. Mann, he believed, liked the world as it was too much and so was liked by the world in return. Musil declared that he possessed precisely the opposite attitude: he liked hardly anything in the world. In his diary, he noted: "Thomas Mann and people like him write for people who are here; I write for people who are not [yet] here."[9] Perhaps it was in recognition of this fact that he entitled his last collection of short stories, published in 1936, *Nachlass zu Lebzeiten* (Posthumous Works in my Lifetime).

The Search for the Balanced Life

The exploratory nature of Musil's quest as a writer is suggested in a question asked by Ulrich, the protagonist of *The Man without Qualities*: "a man who is after the truth sets out to be a man of learning; a man who wants to give free play to his subjectivity sets out, perhaps, to be a writer. But what is a man to do who is after something that lies between?"[10] If one chooses to emphasize the side of "truth," one is led directly to the exact learning of the

scientist and the scholar; if subjectivity is emphasized, one is drawn to dream, literature, and art. Musil was a writer perpetually searching "after something that lies between." As a writer, he wanted to be like one of those men whom he termed "masters of the hovering life," for "their domain lies between religion and knowledge, between example and doctrine, between *amor intellectualis* and poetry, they are saints with and without religion, and sometimes too they are simply men who have gone out on an adventure and lost their way."[11] A constant oscillation between the two worlds of reason and mysticism is the fundamental characteristic of Musil's mind as well as of his art.

The dialectical structure of Musil's work facilitates, first, the fullest possible exploration of each of the two extremes of reason and mysticism, extremes into which the mind of man seems forever forced when attempting to comprehend the essence of life. His fiction is, however, ultimately directed toward a synthesis of these opposites, for such a synthesis, Musil assumed, would reveal the presence of a unity existing beneath man's dialectically perceiving mind. It was Musil's firm belief that life in the twentieth century would become increasingly decadent, sterile, and consequently unbearable until the ultimate task of synthesis had been achieved. And he set himself nothing less than the accomplishment of this task through his fiction.

The magnitude of Musil's task is thus apparent. He intended his fiction not only to mirror the spiritual, emotional, and intellectual problems confronting man in the twentieth century. He wanted simultaneously to reveal the various false and hence decadent solutions employed by men to overcome these problems; he also hoped to guide mankind along a way designed to lead beyond present-day despair. When Musil regarded everyday reality as a rationalist, he approached the perspective of the nihilist: he perceived a world without God, a world that appeared to have been shattered into meaningless and unrelated fragments under the onslaught of man's analytical attitude. As a mystic, however, Musil believed that man could recapture in mystical states of self-absorption that feeling of unity and harmony with the universe which he had seemingly lost forever when he lost God.

Musil did not advocate— as might seem to be the next logical step—that man escape from his meaningless everyday reality and take refuge in a state of mystical trance. He wanted rather to forge a link between both worlds, for he regarded them as equally important aspects of life. If such a link could be achieved, everyday reality would become infused with a sense of wholeness and meaning that it now lacked; at the same time, man's emotional life would become more comprehensible under the searching eye of reason. Decadent solutions to life's problems are for Musil those that tend toward the one extreme while rejecting the other. Hence, Musil believed that the pseudomystical romantic, who despises reason as being superficial and sterile, is really only a dim-witted sentimentalist and pretentious fraud; but he also regarded the pedantic rationalist, for whom the emotions represent nothing more than the vague intuitions of an infantile personality, as a frightened fugitive from the complexities of life.

When regarded in the light of his search for the balanced life, Musil's several changes of profession over a period of twenty-five years become not only comprehensible but also demonstrate a certain logical progression. For Musil, the balanced life is one in which the individual recognizes the necessity of reason and mysticism operating simultaneously within the human mind as it apprehends reality. Since these extremes possess equal validity, man must try to resist the temptation of placing one of them at the center of his life at the expense of the other. In practice, however, a search for the balanced life must usually involve a thorough dialectical investigation first of the one extreme and then of the other. The ultimate synthesis Musil termed "das rechte Leben," the creative or right life. Thus, when Musil decided to abandon his career as an engineer in order to study philosophy and psychology at the University of Berlin, his decision did not represent a rejection of science and the scientific attitude. He wanted, rather, to augment his experience as a scientist by studying certain areas of human experience that appeared to lie outside the boundaries of strict empirical investigation.

At the University of Berlin, however, Musil found that philosophical problems were examined predominantly within the frame-

work of logical positivism, a movement whose interests and methodology limited its activities to a consideration of measurable phenomena. In holding that all true knowledge is based upon sense experience, logical positivism relegated mysticism to the realm of the nonsensical, since mysticism clearly escapes analytical confirmation by the principle of verifiability. Philosophy, therefore, could not provide Musil with that "something that lies between" for which he was searching.

Musil turned finally to literature as a profession in which he could deal with some of the most important problems and areas of human experience rejected by the then prevailing school of philosophy. Musil thereby accepted a grave responsibility for the writer, for he now believed that fiction alone could provide that area between all extremes, that ground from which all of life could be investigated. Fiction alone seemed able "to hover" over all aspects of modern life that appeared fragmented into mutually exclusive opposites under the dialectic of what might variously be termed intellect and soul, mind and emotions, reason and mysticism. As well as providing that "something that lies between," fiction could also describe the search for the balanced life by capturing and structuring through aesthetic means all the dialectical possibilities in life. And the work itself would then also serve as a formal synthesis of all the opposites described in it.

But Musil was not in search of "something between" all extremes merely because he believed that the resulting vision of the complete and balanced human life was justifiable in itself. He was attempting nothing less than the creation of a new morality for Western man, a morality that had to be founded first of all on the synthesis of reason and mysticism. Once noting that there is a type of man who is aesthetically sensitive, Musil placed his allegiance in the opposite camp: "I am morally sensitive," he proudly declared.[12] It was for the sake of calling into existence a new and creative morality that the synthesis of reason and mysticism had to be regarded as the most urgent task facing mankind in the twentieth century.

As seen by Musil, the history of Western morality reveals a

continuing pattern in which the inner needs of the individual have always been in a state of imbalance with the external claims imposed by society and the church. Quite aside from the imbalances that exist between reason and mysticism within the individual himself, Musil also asserted that morality has too often suffered unduly from the compulsions of social codes imposed on the individual from without. In his fiction, the influence of the various rules and regulations for daily conduct, whether social or religious, have little effect upon the thought and action of the typical protagonist, who remains indifferent to any claims made upon him other than those claims arising from within himself. Since the fire of religious enthusiasm seems to Musil to have long ago been extinguished, the church represents in his work but another secular institution whose moral teachings merely justify and reinforce the prevailing codes of social behavior. On a more fundamental level, Musil's rejection of the Christian God meant a concomitant rejection of the metaphysical presupposition that had supported Christian morality for the last twenty centuries. With the resulting collapse of Christian values in the West, all standards for practical behavior once considered objectively valid and universally binding seemed to Musil to be arbitrary and merely subjective. The new morality that Musil sought to create would therefore have to be based neither upon social compulsions nor upon God-given imperatives, but solely upon those potentialities latent within the individual himself. The thrust of Musil's work is therefore forward, directed toward the achievement of a morality that can be realized only after much experimentation, whether the experimentor be Ulrich alone or all of society following in his footsteps. The intellectual and emotional horizons of Musil's fiction are open, his attitude experimental, and his hopes utopian.

　　If Musil did not become a writer out of primarily aesthetic considerations, why did he nevertheless choose fiction as the means for pursuing his investigations on the nature as well as the future of Western morality? Why did he not instead decide upon a university career as a professional philosopher, where he could have pursued such problems in a more direct fashion. This question is not

adequately answered by referring to Musil's disappointment with the restrictions of philosophy as practiced at the University of Berlin.

Synthesis: the Special Task of Modern Literature

Although philosophical writing might have provided Musil with a more direct means of exploring and solving certain questions than did literature, he chose the indirectness of literature because it seemed to him more like the indirectness of life itself. He wanted specifically to "animate" certain problems that have usually been treated in abstract philosophical form. In this way, these problems could be "argued" to a conclusion by means of the thoughts and emotions of a particular individual living at a particular time. The problem as well as its solution had to arise out of the complexities of the human condition; and literature alone seemed to Musil (as it also did on occasion to such philosophically oriented writers as Camus and Sartre) to be able to present the human condition in all its contradictory aspects.

Related to Musil's search for the right or good life ("das rechte Leben"), as he hoped it would one day appear in the living laboratory of his fiction, are his various analyses of how not to live. Literature was also able to provide him with an opportunity to present a large cast of characters through whom he could satirize various decadent ways of living. When these decadent characters are set within their particular cultural and historical context and contrasted with the lives of his protagonists, the result is a much more complex evocation of Austrian life on the brink of World War I than could have been achieved by logical philosophical discourse.

The most important reason for choosing literature as his vehicle was, however, his belief that only in the novel and short story could he give full and equal expression to two seemingly opposed capacities, both of which he possessed to a highly developed degree. In the novel, Musil could first of all investigate and describe mystical states, and secondly he could do so without sacrificing his

strongly developed sense of reason. In this way, he could at once
"unearth" mysticism as an area of human experience worthy of
serious consideration and, by subjecting it to rational scrutiny, res-
cue it from the romantics, religious fanatics, and sentimental idealists whose sole property it had been for too many years. Musil felt
himself to be equally a poet and a scientist, a mystic and a rationalist.   Thus it was only by means of the novel that Musil believed
he could become like one of those "masters of the hovering life,"
whom he so much admired. (Although Musil does not give the
names of such "masters," he may well have had in mind such men
as Pascal, Novalis, and Nietzsche.)

Musil's life and thought present a seemingly paradoxical com-
bination of elements often thought to be mutually exclusive. He
declared himself to be a writer who was not sensitive to aesthetic
problems but, rather, one who wished to pursue problems usually
considered to lie within the domain of philosophic investigation.
He was a rationalist but also a mystic, who wished to force reason
to its most rigorous extreme in order to recover mystical states in
their purest and most powerful form. A mystic but also a nihilist,
Musil believed that the universe was without inherent meaning
and that beneath man's feet there yawned a dizzying abyss. Having
now considered Musil's intentions, we may with some curiosity
examine the nature of Musil's literary style, the form of expression
chosen by this self-declared moralist, rationalist, mystic, and nihilist.

Musil's prose reveals a high degree of abstraction from everyday reality as it is experienced in all its concreteness and triviality.
This abstraction is manifested in two ways. First, Musil's fiction
often includes a large amount of intellectual material; the reader is
immediately aware that Musil's preoccupations and his manner of
considering various problems are generally philosophical. Ideas
are often explored at great length by an omniscient narrator who,
for the reader's benefit, offers his own interpretations directly and
in an extremely analytical fashion. Such a didactic style results in a
generalizing tendency noticeable throughout Musil's fiction.   He
seems always to be working away from the presentation of particular events and relations and toward more general statements and

observations.   It is for this reason that his characters often seem to represent nothing more than the embodiment of various philosophical positions. Musil intends that the reader always be fully aware of the more than merely personal significance of the characters and their lives in his work.

The second kind of abstraction in Musil's fiction also leads away from daily reality but in a totally different direction. His exploration of mystical states of being results in a style through which he attempts to render the most subtle and minute shades of feeling. In place of plot, a mainstay of the more traditional novel, the reader finds a dense web of metaphors. These metaphors evoke a complex internal world of emotions—vague, diffuse, and ambiguous. In those works where mystical states are directly described, Musil's style is not analytical. Nor does the work progress in the direction dictated by a narrator's logical explanations. Instead, the reader is plunged into a churning sea of feeling without visible horizons. He is left to swim (or sink) as fleeting sense impressions, half-completed thoughts, and momentary waves of emotion circle about him.

Both kinds of abstraction result in the relative absence in Musil's work of the two most common characteristics found in the traditional novel and short story: description of the external world and the unfolding of a plot. Musil's fiction, with few exceptions, reveals a striking lack of precise description: houses, streets, clothing, people, and faces seem rather spectral. From the point of view of the protagonist as well as the reader, the outer world appears to lack a sense of form, solidarity, and stability. Thrown either upon his endlessly fertile intellect or upon her complex and formless emotional life, the protagonist (respectively male and female) possesses an unsettling intuition of a void existing above and below him. Outer reality is not denied, but it enters Musil's fiction only as far as it impinges upon the protagonist's intellectual and emotional life, and the intellectual and emotional life of the Musil protagonist is self-sustaining and self-sufficient in the extreme.

Since either emotion or intellectual reflection dominate, Musil's work tends to lack a plot, a sense of progression from event to event. Indeed, such action as does occur is often retrospectively

reported. What is important in Musil's fiction is not what has happened or does happen, but what might have happened and what might yet happen. Musil is particularly interested in those unrealized possibilities that still exist in the human mind. The endless possibilities arising from the rich inner life of the protagonist supplant any single possibility that has been realized by means of action in outer reality. The subjunctive mood hovers over much of Musil's fiction. Possibilities, perspectives, alternatives structure the narrative, not the single story-line of external events.

Musil's first novel, *Young Törless* (1906) contains minimal plot and scant description of the external world because Musil is primarily concerned with the protagonist's experience of certain mystical (dionysian) states which, in a rather frightening fashion, seem to fall upon him without warning, threatening first his reason and finally even his sanity. An omniscient and extremely rational narrator comments upon these states through blocks of explanation that are not directly integrated into the text but seem to function as analytic footnotes to Törless's experiences.

In Musil's next major work, two short stories collected under the title *Unions* (1911), there is an almost total absence of plot and description of the environment. Moreover, the omniscient male narrator with his analytic comments is also absent because Musil here undertook a radical experiment: the fullest evocation of various mystical states as untouched as possible by the powers of reason and intellectual reflection. The narrative perspective is one that resides exclusively within the psyches of two women who are undergoing profound emotional disturbances. After completing "The Perfecting of a Love" and "The Temptation of Quiet Veronica," Musil never again submerged the narrative viewpoint in the emotional life of his protagonists, because such a device totally sacrificed the rational framework.

The collection of three short stories entitled *Three Women* (1924) represents for Musil an unusual experiment with more traditional narrative techniques. Musil demonstrates unexpected concern for his descriptions of the external world as well as for the relationships between the various characters. Each of the three works is a story with a beginning, a middle, and an end. The

narrative point of view is again essentially that of a man, respectively an engineer, a soldier, and a scientist. All these men, who represent a predominantly rational attitude toward life, attempt in various ways, as did Törless, to come to terms with a mystical world. In each of the stories, "Grigia," "The Lady from Portugal," and "Tonka," this world is embodied by a woman who appears in their lives as a silent, shadowy, and mysterious creature existing on the edge of rational male culture.

Musil's *The Man without Qualities* (1930-1943) reveals a greater concern with the social world surrounding the highly introverted protagonist than does any previous work. Through his descriptions of the so-called Collateral Campaign, Musil attempts to evoke an ironic picture of a large segment of Austrian society, from chambermaids to princes, all of whom are preoccupied with their various trivial or grandiose schemes as the Empire totters on the verge of collapse. But his evocation of Viennese society in the year 1913 nevertheless retains a rather spectral quality when compared, for instance, with Tolstoy's description in *War and Peace* of Russian society during the Napoleonic wars. All of Musil's peripheral characters represent various alternatives in living that gain their significance only in relationship to Ulrich's life.

This novel centers, as do all of Musil's works, on the individual psyche, in this case on the protagonist's experiences of the dialectic of reason and mysticism. By exploring both of these themes in Ulrich's life in a manner more rigorous and comprehensive than ever before, Musil hoped in his last novel to be able to arrive at a final synthesis. It is in *The Man without Qualities* that Musil's dialectical vision achieves its most appropriate stylistic consummation: the essay. Ulrich calls "the masters of the hovering life" the great essayists of life. The essayist, Ulrich reasons, has to live in a realm between extremes, for he is in search of a synthesis that would, if achieved, represent a connection between the exact and the nonexact, between precision and passion. He must therefore possess an attitude that is at once cold-blooded and fanciful. As such, the essayistic attitude incorporates the precise attitude of the scientist and the subjective attitude of the artist. Ulrich is attracted by the idea that, according to his definition, the essay pur-

sues a particular theme from many points of view without bias and does not assume that total comprehension will immediately result. He decides to apply an essayistic attitude toward his daily life: to accept no one point of view as being more than partially true.

As Ulrich thinks in terms of the essayistic attitude, Musil writes his novel under the guiding principles of the essay form. Thus Musil interjects essays directly into the novel and sets them off from the main body of the text as separate chapters with such extraordinary titles as: "If there is such a thing as a sense of reality, there must be a sense of possibility"; "Ideals and morality are the best means of filling the big hole that one calls soul"; "From Koniatowski's critique of Danielli's theorem to the Fall of Man." Although the topics of these essays are more or less related to Ulrich's intellectual and emotional life, Musil's philosophical reflections and analyses have in this novel also achieved an existence almost independent from the life of the thinking protagonist. In fact, by means of his essayistic style, Musil has written the most directly philosophical work in the history of the novel.

Musil's death in 1942 left the novel without a final synthesis between reason and mysticism. The novel also lacked an unambiguous resolution of Ulrich's mystical experiment with his sister. But Musil's work on the novel had already reached an impasse before his death. His failure to write a conclusion to the novel was not in the first instance to be explained by his death; death merely stopped him from writing ever further interpolations which did not serve to move the narrative forward in time. Of course, had he lived he might eventually have broken through this impasse and completed the novel, since he continued to write every day with soldierly dedication. As matters stood in 1942, however, he could not forge ahead chronologically in the novel, that is to say, he could not bring Ulrich significantly closer to the final catastrophe, the outbreak of World War I.

In 1932, Musil had stated that although he had as yet no precise idea of Ulrich's final position, he was certain that Ulrich was not destined to end his days in pure nihilism and despair. But even ten years later Musil had still not developed a clear idea of what Ulrich's fate was to be. Musil could not change the advent of

World War I, nor apparently could he effectively deal with it. Since he regarded Ulrich as a representative of his culture, as Mann regarded Hans Castorp in *The Magic Mountain*, Ulrich was destined in spite of his uniqueness to be swallowed up by the war at least for a time. Ulrich was definitely intended to survive the war, however. Musil left behind plans to present Ulrich many years after the war in the novel's final section, to be entitled "A Sort of Conclusion." But while writing in 1942, Musil seemed to recoil from a confrontation with the historical outbreak of World War I. Thus, he did not allow Ulrich's life to progress to the date of the General Mobilization, July 28, 1914. Instead, Musil busied himself with writing chapters that seem to exist outside of time. These chapters take the form either of conversations between Ulrich and his sister Agathe or of essays concerning "the right way of living."

The tragic nature of this impasse becomes clear when we recall that Ulrich's solution was also to function as a form of salvation for decadent Western culture on the edge of moral and spiritual chaos. Musil considered himself a self-appointed artist-priest, who would by means of the novel show Western man the way beyond nihilism. The individual and society would thereby be purified and renewed. Everything in Musil's life and fiction was focused on this goal. Toward the end of his life, however, Musil admitted: "The solution goes beyond the abilities of Ulrich and therefore also beyond those of his creator."[13]

Unlike that of Mann and Broch, Musil's life and work remain a great fragment, an uncompleted mission. In connection with an application made in 1941 for a foundation grant that was denied as usual, Musil called himself (paraphrasing Nietzsche's "*Nur* Narr! *Nur* Dichter!"): "Only a fool, only a poet."[14] All the seriousness and tragedy of Musil's life is expressed in this ironic self-description. His high regard for his own mission as a writer in the twentieth century was countered by the idea that it was perhaps sheer foolishness to have assumed such a difficult, if not impossible task. We recall that Musil wrote of those masters of the hovering life that often they were "simply men who have gone out on an adventure and lost their way."[15]   It will be left to Musil's readers to

decide for themselves whether or not Musil was one of those who risked too much, who hovered too high, who set himself only the most absolute of goals and went hopelessly astray. Although the adventure was not completed, Musil's boldness, dedication, and courage cannot be denied.

The Critical Context

There exist any number of critics today who have attacked Musil's achievement, and their objections are often valid. There are also an ever-growing number who have praised his works in the most extravagant fashion, ranking him with Proust, Joyce, and Kafka. The approach of the following study of Musil's major fiction is based on the assumption that his qualities as a writer will be seen most clearly if the critical analysis is untainted by extremes of either praise or censure. As F.L. Lucas once wrote of the English dramatist John Webster: "It is too easy to pile mere flowers of speech on a grave; in a day or two it is the flowers that are dead. The essential is not to praise, but to try to understand."

In order to facilitate such an understanding, this study will regard Musil's fiction from various perspectives, both philosophical and psychoanalytic. In fact, one major purpose of the present study is not only to illuminate Musil's texts but, quite specifically, to set Musil's literary preoccupations in the broader context of European intellectual history. (The form and style of Musil's fiction are studied, but only to the extent that they represent a natural and—for the critic—illuminating accommodation and outgrowth of Musil's subject matter.) Given the obvious philosophical nature of many of Musil's works as well as his profound knowledge of and great admiration for the thought of several important philosophers, such an approach need not be defended. However, this study will not only draw upon those philosophers whose works Musil undoubtedly knew well. Comparisons will also be made with some central problems explored by Kierkegaard and Camus. Though Musil probably had little or, in the case of Camus, no direct knowledge of the work of these philosophers, the nature and

location of Musil's spiritual journey in fiction can be more clearly assessed when viewed in the perspective of their thought. Moreover, Musil did not believe that his own work existed in an intellectual vacuum, but rather that it represented a new formulation and (he hoped) a higher synthesis of perennial problems in the history of Western man. Although Musil would probably not have objected to having some of his preoccupations placed within the broader perspective of existential thought, it should immediately be added here that he was not a religious existentialist as was Kierkegaard, nor does his *Weltanschauung* reveal the often uncompromisingly bleak vision of Camus. While rejecting the concept of God, as did Camus, Musil nevertheless remained in a fundamental sense a late romantic: he never ceased to hope for a utopian synthesis of analytic reason (which reveals a world without coherence and order) and the mystical impulse (which could restore a feeling of meaning and wholeness to daily life). In certain respects the possibility of such a synthesis represents a secularization of the Kierkegaardian hope that man's daily life will be revitalized and unified by his achievement of the profound mystical state that is belief in God.

Musil's fiction has been declared off-limits to psychoanalytic interpretation, and so it is only with some trepidation that a critic dare raise the question of a psychoanalytic approach to Musil's work. Such an approach must be defended not only against Musil's critics but also against the quite unambiguous objections that Musil himself made to the theories of Freud and Jung. Karthaus, in his report "Musil-Forschung und Musil-Deutung," declares: "It was recognized quite early that Musil was not concerned with questions of psychology or depth psychology."[16] And he supports this observation by referring to the critical studies of Beda Allemann and Gerhart Baumann, who also arrived at the same conclusion. Musil's profound aversion to (possibly even fear of) psychoanalysis is clearly evident. In the years 1928 to 1930, Musil underwent psychoanalytic therapy under the direction of a disciple of Alfred Adler. Although almost nothing is known of this episode in Musil's life, references to Freud, Adler, and Jung begin to appear with greater frequency in his diaries after 1930, and almost all

of them are negative. Musil admitted that although Freud did contribute insights of great importance to Western culture, these insights were often unfortunately confounded with much that
seemed untrue and totally one-sided.[17] Not long before his death,
Musil declared that it was "flat" experimental psychology rather
than depth psychology that had always interested him.[18] What is
quite clear is the fact that when Musil did read psychological literature, he did not read the works of Freud, Adler, or Jung. For he
felt not only a lack of interest in them, but apparently a positive
dislike for their way of describing the workings of the inner life.
(Thus Harry Goldgar's analysis of *Young Törless* from the perspective of Musil's knowledge of Freud's work is unconvincing.[19] In a
frontal assault upon Goldgar's article, Annie Reniers demonstrates
that Musil could have had absolutely no knowledge of Freud's
theories in 1905, the year in which he was working upon *Young
Törless*.[20]) Musil particularly objected to psychoanalysis because to
him it represented a form of intellectual dictatorship.[21] Its disciples
attempt to explain the whole world with a dozen concepts. Musil
argued that one could just as easily achieve the same (oversimplified) coherence if one interpreted the world within the perspective
of a totally different system.[22] Lida Kirchberger's interpretation of
Three Women, in which she fits "Grigia" (the primeval world),
"The Lady from Portugal" (the medieval world), and "Tonka" (the
modern world) into Freud's descriptions of the Id, the Ego, and the
Superego, respectively, has been attacked by Ulrich Karthaus and
Elizabeth Boa.[23] Both critics (in essence) accuse Kirchberger of
applying the "intellectual dictatorship" of Freudian theory to the
text.

The use of the thought of Freud and Jung in the present study
does not presuppose that psychoanalytic theory holds the key either to truth in general or to the secrets of Musil's work in particular. Psychoanalytic theory will be utilized only to provide a more
readily accessible framework within which some of Musil's more
opaque works may be examined. Psychoanalytic thought has not
been used in any systematic fashion in the analysis of Musil's two
works dealing with the male protagonists Törless and Ulrich, but
has been found to be especially illuminating in a consideration of

the five short stories about women. In these short stories, the theme is either the nature of the feminine psyche (*Unions*) or the masculine attitude toward women (*Three Women*). In the former case, Freudian theory has proved singularly useful and in the latter, Jungian theory. However, in neither case is psychoanalytic theory presented as providing more than merely one, though one particularly instructive, way of comprehending works which often seem to verge on the incomprehensible. Musil's fiction remains more subtle than the psychoanalytic concepts through which it is viewed. In his five short stories, Musil was primarily concerned with presenting the workings of the irrational mind and therefore employed a series of metaphors not meant to be analytically comprehended and discursively described by the narrator. In this respect he obviously differed from Freud, who directed his energies toward a rational comprehension of the irrational mind.

Two objections to the use of psychoanalytic theory in the interpretation of Musil's work must nevertheless be directly confronted. First, Musil's grasp of Freud and Jung was minimal and, second, Musil's technique and style of literary expression is often strikingly "unpsychological." To reject the use of psychoanalytic insight in criticism where no psychoanalytic influence exists, or can be documented to exist, is, however, to misunderstand the applicability of psychoanalytic theory to literature. Freud attempted to describe the operations of the human psyche, and this is the same psyche of which Musil writes, albeit from a quite different point of view. As Jung wrote: "It is obvious enough that psychology, being the study of psychic processes, can be brought to bear upon the study of literature, for the human psyche is the womb of all the sciences and the arts."[24] The crucial question for the critic is, therefore, whether Musil's treatment of the human psyche permits and is illuminated by comparison with a parallel, although scientific, interpretation of the human psyche. If so, then the proper use of psychoanalytic interpretation is a matter of degree and a question of the critic's literary sensitivity.

Concerning the second objection, it must be admitted, as argued above, that Musil's fiction tends toward two extremes, neither of which is "psychological": one is the abstract and highly intellec-

tual style of those works dealing with the male protagonist, and the other is the endless stream of metaphors in those stories describing the inner lives of his female characters. (Of course, this dichotomy of style is not absolute. To the extent that mystical states are treated in *Young Törless* and *The Man without Qualities*, Musil uses metaphors to describe that which lies outside the domain of rational and discursive language. The style of *Three Women* tends toward a balance between these two extremes.) However, it is precisely Musil's aversion to psychologizing in his works that opens them to meaningful psychoanalytic interpretation. In this regard Jung argues that "the so-called 'psychological novel' is by no means as rewarding for the psychologist as the literary-minded suppose. Considered as a whole, such a novel explains itself. It has done its own work of psychological interpretation, and the psychologist can at most criticize or enlarge upon this."[25] It is for this reason that a novel which "is apparently quite devoid of psychological intentions is just what interests the psychologist most of all. Such a tale is constructed against a background of unspoken psychological assumptions, and the more unconscious the author is of them, the more this background reveals itself in unalloyed purity to the discerning eye."[26] Such a mode of artistic presentation may positively invite psychoanalytic interpretation. Here Jung made a distinction between "psychological" and "visionary" literature and it is, not surprisingly, visionary literature which he believed provides the best opportunity for psychological interpretation. Jung offered a further distinction concerning the different kinds of material that each form of literature draws upon. Psychological literature takes its material essentially from conscious human experience and everything that it deals with belongs to the realm of the understandable. The materials which inform visionary literature, on the other hand, are drawn directly from the unconscious and make their appearance more or less unmediated by abstract thought. Such material generally expresses itself in the form of metaphor and symbol. Of such literature Jung wrote: "We are reminded of nothing in everyday life, but rather of dreams, night-time fears, and the dark, uncanny recesses of the human mind. The public for the most part repudiates this kind of literature."[27] Such material

arises from "the hinterland of man's mind."[28] It is not surprising, therefore, that a Jungian approach to the "dark visions" of women, as they arise out of the psychic hinterland of the three masculine protagonists in *Three Women*, is a particularly illuminating one.

The universal rejection of and snobbish disdain for psychoanalytic interpretation may arise in part from the critics' belief that Musil's fiction may be unable to withstand the scrutiny of psychoanalysis and must, consequently, be protected from its cold and relentless eye. But there is no danger that Musil's life's work will shrivel away under the impact of psychoanalytic interpretation, leaving behind only a series of artistic rationalizations for the author's personal pathologies, which he wished to hide from the public and himself by obfuscating his inner life through complex philosophical analyses and opaque streams of exotic metaphors. Psychoanalysis is not called upon, nor is it able, to evaluate and judge a work of art. Consequently, there is no possibility that a work of art will be "reduced" by psychoanalysis, for when psychoanalytic interpretation has run its course, the artistic achievement of a work of literature remains yet to be assessed.

In support of the appropriateness of psychoanalytic interpretation, it will be shown in this study that Musil's work, whether functioning on the level of metaphor or of reason, does not ignore and therefore violate psychological reality. The characters in his fiction are particularly prone to nervous breakdown, psychotic regression, and suicidal impulses. When psychological conflict becomes too great for the protagonist, he seeks some form of psychological escape. Musil's brilliant descriptions of the various forms of such escape reveal that he had, indeed, a unique grasp of man's psyche in states of highest stress.

A final word should be added on the amount of space that will be devoted to each of Musil's works. More space will be given to the shorter works because they present more difficult critical problems. They have also received the least attention from critics to date. *The Man without Qualities*, which is about 1,600 pages long, will receive hardly more analysis than the two short stories in *Unions*, which together comprise 54 pages. The themes and problems treated in *The Man without Qualities*, Musil's most frequently

scrutinized work, are expressed within the book itself in an objective, discursive style, one not unlike that of the literary critic. Like Thomas Mann's *Doctor Faustus*, this novel to a great extent contains its own interpretation within itself.

The critic's task in Musil's novels, at least initially, is one of coming to terms with the obvious complexity of intellectual material. But the themes which Musil explores in *Unions* are presented largely through a series of highly personal metaphors and associations that require extensive analysis in order to bring to light their inner meaning, coherence, and relationship to the author's less obscure fiction. Because Musil's vocabulary in the short stories is so personal, it is particularly useful to employ the psychoanalytic approach, a different but parallel "vocabulary" that deals on a more intellectual and less metaphoric level with the workings of the psyche than did Musil himself. It is hoped that this investigation of the author's esoteric short stories will correct an obvious imbalance in Musil criticism to date without, however, slighting the two more exoteric and accessible novels.

II ✆

Trapdoor into Chaos: *Young Törless*

ALTHOUGH MUSIL'S SECOND and last novel, *The Man without Qualities*, is regarded as one of the longest and most complex literary works of the twentieth century, his first novel, *Young Törless*, is in certain ways more difficult and elusive. In his last novel, Musil allowed himself more than 1,600 pages to explore at leisure any given topic from numerous points of view. In *Young Törless*, however, he was at pains to compress his treatment of the protagonist's intellectual and emotional crisis into fewer than 150 pages. The result of such compression is a gripping and streamlined novel. But *Young Törless* is also a work in which Musil omnisciently presents some of his own philosophical interpretations in a fashion too highly elliptical to be readily comprehended by the reader. Therefore, the reader is himself forced into providing the meaningful connections between Törless's actions (which constitute the plot of the novel) and Musil's own highly condensed and interpolated philosophical observations upon Törless's activities and mental condition.

The plot is, in fact, meagre. The novel describes the final months spent by the 15-year-old Törless at a military academy located in a remote corner of the Austrian Empire. After the failure of a brief friendship with an ethereal young prince, Törless falls under the influence of two totally ruthless but energetic classmates, Beineberg and Reiting. Together, they force a fourth student, Basini, whom they have discovered stealing money from the school lockers, into a position of obsequious servitude under threat of public exposure. Under the pretext of punishing the thief themselves, each of the three boys carries out his own particular experiment on the frightened and cowed Basini. When the affair eventually becomes public, Basini is suspended and Törless is dismissed from the school as being too emotionally unstable to continue in

such an environment. Beineberg and Reiting apparently suffer no ill consequences at all, remain at the school, and continue their studies.

The recounting of these few external events in the plot reveals little concerning the central issues of the novel. Although Musil's evocation of the school, the village, the teachers, and the various students is on occasion vivid, *Young Törless* is essentially a novel of ideas. The plot remains without meaning until the critical reader exposes to view the often half-expressed ideas beneath external events, studies the development and interrelationship of these ideas, and clarifies Musil's intellectual presuppositions with regard to the novel as a whole. The plot serves as a framework for the exploration of those ideas that have perennially occupied the adolescent in Western Europe: the nature of reality, the limitations of reason, the terrors of sexuality, and the hollowness of traditional morality.

Adolescence and the Illusion of Character

Adolescence is regarded by Musil as that period which exists just before the individual has managed to construct the fiction of character.[1] The adolescent Törless "had no character at all."[2] He seems to live without "this ultimate, immovable background" that is called "character or soul, a person's inner contour or aura" (15). One day, however, Törless begins to become aware of a "nothing-ness," an "emptiness in himself;" Musil states plainly that "in young Törless's soul was a void" (10).

In Musil's psychology, the inner void must be concealed if character is to develop. Once character has been achieved, as in adulthood, it acts as a permanent and opaque "floor" over the void within. Therefore, the dangerous time of life is that period in which the individual first leaves behind him the unexamined security of childhood and begins to construct his own character on the way to the equally unexamined security of adulthood. Musil believes that schools have essentially two ways of concealing the inner void during this particularly dangerous time. On the one hand, the student

is encouraged to read literature as a means of strengthening the "floor" of character. By submerging himself in the adventures of some heroic figure, the adolescent is readily able to borrow by means of identification the character of some fictional protagonist, particularly that of the romantic hero. On the other hand, the student is encouraged to take up sports, for sports keep the adolescent in a constant state of exhaustion, which leaves him neither the time nor the energy for introspective examination. Törless, however, finds himself in the dilemma of being at once too intellectually inclined for sports but also totally uninterested in literature, which he considers a form of emotional fraud. Alone among his peers, he begins to gaze compulsively into "this nothingness, this emptiness in himself" (10). He thereby finds himself in precisely that psychological condition of which Musil warns: should an adolescent be unfortunate enough to attain a complete view of his inner self (or rather of its absence), whatever "floor" he may have tentatively begun to construct would give way under him. He would plunge downward, experiencing the world like a somnambulist who, upon awakening, sees only emptiness around him (14).Törless does fall into this psychological void, and the novel describes his desperate attempt to comprehend the nature of his fall.

A major assumption that Musil asks the reader to make entails the recognition of a tragic discrepancy between the demands of truth and those of psychological necessity: in reality, man does not have a character, but the illusion that he does have a character is a necessary fiction if the child is to develop into an adult, if indeed he is not to lose his sanity during transition over the void and into the adult world. What, then, is this "character," whose actual and powerful presence within himself man so vehemently affirms as a reality and Musil so adamantly denies? In what way does its presence stabilize life?   For Musil, character is merely a conceptual synthesis. Indeed, the very word "character" can be defined as an abbreviated formula for that mechanism of simplification that limits man to a single perspective of seeing. If, in this context, strength of character may be said to result from a restriction of perspectives upon life, and consequent lack of ambivalence,

then a strong character is indicative of a decided will to stupidity. A man possessing such a character lacks knowledge of the many possibilities and directions for action; his intellect is fettered and restricted. But Törless's intellect is still free, not because he possesses, as does Ulrich in *The Man without Qualities*, a will to truth at all costs that destroys the illusion of character, but because he is still too young to have developed this fictional synthesis. Because Törless has at most only a weak character, his intellect remains unfettered and thus powerful enough to regard life from many varying perspectives.

Because of Musil's presuppositions concerning the nature of adolescence and the illusion of character, *Young Törless* represents more than yet another novel about the initiation of an adolescent into his society. Since Musil describes Törless as an adolescent who refuses to accept various comforting illusions adopted by the world of adults, his process of initiation into the adult world is in jeopardy from the very beginning. Törless perceives that age brings not wisdom but hypocrisy. Musil characterizes the adults of Törless's society as benevolent ignoramuses or self-deceiving frauds; therefore, all possible models for the adolescent's emulation are absent. These adults have become skilled in creating self-sustaining myths that provide their lives with structure and meaning. Törless comes to discover the precise nature of that legacy which his parents' world has bequeathed him: he discovers a world in a state of total intellectual, moral, and spiritual bankruptcy. Musil's fundamental assumption is that the social world into which Törless is being initiated is not worthy of being entered.

Fantasy Becomes Reality

It is Törless's great misfortune to become aware of the psychological void within himself at that very fateful period when the sexual impulse "began to rise up in him, darkly and steadily" (13). The void beneath character becomes inextricably connected with sexuality.

Törless's sexual fantasy world, as Musil directly describes it to

the reader, is comprised of environments of filth and darkness, of small rooms with oppressive atmospheres, entered by means of narrow stairs and doors. He imagines himself imprisoned behind high walls and subjected to the lure of some shadowy and monstrous woman. These fantasies are pervaded by a paralyzing sense of terror and a desire to be completely destroyed by a beastlike sensual creature.

In these fantasies all bourgeois codes of accepted behavior are broken. In fact, any experience in the external world that appears to transgress the bourgeois codes of his parents becomes sexualized for Törless. For example, dark, dirty, confining spaces, which he feels invert the ordered and spacious world of middle-class houses, seem to take on a sexual aura. All irregular behavior, from the *faux pas* to the blatant criminal act, is similarly sexualized by Törless, since such actions are viewed by him as transgressions against strict middle-class morality.

In opposition to this newly discovered dark and dangerous fantasy world, Törless also feels the presence of what he interprets as the rationally controlled world of everyday reality, and he desperately attempts to cling to the latter. These two worlds, as Törless experiences them, arise from an endopsychic conflict within Törless himself. That is to say, he unconsciously projects these two conflicting worlds into the external world in a state of mutual exclusivity. Due to a "change of inner perspective" (130), Törless sometimes perceives the world "with the eyes of reason" (170); at other times he perceives the world through eyes "as if only his soul saw" (67).   Musil himself analyzes Törless's schematic division of reality into two halves as follows: "He felt as though torn between two worlds: one was the solid everyday world of respectable citizens, in which all that went on was well regulated and rational, and which he knew from home, and the other was a world of adventure, full of darkness, mystery, blood, and undreamed-of surprises. It seemed then as though one excluded the other" (50). This contrast can be expressed in general terms from any number of points of view. Socially: the bourgeois world versus an underground world of criminals and social outcasts. Metaphorically: day versus night, light versus dark. Emotionally: restraint, prudence,

and calm versus lack of control and absence of judgment and proportion. Intellectually: logic versus instinct, and consciousness versus unconsciousness.

Törless expresses the precarious nature of his psychological situation by employing the metaphor of a trapdoor that can open up at any moment and precipitate him into a dark dionysian world of chaos and madness below. In Musil's view, it is only during early adolescence that the trap door is likely to open in that place termed the "floor," where strong character later develops in adulthood. For as the individual grows older, the "floor" is continually thickened and strengthened by prejudices, eccentricities, and numerous self-deceptions.

What, then, is the nature of this void into which Törless feels he may fall, this void in which the bourgeois world of his parents appears as an inverted reflection? Why does he call this state an abyss rather than a fulness? In his diaries Musil associates this void with a form of mysticism, a dionysian mysticism in which the self is absorbed and extinguished. All energy that had formerly been used by the individual to think, perceive, and evaluate is transformed into intense physical activity.[3] Many students might welcome such an extinguishing of the self in dionysian states such as those induced by sports or sex. But for Törless, such states are threatening and dangerous because his concept of himself is so frail that he cannot afford to give up (however temporarily) any degree of his ego, rudimentary though it may be, in the pursuit of sensual or physical activity.

Because Törless is unable to utilize as stabilizing forces either a belief in character or in the firm moral guidelines of any social or religious code, he precipitates himself into a situation in which his confused feelings represent the sole reality of his life. In one sense, *Young Törless* may be regarded as a literary experiment in which Musil explores what happens when, in a world where all social and metaphysical values have been implicitly rejected, sexual fantasies become the primary reality.

Musil implies that the various elements of Törless's sexual fantasies had already existed as nightmarish images in his mind even before the novel opened, but they existed totally disconnected

from any corresponding state or object in reality. On the day the novel opens, these sexual fantasies all at once begin to find external correlatives in Törless's physical environment. The metaphoric trapdoor first opens slightly when Törless is walking by the huts of some local peasant women, later that same day when he visits the town prostitute Božena at the local inn, and then repeatedly in the red attic room at the school where Basini is tortured. With the onset of puberty, Törless begins involuntarily to project his fantasies onto real persons, real places, and even onto ideas, bestowing upon them the power that is able to undermine his self-control. In other words, people, places, even ideas, which are in themselves totally neutral, become transformed by Törless's fantasies into representatives of a threatening world of dionysian chaos. Törless initially fails to recognize, however, that it is his fantasies that are constantly adding the dionysian element to the outer world. It is he who associates the small filthy houses, narrow doorways, heavy atmospheres, dirty clothes and bodies of his fantasies with the peasant women outside their huts, with Božena in her bedroom, and with the events that take place in the attic room. Whenever any one of the descriptive elements of his fantasy world coincides with something that is actually present in the external world, Törless is overwhelmed by feelings of sexual desire, terror, and masochistic surrender to destruction. Merely the element of darkness outside a café window stimulates Törless's terrifying sexual fantasy of being abandoned and locked into a dark house at the complete mercy of the monstrous mistress of his imagination.

At first, Törless's fantasies merely provide him with mysterious and fascinating moments that help to relieve the monotony and boredom of daily routine. Although the peasant women and Božena are representatives for him of a dark, mysterious, passionate world, this world exists safely outside the sphere of his social class and school environment. At this point in his life, where the trapdoor opens only partially from time to time, the dionysian realm is associated with poor country people, whose physical environments coincide with the oppressive environments of his fantasies. But one night as Törless is looking at Božena, he is puzzled and revolted to discover that he cannot stop thinking of his

mother. The prostitute Božena seems in some way to be disturbing Törless's previous concept of his mother as a calm and rationally comprehensible being and dragging her toward a shadowy and chaotic Other World [4] to which the peasant women belong. It now becomes Törless's most urgent need to recapture and hold fast to the image of his mother as a Madonnalike figure, secure in a world that is serene and innocent.

Törless's need to hold the dionysian realm at a distance is made impossible by Basini's "fall." It may be recalled that the breaking of any social code stimulates sexual fantasies in Törless's mind. Had Basini not broken the social code by his petty thefts of money from his fellow students' lockers, Törless's fantasy would not automatically have turned him into a representative of that other frightening world. Törless does not become sexually involved with Basini because he is attracted primarily to the physical body of this effeminate young boy. What arouses interest and desire in Törless is the sexuality of Basini's entire being, a sexuality that for Törless proceeds immediately from Basini's criminal behavior. The existence of that other, dark, immoral, and chaotic world, which had previously been a more or less imaginary quantity outside his everyday life, now all at once "shifted out of the imagination into life itself and became a menace" (74).

Törless's compulsive interest in Basini arises from his need to save not only his mother but also himself from contamination by this Other World. Thus Törless is desperate for two reasons. First, if Basini could without warning fall through a trapdoor into that Other World, then this world must exist not only for people such as the peasants and Božena but for Törless as well. Törless at first wants Basini to be expelled from school. He denies that Basini ever was his peer. But unlike Božena, Basini is part of Törless's world. Törless finally admits this truth: "It was a reality. Yesterday Basini had been the same as himself. Now a trapdoor had opened and Basini had plunged into the depths" (56). Hence Basini's fall reveals the possibility of Törless falling too. Moreover, if Basini could be both a thief and a social equal, then Frau Törless could be both a woman like the prostitute Božena as well as his mother. Whereas Törless had previously been able to keep the two worlds

apart by associating the dionysian realm only with a socially inferior class, they now lose their separateness and meet in the upperclass thief Basini. They also come together in his mother and in Törless himself. With the revelation of a fellow student as a thief, Törless's perception of himself now begins to fragment. Part of himself seems to move off into the void, as did the image of his mother that night in Božena's room.

A Vision of Nothingness

Not many days after Törless has been plunged into a state of desperation by the discovery of Basini's theft, he makes another discovery that complicates and extends his despair into the very heavens. Lying alone one day on the grass in the school park, Törless becomes aware that "straight above him, shining between the clouds, [there] was a small, blue hole, fathomlessly deep" (76). He becomes frightened and attempts to calm himself with the thought: "Of course there *is* no end, . . . it just keeps going on and on forever, into infinity" (76). But Törless nevertheless feels overcome with anguish. It seems to him as if suddenly something destructive and malevolent in the heavens is confronting him. For the first time, he becomes aware of an infinite depth in existence, a depth without the presence of God to reassure and protect man.

Törless's experience in the park is reminiscent of man's situation in a nihilistic world as described by Nietzsche's madman in *The Joyful Wisdom*, a book that Musil read while working on *Young Törless*. The madman, who appears in the marketplace with a lighted lantern at noon, at once announces the death of God and describes the new world in which man will henceforth have to live. By destroying the concept of God, man has swept away the comforting horizon surrounding his life and is, therefore, no longer able to avoid perceiving a new and frightening world of nothingness above him. Surrounded by infinite empty space, man will soon (so warns the madman in 1882) find himself overwhelmed by terror and anguish.[5] Having discovered the void in the sky, Törless feels overcome by terror and conceives of himself as now being nothing

more than a small speck of life upon the surface of the earth who must henceforth continue to exist beneath the gigantic transparent corpse (!) in the sky.

Musil believes that the absence of character is in some way related to the absence of God. In a short story entitled "A Man without Character," Musil, paraphrasing almost to the point of exact quotation Nietzsche's parable of the madman, described how his [Musil's] madman went to the marketplace at noon with a lighted lantern seeking not the God, who has vanished, but rather character, which seems also to have disappeared.[6] This paraphrase, which intimates a direct connection between Musil's own concept of man without a character and Nietzsche's concept of man without a God, also suggests a further psychological and historical consequence of the death of God.

Musil's reworking of Nietzsche's parable represents first of all a shift from the outside to the inside: just as Nietzsche felt that man conceals from himself the void above by his belief in the philosophical fiction of God, so Musil felt that man conceals from himself the void within by his belief in the psychological fiction of character. Thus for Musil, the nihilistic *Weltanschauung* that asserts the absence of God necessarily possesses a psychological corollary: the absence of character. Ulrich, the protagonist of *The Man without Qualities* and a more mature version of Törless, defines the nihilist (e.g., himself) in psychological terms as a man who lacks character.[7]

As for the historical development of man's spiritual and cultural condition after the disappearance of God, Musil's paraphrase suggests that the death of God is the prerequisite and eventual cause of the dissolution of character. By reducing the concept of God to the level of a dispensable metaphysical fiction, man not only removed God from the heavens, thereby exposing his own existence to the void above, but also removed himself from the center of God's creation. When man is no longer able to regard himself as the purpose and the glory of creation, he will also be unable to continue to support the illusion of possessing a character. In his novel *The Man without Qualities*, Musil expresses the psychological consequences of philosophical nihilism as follows: "It is

probable that the dissolution of the anthropocentric attitude (an attitude that, after so long seeing man as the centre of the universe, has been dissolving for some centuries now) has finally begun to affect the personality itself."[8] By murdering God, man unknowingly also murdered the host upon which his character lived. Just as Nietzsche's madman prophetically announced in 1882 that man's future condition of life was to be an existence without God, so Törless is regarded by Musil in the early 1900s as a precursor of that type of man who will one day be able to live in an empty universe without the comforting illusion of character.

Mathematics as a Bridge over the Void

As Törless uses the metaphor of a trapdoor in connection with his experience of the void within, he finds a second metaphor, that of a bridge, to give expression to his experience in the park of the void above. Musil summarizes Törless's experience of looking through the hole in the sky with a single word: " 'Infinity!' Törless had often heard the word in mathematics lessons" (76). And shortly after the experience in the park, Musil writes of Törless: "He felt the urge to search unceasingly for some bridge, some connection, some means of comparison between himself and the wordless thing confronting his spirit" (79-80).

Led astray by language, Törless concludes that since mathematics often deals with concepts of infinity in its calculations, mathematics may not only hold the key to the threatening experience of infinity in the sky but may also indicate a means by which he might be able to control it. He reasons that mathematical equations both begin and end with solid and real numbers. But the mathematician is quite prepared to employ such concepts as imaginary and irrational numbers and even the formula for infinity to deal with the area in between. Törless concludes: "But these two lots of real numbers are connected by something that simply doesn't exist. Isn't that like a bridge where the piles are there only at the beginning and at the end, with none in the middle, and yet

one crosses it just as surely and safely as if the whole of it were there" (90).

A further step in Törless's confusion is caused by his sudden inspiration that the irrational element in mathematical calculation is in some way similar to the irrational element in Basini's behaviour. In essence, Törless now incorporates into his psychological metaphor of the trapdoor over the inner void the new metaphor of the bridge, which functions primarily as a means of giving expression to a philosophical interpretation of reality. That is to say, Törless's experience in the park, which he connects with the bright void in the daytime sky, quickly becomes associated with the dark void he perceives in Basini. He now begins to think in terms of building a bridge across (as opposed to a floor above) the void within by means of mathematics.

With this new metaphor, Törless begins to think not simply in terms of preventing a fall into the void, but of crossing it, of getting from one side to the other. He believes that as mathematical calculations begin and end with real and solid numbers, so does man's psychological life begin and end with the security, respectively, of childhood and adulthood. The illusion of character, a totally imaginary concept that he rejects as a cowardly fraud, Törless now regards as being only one possible solution to the problem of creating a floor over the inner void.

Mathematics might serve as another solution because, although it uses irrational and imaginary numbers in the middle of its calculations, it nevertheless manages to reach the other side without committing intellectual fraud. This is due to the fact that irrational and imaginary numbers are used only over the void (as it were) and cancel themselves out before the equation reaches its end, an end which is as real and concrete as everyday life. Mathematics is a science of pure reason, Törless surmises, and yet it is able to control and use irrationality for its own purposes. To cross the void by means of mathematics is, therefore, the honest route as opposed to the fraudulent route of character. He thus decides that if he can fully comprehend the nature of irrational numbers in mathematics, he may be able to comprehend rationally the irrational element in Basini's soul that caused him to fall into the void.

For this reason Törless makes an appointment with his mathematics teacher.

Törless is informed by his teacher that the problem of irrational numbers and their relationship to everyday life involves a controversial question: the intervention of "transcendent factors" (94) into daily existence. The teacher does not consider himself sufficiently qualified to speak on such a matter. More important, he is unwilling to discuss any subject that might lead to controversy between himself and his colleagues, particularly the school chaplain. He is only prepared to continue the discussion if Törless can agree to limit conversation solely to a consideration of the irrational element in mathematics itself. He adds, however, that Törless would really have to know at least ten times more about mathematics than he does at present in order to be able to comprehend the sophisticated mathematical arguments that such a discussion would involve. With the imposition of such a limitation, Törless, of course, immediately loses all interest in mathematics. Making an analogy to mathematics, however, the teacher suddenly begins to talk about Immanuel Kant.

The Kant Experience

In Kant's philosophy, the teacher asserts, the reader is continually encountering certain principles that are inherent in the nature of thought and yet are not rationally comprehensible. The same situation occurs in mathematics. But although we cannot comprehend the irrational fully, we nevertheless continue to incorporate and use it in our philosophical and mathematical deductions. Referring to a book by Kant that he is holding in his hand, the teacher concludes the discussion with the observation: "For the present I think it would still be a little beyond you" (95). Törless is not prepared to wait until he is older to examine Kant's work, since it is now that he desperately needs to comprehend rationally the irrational world into which he has plunged. Törless is attracted to Kant because he regards this philosopher as a supreme rationalist who nevertheless managed to include irrational

elements of life (as does mathematics) within the boundaries of his rational thought.

Törless now initiates what can only be regarded as a pathetic experiment designed to throw the brilliant light of Kant's power of reason upon the darkness of the dionysian world: with one eye literally upon the pages of Kant's work and the other eye on Basini as the representative of the dark world, he thinks he will be able to comprehend rationally the irrational world. Only in such a way, Törless believes, should one attempt to capture truth, a way in which the threatening and questionable aspects of life are never (literally) lost sight of. But when illumination fails to occur, Törless immediately loses all interest in Kant's philosophy, and his interview with the mathematics teacher merely confirms his rejection of the philosopher and his work. Since Kant's philosophy has failed the test, Törless reasons that it must be regarded as existing solely within the narrow limits of the everyday world where everything is correct and ordered but completely unimportant. And a dream provides a most striking imagistic embodiment of Törless's decidedly negative opinion: Kant appears to Törless not as a philosopher thinking about the profound problems of existence but as a caricature of a pedantic scholar who is cheerfully studying the pages of a great tome rather than the darker aspects of life. For Törless, Kant's philosophy seems to reveal merely the history of a highly developed intellect rather than the tortured (hence interesting) biography of a living, complicated, and problematic existence.

Törless believes that he has in fact managed to win a victory over Kant and his impoverished way of comprehending reality. Törless's self-congratulations reflect his belief that it is precisely because of the profundity of his own (dionysian) sensibility that he has managed to escape from the clever superficiality of all rationalists such as Kant, his own teachers, and adults in general. He asks himself whether such clever little men have ever in their lives had such experiences as he has had when people, things, and even ideas appear to fall out of the everyday world and into that Other World, producing with their fall a feeling of sexual excitement that threatens one's sanity. No, is his answer. Such people are so terrified by the prospect of complications and the problematic aspects

of life that they have had to erect a bulwark of rationality against the dark truth. Their lives are bright, cold, careful, and narrowly conscious, and thus protected from the dangers of sexuality as well as from the experience of the void above. In a word, such people hide behind character and reason.

The fifteen-year-old Törless comes to regard reason as at most a form of self-protection; it is certainly not a means of plumbing the depths of being. Reason is cowardice. Thus Törless's Kant experience serves first to reconfirm the opposition between himself and the adult world of reason, and second to extend this opposition into the realm of learning and philosophy, which he also now rejects as being superficial and uninteresting. As Törless comes to regard the world of the passions as the only reality, the everyday world of teachers, parents, and school seems to become by comparison ever more stupid, boring, and trivial.

The Failure of Reason

Why should reason be unable to comprehend and express reality? Why must the theoretical man be doomed to remain a superficial observer of life, to remain profoundly ignorant, however great his knowledge and intelligence may be? Not only does Törless make such assertions in carefully formulated reflections, but Musil himself shares Törless's belief in this instance. It is therefore necessary for a comprehension of the novel to examine the logic of Musil's indictment of reason and consciousness.

A key to the understanding of Musil's belief in the inadequacy of reason and consciousness lies in his concept of the nature of language as revealed in the motto with which he has chosen to preface *Young Törless*. The motto reads:

> We believe we have dived to the uttermost depths of the abyss, and yet when we return to the surface the drop of water on our pallid finger-tips no longer resembles the sea from which it came. We think we have discovered a hoard of wonderful treasure-trove, yet when we emerge again into the light of day we see that

all we have brought back with us is false stones and chips of glass. But for all this, the treasure goes on glimmering in the darkness, unchanged. (Maeterlinck)

For Musil, Maeterlinck's words function as a metaphor for Törless's internal world. The scene he describes illustrates Törless's divided psychological state in which, metaphorically, the surface of the water has little relationship to the bottom of the sea. Later Musil actually paraphrases the motto within the novel by defining the upper and lower levels of water in terms of the relationship (or rather lack of relationship) of reason and consciousness on the surface to emotion deep below (111).

Along with the lines from Maeterlinck quoted above, Musil also included in his motto a further thought of Maeterlinck—one that transforms the metaphor into an allegory: "In some strange way we devalue things as soon as we give utterance to them." The metaphor thus not only expresses Maeterlinck's and Musil's pessimism concerning the failure of language to give adequate expression to the reality that lies in "the uttermost depths of the abyss," it also seems to forecast that the theme of the novel to follow will involve some heroic attempt as well as an inevitable failure: Törless's unsuccessful attempt to express in language some symbolic treasure of great value that exists "in the darkness" of his soul.

The failure of language is due to the inability of consciousness to circumscribe and comprehend the emotions. Nietzsche's concept of the function of language and the nature of consciousness provides an illuminating parallel. Nietzsche regarded consciousness and language, which are directly related to each other, as social products and, for this reason, unsuitable as a means of capturing the dionysian experience of the single, unique individual.[9] Thus consciousness is not a state that "belongs" to the particular individual himself; it is rather a state of mind collectively shared and represents a connecting link between man and man; its strength depends upon the degree of its social utility. Consciousness, which has developed in direct proportion to man's need to communicate with other human beings, can register only the communal and nonindividual aspects of man, since it immediately translates all

thoughts into the perspective and language of the herd. Thus everything that finally becomes conscious and receives expression in language has been simplified, regularized, straightened, and made safe.[10] Consciousness and language can never, therefore, reflect the truth, which is complicated, irregular, and frightening. Just as Maeterlinck's "false stones and chips of glass" fail to resemble the "treasure . . . in the darkness," so do thoughts in the conscious mind fail (in Musil's opinion) to reflect the emotional realm far below.

What happens to Törless when he makes various attempts to articulate his visions of the newly discovered dark world to his teachers and his fellow students? And more important, what happens when he attempts to formulate these visions for himself in order to comprehend them? Passages of the following type occur with frequency in *Young Törless*: "But it was no use; words meant nothing, or rather, they meant something quite different . . . ." (76); "It was the failure of language that caused him such anguish, a half-awareness that words were merely accidental, mere evasions, and never the feeling itself" (79). Törless himself eventually comes to believe that there is some connection between the irrational nature of his dionysian experiences and the inability of language to articulate these experiences. He states: "the whole thing seems altogether to have had very little to do with my reason" (172). By the time his experiences are "processed" by reason and expressed in language, they have lost whatever unique and frightening elements they might once have possessed.

The difficulties that Törless encounters when he attempts to give verbal expression to his deviant experiences (i.e., to those experiences that are unintelligible in relation to society's concepts of the nature of reality) make such experiences seem equally unintelligible to himself. Thus Törless now and again thinks that he must be losing his mind. He becomes obsessed with the fact that he is not only unable to communicate the unique elements of his inner life to others but that he is equally unable to grasp them in his own thoughts. He therefore comes to the final conclusion that reason and thought are limited, unable to do more than merely lead one toward that world in which everything is ordered and calm, but

ordinary and unimportant. Törless's inability to explain to his teachers, who want a rational and coherent explanation, the nature of his strange experiences results in his being asked to leave the school. After Törless's great abortive attempt to communicate his frightening encounters with Basini, mathematics, and infinity, Musil simply writes: "He fell silent" (170).

The Experimentor as Psychologist

Having been unable to find any way to dispel his confusions, Törless decides to launch an experiment with Basini's soul as the object of his investigation. His experiment is obviously not motivated by a spirit of disinterested inquiry, for he feels himself gripped by a compulsion to stare into the darkness within himself. His "vivisection" of Basini's soul reflects his need to regain possession and thus reunite the two halves of his own soul; for it was Basini's theft that caused a division within himself between that which is irrational and that which is rational: "And what about Basini? The thought of what was happening to Basini had rent Törless in two" (77). The experiment, expressed in general terms, is primarily concerned with Törless's attempt to understand rationally—so as to be able to control and prevent—the way in which people (particularly himself) can and do fall involuntarily through a trapdoor into that Other World where Basini now seems to have taken up permanent residence.

Musil never reveals the exact details of Törless's experiment upon Basini, probably so that Basini's plight will not distract the reader and draw his attention and sympathy away from Törless's various attempts to resolve his own confusions. All the reader learns is that the three students, Törless, Reiting, and Beineberg, have apparently been sexually abusing as well as systematically beating Basini nightly in the attic room. Törless has gotten no nearer to solving his problems in this fashion than he did by reading Kant's works. Finally, Törless decides to question Basini directly in order to find out what it is like to live daily within that Other World, the world of thieves and the sexually abused. He asks

Basini what happens inside himself on occasions when he commits a theft or is abused by others. Doesn't he feel his inner self split into two halves? Törless says to him: "Yes, I'm tormenting you. But that's not what I'm after. There's just one thing I want to know: when I drive all that into you like knives, what goes on in you? What happens inside you?" (128). Törless explains to Beineberg and Reiting that he is searching "for something behind it all" (154).

Basini, of course, has not even the remotest idea of what Törless is talking about. Nothing is happening to him. Therefore, when Törless finally accepts Basini's assertion that neither the theft nor the sexual abuse caused him to fall into an Other World, his experiment with Basini suddenly seems senseless. He realizes now that all the while he has been investigating and looking for something that does not exist. Törless comes at last to realize that it is he alone who has been adding the irrational dimension to things, places, and people and he concludes that the whole problem of two worlds was an illusion. His "dark visions" do not represent a breakthrough to a truer, more fascinating, and more meaningful external reality. Reality is composed, at most, of numerous levels. One can never "get out" of the (boring) world of appearance and into another (fascinating) world beyond or beneath it. The illusion of depth injected into the flatness of life is caused solely by the strength of emotional interest directed toward appearances, which was very great in Törless's case because of his desperate state of mind. There are no dark enigmas in life, Törless concludes. Things just happen. Nothing more than that exists. He summarizes his final attitude toward life with the fundamentally nihilistic declaration: "I don't believe in anything at all" (146).

Törless nevertheless comes to the conclusion that there does exist an irrational world beneath reason. He no longer believes that it exists in the outer world as a threat, but he does recognize the presence of a world within himself that is far richer, more beautiful, and more powerful than the world of intellectual concepts. However, he remains uncertain as to how to come to terms with this insight, and Musil himself stresses simply the fact that Törless has awoken out of his nightmare.

Musil does not consider it sufficient merely to allow Törless to discover his error. He formulates a kind of psychological law for the reader's benefit to describe the dynamics of the situation which misled Törless:

> It was this mental perspective that he had experienced, which alternated according to whether he was considering what was distant or what was near-by; it was this incomprehensible relationship that according to our shifts of standpoint gives happenings and objects sudden values that are quite incommensurable with each other, strange to each other . . . (172)

Musil connects that which is distant with "the life one feels" and that which is close with "the life one lives." That is why those things that are metaphorically in the distance appear "so great and mysterious" and look like a "misty sea full of gigantic, everchanging forms" (130). But when that which was far strikes one's life and becomes experience—which means for Musil that it has metaphorically squeezed through a narrow gate and become tightly compressed so as to be able to pass into man—it suddenly shrinks and looks "clear and small, human in its dimensions and human in its outlines" (130). This law explains how Basini's theft changed him in Törless's eyes into a mysterious, fascinating, and threatening being.

While Basini has committed the theft and thus made it part of his experience, Törless sees the theft only at a distance, as it were. Even acts of sexual degradation, which Törless initiated for the purpose of observing and investigating at first hand how a person feels when he falls into the dark world, are experienced by Basini simply as events without any complications. Thus the dark and fascinating world that Törless has been investigating suddenly seems to lose all its romantic aura when it "collides with life" and becomes translated into experience and activity. According to this interpretation, Maeterlinck's "treasure," which is glimmering in the depths, has never really been anything more than "false stones and chips of glass." It looks like treasure only when viewed from the distance.

Just as Törless had rejected the floor of character as a fraudulent psychological construct even when used like a bridge to pass from the security of childhood over the perceived void to the security of adulthood on the other side, he now comes to realize that there is, in fact, no connection between the two perspectives of reason and mysticism. Expressed in terms of Maeterlinck's metaphor: man can exist either at the surface of the ocean or at the very bottom; there is (for some unexplained reason) no middle area in which one can live. Törless comes to such a conclusion after many attempts to catch and hold both of the perspectives simultaneously at the moment when one shifts to the other. But all he perceives is a "faint click in the mind" (130), followed by a sudden, spasmodic change to the other extreme. Musil believes that total incompatibility reigns between the two extremes. Törless later summarizes this conclusion as follows: "I shall probably go on forever seeing them [things, events, ideas] sometimes this way and sometimes that, sometimes with the eyes of reason, and sometimes with those other eyes. . . . And I shan't ever try again to compare one with the other . . ." (170). Between the two perspectives there can apparently exist at most only an aesthetic relationship.

The Experimentor as Metaphysician

Two other experiments, besides that of Törless, are being carried out simultaneously upon Basini, who actually even terms himself an experiment. All three experiments are concerned with the same fundamental problem: how to live in a nihilistic world, that is, a world without divinely sanctioned values and therefore a world in which man must find his own way through endless political, moral, and intellectual experiments. Reiting explores Basini's psychological reactions to his bullying in order to discover how people can be most effectively manipulated politically. As opposed to the more intellectual Törless, who is always submerged in a sea of possibilities and unable to realize any one of them in action, Reiting is nothing but a man of action. Musil does not devote much attention to Reiting's experiment, since he no doubt consid-

ered Reiting's response to life as one that was too uncomplicated to warrant fuller intellectual presentation in the novel. (The historical events in Germany in the 1930s and 1940s reveal, however, that it was precisely the Reiting mentality that came to dominate German political life and to destroy the intellectual life of the nation, forcing such novelists as Musil, Mann, and Broch to flee for their lives.)

Musil does, however, devote a great deal of attention to Beineberg, who quite consciously calls his tortures of Basini "a sort of experiment" (143). On the practical level of his experiment, Beineberg wants to induce in Basini a semimystical trance. If one can succeed in killing the desires of the body, in stripping away the mere physical semblance of the flesh, then one will be able to have direct intercourse with the soul. By inducing a trance, Beineberg hopes to observe how Basini will enter into that higher spiritual realm described in the books of Indian ascetics. In such a condition, the souls of Basini and Beineberg will be able to have intercourse with each other (125), an idea that foreshadows the relationship between Veronica and Johannes in "The Temptation of Quiet Veronica."

Beineberg alone of the students and teachers at the military academy has some intellectual comprehension of the general nature of Törless's nihilistic view of reality, that is to say, a reality without psychological or metaphysical absolutes. His experiment, too, is concerned with a comprehension of the void. Like Törless, he also uses such terms to describe this void as "black hole," "nothingness," and "the fathomless abyss that we fall into" (149). And, like Törless, Beineberg also recognizes the inadequacy of reason to comprehend experiences of the void. An illuminating parallel to Törless's and Beineberg's experience of the void can be found in the work of Blaise Pascal (1623-1660), considered by many to have been the first existentialist. Pascal perceived man as existing in a "middle station" suspended between a void above and a void below. Man floats along. Nothing stands still for him. In his "pensée number 199," Pascal wrote: "We burn with desire to find a firm footing, an ultimate, lasting base on which to build a tower rising up to infinity, but our whole foundation cracks and the earth opens

up into the depths of the abyss."[11] This prospect filled Pascal, as it does Törless, with terror: "The eternal silence of these infinite spaces fills me with dread."[12] For Pascal, reason could not solve this problem; only the Christian's faith in the reality of Christ was able to save man from being driven to despair in such a universe.

On this point, Beineberg stands philosophically quite close to the ideas of Pascal. For, in Beineberg's view, man is protected from despair through his intuition of a metaphysical entity which he calls the world-soul ("Weltseele"). This world-soul functions for Beineberg as the metaphysical equivalent of what has here been termed the "floor" of character. As opposed to Törless, Beineberg does believe in character. For him, the strength of a man's character is directly related to the strength of his belief in the idea of a world-soul. Since the world-soul is a metaphysical concept, Beineberg's view is reminiscent of Musil's assertion that there is a direct and necessary connection between man's belief in God and the existence of character. According to Beineberg, if a boy like Törless loses his connection with a metaphysical entity such as the world-soul, "he loses himself" and becomes "an empty form" (68). But for Törless such an explanation is sheer nonsense.

Törless rejects a metaphysical interpretation of reality for the second time during an interview with his exasperated teachers, an interview that leads directly to his dismissal from school. The divinity teacher and the school director, vainly attempting to comprehend Törless's confused explanations of his fall into the void, suggest that perhaps Törless has simply experienced the profound insight that reason has its limits. They further suggest that Törless's new understanding of reality seems to justify the final necessity of man's irrational acceptance of the supernatural, a fundamental idea in Christianity. But to the director's question: "Have you an inclination to look behind events or things . . . seeking the religious background?" (167), Törless responds in a decidedly negative manner.

The difference in the interpretation of reality that arises between Beineberg, as an embryonic metaphysician with his concept of the world-soul, and Törless, as an embryonic psychologist with his exploration of Basini's psyche, may be expressed in another

fashion. Although Beineberg and Törless are both concerned with
the irrational, Beineberg feels that it is necessary to call upon a
supernatural construct (the world-soul), whereas Törless feels that
an explanation must lie within the realm of that which is natural.
As Törless tells Beineberg: "I'm looking for something quite different behind it from what you are looking for. What I'm after isn't
anything supernatural at all. It's precisely the natural—don't you
see? nothing outside of myself at all—it's something in me I'm
looking for! something natural, but, all the same, something I
don't understand!" (102-3). From Törless's point of view, Beineberg's mysticism as well as the divinity teacher's Christianity seek
for a "something" that is both irrational and supernatural, whereas
he himself is searching for a "something" that is quite natural,
however irrational it may also seem to the mind of man.

The psychological approach to the problem of the irrational
in life, which is expressed in Törless's probing of Basini's feelings
when falling into the Other World, at least achieves the result of
destroying man's illusions about himself and his world. Basini's
answers reveal that Törless's concept of the trapdoor into chaos
was false. On the other hand, the metaphysical approach will never
lead to results that can be disentangled from falsehood, for such
metaphysical concepts as Beineberg's world-soul will always remain beyond examination. From the point of view of Beineberg's
experiment, therefore, the negative conclusion of Törless's experiment represents a positive achievement, for it brings him back to
reality.

Living or Perspectives on Living

Throughout the novel, Törless has been presented as the perspectivist in embryo, i.e., as an individual who regards every aspect
of life from numerous intellectual points of view: "For Törless's
mind was the most subtle. Once he was set on a trail, he was
extremely ingenious in thinking out the most abstruse combina-
tions. Nor was anyone else so exact as he in foreseeing the various
possible reactions to be expected of a person in a given situation"

(49). Even Beineberg is quite conscious of this special talent that Törless possesses, and he cautions him to stop forever playing with the mind in such a fashion. Looking at every event from several points of view is, for Beineberg, nothing more than mental gymnastics that can never lead to anything concrete.

Musil suggests the antithetical relationship existing between Törless's perspectivism, on the one hand, and the realization in action of any one possibility, on the other, as follows: "Only when it was a matter of reaching a decision, of accepting one of these psychological possibilities as the definite probability and taking the risk of acting on it, did he fail, losing both interest and energy" (49). The perspectivist ignores actual life either because he finds himself unable to choose one out of many possibilities to realize or because he loses all interest whenever the nonintellectual aspects of daily living must be considered.

It is Basini's seduction of Törless that destroys Törless's experiment. Törless tells Basini: "Whatever else I wanted from you before, I've forgotten since you got in the way of it with your lecherous desires. I wanted to find a point remote from you, to look at you from there. That was my interest in you. You destroyed it yourself" (158). This opposition between perspectivism and experience is also strikingly revealed within Törless himself when it seems likely that, instead of being able to carry out his experimental observations on Basini from a safe and aloof point, he will himself become the object of Reiting's and Beineberg's sadistic experiments. Törless then thinks: "Here was no more idle drifting along, no more toying with enigmatic visions—this had hard corners and was tangible reality" (123). The threat of life breaking sensually in upon him either in the form of sexual experience or physical pain destroys Törless's perspectivism.

Musil has thus provided in *Young Törless* the rationale for the perspectivist's active exclusion of the dionysian aspects of life, which is tantamount to the excluding of life itself. It should be emphasized that Törless affirms sensuality only when it remains in the realm of the imagination. In reality, sensuality is felt to be a danger. This interpretation proves to be of decisive importance for Ulrich's first and second experiments in *The Man without Quali-*

ties, for both of his experiments attempt to exclude the influence of sexuality and living in the everyday world.

The Morality of Self-Growth

Young Törless is not simply an objective case study of an adolescent's psychological crisis in which, disoriented by extreme confusion, he became a sadist, although perhaps out of the highest motives. It is clear that Musil believed Törless's torture of his fellow student to have been justified on intellectual and moral grounds. Looking back at the Basini episode at school, Törless admits many years later that it may well have been a degrading affair but it was nevertheless one which could be justified by the fact that it eventually led him to a higher form of self-awareness. He became, Musil wrote, a man "whose mind was both subtle and sensitive" (137). Even though Törless later comes to view these few weeks in his own adolescence as a form of illness, this fact does not necessarily imply for Musil a criticism of Törless's behaviour toward Basini. For Musil, health and illness are concepts relative to the particular individual: some individuals may require illness in order to grow. Before a negative moral judgment can be made concerning such illness, it is first necessary to learn something of the individual's spiritual horizons, intellectual powers, and emotional needs, as well as of those ideas that motivate his actions.

Musil's justification of Törless's behavior is based upon a Nietzschean morality. An individual's cruelty toward a weaker human being is acceptable to Nietzsche when it is merely an ancillary result of his striving for greater clarity and knowledge. Because such Faustian striving justifies any means an individual may use to achieve enlightenment and growth, Nietzsche's morality does in certain circumstances also sanction the decadence of the striver. If an individual's decadent condition does not go beyond the mere generation of thoughtless acts of cruelty, then it is a decadence that remains negative and uncreative (as were Beineberg's and Reiting's experiments.) But if an individual's decadent condition forces him to summon all his emotional and intellectual energies to over-

come this condition, then it is positive, since it leads the individual to a higher state of health.

Törless had fallen into a decadent state as defined by Nietzsche. He had become confused, uncertain, emotionally exhausted, and unable to control his mental and emotional processes. Musil nevertheless affirms Törless's state because, like Nietzsche, he stresses the courage and intellectual honesty of the striver rather than the suffering of the inadvertent victim. In fact, the reason that Nietzsche's definition of decadence is so vague and often even contradictory is that Nietzsche cares nothing about the state of decadence in and of itself. The only question he asks concerns the "rank" or "nobility" of the individual experiencing it. From this point of view, the only relevant question becomes: is Törless able to overcome, or does he fall victim to, his confusion, uncertainty, despair, etc.—all of which were caused by his agonizing vision of the void within himself? Does the truth shatter him or does it force him to strip away illusion and to search for a truer and stronger vision of reality.

Törless becomes an example of an individual who possesses what Nietzsche called "the great health," since he was able to give himself over to decadence for a time and yet emerge from it in a state of even greater spiritual health. Musil regards Törless's illness as that force that moved him beyond a crude, immature selfhood and into a more fully human condition where growth represents victory over inner struggle and confusion. Törless's health presents a contrast to the untested healthiness of the lower animals and even to that of his teachers. The teachers are decadent in a totally negative sense: they have achieved their apparent health (a feeling of order, stability, and self-confidence) only by denying, rather than including and transcending, the hard, gruesome, evil, and problematic aspects of existence.

At the end of *Young Törless*, however, the reader may well ask himself what effect this episode has had upon Basini's soul. But Musil does not comment upon this point. Even the adult Törless apparently finds it irrelevant to consider the question of whether it is permissible to cause perhaps permanent psychological damage to someone else. Evidently, the individual's search for self-knowl-

edge and spiritual growth carries its own justification. Like Ulrich in *The Man without Qualities*, who respects people only when he respects the power of their ideas (which is rare), Törless apparently believes that Basini is not worthy of humane treatment, for Basini lacks the will to use and therefore to overcome his own decadence. Decadence had, as it were, not made Basini into a human being; it had prevented him from passing beyond—or had even reduced him to—the state of a lower animal. But in Törless's case "the poison" generated by the episode acted like "that small admixture of a toxic substance which is needed to rid the soul of its over-confident, complacent healthiness, and to give it instead a sort of health that is more acute, subtler, and wiser" (138). Basini was simply poisoned.

The conflict between a morality of self-growth as opposed to that of Christian compassion receives forceful expression in Törless's inhuman behavior toward Basini. The most striking feature of Törless's experiment with Basini is its total lack of pity. Törless's experiment, designed to yield knowledge of himself, reveals Musil's agreement with Nietzsche's morality of the "free spirit," in which Christianity, as a religion of pity, represents a position directly opposed to that of knowledge and truth.[13] For the sake of knowledge (Musil implies) the morality of self-enrichment must stand beyond the Christian values of compassion and pity. Nietzsche believed that the "free spirit" is under no obligation to treat his neighbor better than himself. Since he would sacrifice himself in the search for knowledge, he also has the right to sacrifice his neighbor. Törless feels that his self-growth alone "made up for all that had happened"; "Törless felt no remorse for what he had done" (162). Thus when Törless does stop torturing Basini, it is not because he has belatedly been overwhelmed by a sense of compassion and regret. At this point he says to Beineberg and Reiting: "You two make me sick! Your beastliness is utterly senseless! That's what's so revolting about you" (157). Törless stops only when he realizes that his experiment is senseless because it can never yield any true knowledge.

Musil seems to accept here the essentially Nietzschean position that the roots of knowledge are often to be found in evil, as

defined from the Christian point of view. He who investigates must therefore accept the fact that he will be regarded as immoral. The greatest man will always be the one richest in cruelty and evil, for the devil is the oldest friend of knowledge. Since evil means growth, man must grow ever more evil. It is because Musil accepted (apparently without reservation) these Nietzschean ideas that Törless feels no guilt: spiritual and intellectual growth is an absolute good, while the Christian concepts of compassion and love for one's neighbor are trivial concerns for trivial minds.

Rejuvenation and Challenge

At the end of the novel, Törless experiences a spiritual and emotional rejuvenation which he observes (as is his nature) with a certain amount of objective and analytical curiosity. He feels as if he has awakened after a long illness; the suffering, the despair, and the confusion have passed, leaving him in a state of coolness and indifference toward the world. For his teachers, who were unable to comprehend the nature and positive value of his illness, he feels only contempt. (They had dismissed his problem with the comment that he was obviously suffering from a pathological tendency toward hysteria.) Musil himself suggests that Törless's overcoming of his illness is natural, as natural as the growth of a tree; and a tree can grow great and strong only if it has first been subjected to bad weather and violent storms. Törless feels he has now passed through a violent but necessary stage in his development: "One phase of the development was at an end; the soul had formed another annual ring, as a young tree does" (162). He also feels as if his soul were rich black earth beneath which he can already detect the stirrings of seeds about to sprout. Törless thinks of himself as a gardener who must water his flower beds every morning and tend his plants with steady, patient kindness. Musil's use here of the tree and gardener images reveals his own belief that Törless's illness and behavior to Basini were productive and therefore justifiable.

If an "increase in soul" is one highly positive result of Törless's self-healing, there is yet another result, one that suggests a

higher state of consciousness rather than the health of natural growths such as trees or plants. It is a condition associated only with the individual whose maturity represents not merely a victory over self-confusions and worldly illusions but also the final destruction of all comforting fictions. Törless is left with an attitude of pessimism toward human life. He feels a faint, brooding lassitude and a total skepticism. For although he now realizes that there is no dark and threatening world out there beyond himself, he has learned of the precarious instability of the human condition: "that there were fine and easily effaced boundary-lines around each human being, that feverish dreams prowled around the soul, gnawing at the solid walls and tearing open weird alleys—and this memory had sunk deep in him, sending out its wan and shadowy beams" (173). Thus Törless's overcoming of his youthful period of decadence also brings with it the unpleasant and disturbing effect of forever undermining whatever childlike feelings of security he may once have possessed toward life and the world. Because Adam ate from the Tree of Knowledge in the Garden of Eden, he was expelled; and the way back to the other tree in the Garden, the Tree of Life, was barred by a cherub with a flaming sword. Törless, like Adam, has eaten of the Tree of Knowledge, with similar results. He now finds the whole world lying before him, but it is a world in which he must create for himself the right way of living, must discover his own Tree of Life. Life now appears as a challenge, as a problem for which there is no given solution.

III 🎵

The Return of the Repressed: "The Perfecting of a Love" and "The Temptation of Quiet Veronica"

MUSIL HAD EXPECTED to finish the two short stories of *Unions* within a matter of a few weeks. Instead, "The Perfecting of a Love" and "The Temptation of Quiet Veronica" required (as he later wrote) two and a half years of desperate work, almost day and night. He felt that he had nearly destroyed himself emotionally in their creation.[1] Thomas Mann had also at first imagined that *The Magic Mountain* and *Joseph and His Brothers* could be completed within a short period of time. But whereas Mann steadily increased the length of these two novels over the years, Musil continually rewrote what he had already written, making *Unions* denser rather than longer. As a result of this manner of writing, the two stories have a complexity and opaqueness that make them among the most difficult works in modern literature. But, writing in 1940, Musil noted that of all his works, *Unions* (published in 1911) was the only one that he was now and again able to reread.[2]

The style of *Unions* is characterized by an almost impenetrable surface of images and metaphors, directly beneath which teems a world of chaotic emotions. In a quite conscious virtuoso performance, Musil has managed to exclude plot, the physical world, and omniscient intellectual analysis to a greater degree than in any of his other works. In place of a narrative stream of events, he presents a stream of emotions. His aesthetic principle was (as he noted) to achieve a maximal loading of the smallest steps.[3] Musil's loading of metaphors, which describe the most minute sensations and feelings, becomes so dense that the passage of time often seems to come to a complete halt. Musil himself wondered whether *Unions*

could actually be called a book. In fact, he stated that the problem with *Unions* lay in its trying to be a book at all, in having covers, a spine, pages.[4] These stories seem to be constantly striving to take refuge in a world of emotions, to escape not only from the external world of events and from the rational intellect but also from discursive language itself.

"The Perfecting of a Love"

In "The Perfecting of a Love," published five years after *Young Törless*, Musil once again took up the theme of dionysian mysticism or, to be more precise, the relationship between dionysian mysticism, which is characterized by sheer motor activity, and nondionysian mysticism or "contemplatio," [5] in which the individual achieves a condition of pure stasis, a feeling of being one with all that exists. But the narrative perspective has shifted from that of an adolescent boy at school to that of a mother, Claudine, who is taking a train trip alone to visit her child at boarding school. As Törless dropped through a trapdoor after being separated from his bourgeois parents, Claudine begins to lose her balance in a similar fashion shortly after leaving her bourgeois husband in order to undertake a journey by herself. Törless fell into a void that he had never experienced before. Claudine, however, falls into a void which she believed she had overcome and disposed of once and for all in an earlier period of her life. She now experiences a sudden and unexpected attack from the past upon her present tranquil and contented married state.

Marriage as Aesthetic Perfection

In the first scenes of both *Young Törless* and "The Perfecting of a Love," Musil introduces, as an initial point of reference for his reader, prototypical representatives of the bourgeois world; respec-

tively, Törless's parents and Claudine's second husband. Both works describe a departure from a circumscribed world of stability, security, reason, and control, which is followed by a half-resisted, half-yearned-for journey into the vast and undefinable realm of dionysian mysticism.

"The Perfecting of a Love" begins with Claudine and her husband sitting in their living room drinking tea. Musil's description of this scene suggests an impressionistic painting, a still life of fruits and flowers or lifeless puppets rather than of two human beings. With immobile faces and unmoving eyes, the couple is pictured sitting rigidly upright as if laced stiffly into thick gold brocade. Time itself appears to have come to a halt in this room; everything seems to be holding its breath, to be pausing and standing silent and rigid in a cool atmosphere of glittering colors. The scene evokes an eighteenth-century sense of beauty, with balance, symmetry, and tranquility. But this beauty and perfection is lifeless and intimates that the relationship between Claudine and her husband is too precious and delicate to exist anywhere except in its own vacuum, removed from the stresses of everyday life.

Husband and wife are variously described as two tightrope acrobats mutually lending support to one another or as sitting together inside a transparent crystal sphere. They feel nearly "exhausted by the weight of their happiness,"[6] for their marriage seems to be the kind of exquisite relationship that can exist only between two highly intelligent, refined, and civilized human beings, such as they no doubt consider themselves to be. They are positively languid in the bliss of their apollonian tranquility.

But Musil also describes the relationship between Claudine and her husband as "painfully morbid" (18) because of the extreme degree of sensitivity that each partner possesses with regard to the slightest symptom of psychological instability in the other. Moreover, something indefinable and barely perceptible, something like a faint and distant crackling of tensions deep within both Claudine and her husband seems continually to be stirring to life, only to become dormant again. Although together they had always felt a sense of solitude vis-à-vis the outer world, each of them now begins to perceive a further and separate solitude within himself.

Claudine, who has not been away from her husband even for one day since their marriage, is about to leave him the next morning for a short trip. Deprived of his constant support, she is destined to lose her balance and fall from the tightrope of their marriage. The crackling of tensions and feelings of solitude within will suddenly increase, shattering the beautiful crystal sphere of their perfect relationship.

Claudine's daughter Lilli, whom she is about to visit at boarding school, represents the link that connects Claudine's tranquil present with her past, a past marked by sexual promiscuity. Lilli is the daughter of a dentist, whom Claudine visited for treatment while on vacation some fifteen years before. At that time, she had still been married to her first husband but was vacationing without him and expecting the imminent but always delayed arrival of her lover at the resort. It was in a state of impatience and exasperation, and after days of watching the dentist's face hovering above her, that she allowed herself to be seduced. Such brief sexual encounters often occurred in what Musil terms "that first, wasted part of her life" (19). Ever since Claudine acquired her second and present husband, however, her dissolute earlier life has been buried under the heavy edifice of their bourgeois marriage. She has never been unfaithful to her second husband, nor has she wished to be. Their marriage seemed the perfect union.

An Inexplicable Obsession

The past begins to intrude surreptitiously upon Claudine's present life even before she embarks on her trip. In the midst of the serenity and petrified happiness of the tea drinking scene, Claudine inexplicably begins to talk about something ugly, violent, and horrifying. With a certain compulsive interest, she mentions the case of a psychotic murderer and sexual pervert named G., who appears in a novel that she and her husband have recently been reading. The strange and twisted inner life of the murderer seems to exercise an unusually strong grip upon the imagination of this bourgeois hausfrau. G. is described metaphorically (by Claudine)

as a wanderer walking through himself again and again as if through a dark and deserted house, groping for an open door. He lives alone in a cold and vast solitude, in an atmosphere pervaded by melancholy and mournfulness. Looking through murky window panes, he seems to gaze out of a void at his victims from a long way off; his face hovers over them as they bleed to death. Through the commission of his sexual murders, G. enters Claudine's imagination as some alien beast who seems to float off into the void, borne aloft by "the mystery of its solitude" (16).

Claudine wonders whether G. knows he is doing wrong. According to Claudine's interpretation, G. probably simply stares in fascination "at the little scrap of eroticism that faintly flickers in him like summer lightning" (15). He believes that "his actions are good" (15), for within himself all his violent external actions are transformed into a "gentle music" (16), a music that cannot be heard. Heaven sends such things, Claudine decides, and there is simply no comprehending why. In the very intensity of his feelings lies all the justification necessary for the destruction he wreaks. Questions of everyday morality are irrelevant in evaluating actions arising from an inner world of dionysian feelings. With this analysis, Claudine has justified in advance her coming adultery with a stranger whom she will meet on her forthcoming visit to her daughter.

The immediate reason for Claudine's obsession with G. becomes apparent during her tea-time conversation with her husband. Apparently, the thought of G. had first overtaken Claudine with overpowering intensity several nights earlier while she was making love with her husband. G. had usurped her husband's place in her mind and she had been unable to drive him out. With the intrusion of G. into her thoughts that evening, Claudine seemed all at once to have gained a double perspective on her life: in addition to the usual perspective of wife and mother, she perceived her life as if "with an alien gaze" (17). For the first time the thought occurred to her that perhaps she could live without her husband. Claudine was overcome with fear and ambivalence when she glimpsed her life through this other perspective: she attempted to pull her husband back into her thoughts but also to push him

away again. It was in bed a few nights before the story began, therefore, that the crystal of an apparently perfect second marriage had suffered its first crack and that Claudine had begun to lose her equilibrium on the tightrope of her marriage.

Departure from the Present

Claudine sets off by train and travels through a brilliant wintry countryside which, as she notices, is beginning to melt, to loosen up, and to yield under the impact of spring. When she attempts to think back to her husband, all she is able to call to mind is the notion of a dark room where all the windows have been locked. She then experiences a feeling that somewhere within herself a door has been flung open, allowing a convalescent to take her first steps out of doors. Filled with a vague intuition that something is about to burst forth, that everything tight and narrow is opening out into the four quarters of the sky, Claudine perceives within herself the presence of a yearning for some extreme tension, for an ultimate climax. She feels as if she is leaning into a void. From a psychological perspective, it can be said that some undefinable part of Claudine's present emotional life is "leaning back" into her past. She knows that something which is about to happen to her will merely be a repetition of something she had already experienced at some period in her long-forgotten earlier life. But at this point in her journey, Claudine is as yet unable to understand these peculiar sensations or give them any concrete substance.

When Claudine arrives in the town in which her daughter's school is located, a sense of her earlier life becomes overwhelming, for it seems to her that there is in this town "a queer atmosphere of the past, pervading everything" (39). It is as if while traveling physically forward to this town, Claudine's emotional life has been traveling backwards, eventually to arrive at an earlier point in her life. Or, it is as if her past, which has recently awakened under the influence of G., has come to meet her in the present as she steps from the train. She feels overwhelmed by a sense of destiny: "all at once her past seemed the imperfect expression of something that

was yet to come" (28). Claudine realizes with a shock that she is going to have an affair with some stranger, with any stranger. A "stray particle of a love" long suppressed by marriage has now irresistably torn itself loose from an emotional world far below and started off "in quest of its own perfection" (38).

Claudine experiences this newly discovered "landscape of her life," this "sunken realm" from which this particle comes, in terms of a series of metaphors similar to those used by Musil in *Young Törless* for the same purpose, namely, to describe the void within. She feels herself "bending over the brink" (54) and about to plunge into "the blind vastness of empty space" (29). Her soul is groping "for the sake of greater truthfulness, into the void" (59). She associates this Other World with a "ravening, devouring, annihilating force"(52). As Törless used the metaphor of a trapdoor to the dionysian realm, Claudine conceives of the entrance to this realm as "a dark tunnel" (24), "a passage leading underground" (32). Claudine experiences the long sleighride from the train station to her hotel in the town as a journey down a long "dark corridor" (31).

The Double Perspective

The same dialectical vision that informs *Young Törless* is present in "The Perfecting of a Love." The life Claudine had been leading before her trip represents one extreme pole. She had been a captive of routine and convention, chained for years to one place, one city, one house, one man, one sense of herself. Her daily life had been like something hard and bony: every action had been tightly linked to the next, every word related only to the one before and the one after. All aspects of her existence had been designed to form a chain of events without lacuna that had restricted her but had also served to protect her. Her marriage was like a line she had scratched in the ground, an unbroken line that helped her keep her equilibrium in the midst of a silent chaos that she vaguely sensed lying just beyond daily existence, a chaos that was always threatening to fragment and disintegrate her life.

But what if one day the words or the actions should fail to link

up? Then one would be in danger of being swallowed up by the void. Gaps and cracks would then begin to appear with ever greater frequency in the surface of reality. One might gain a glimpse of a realm far below where "one's solitary self floats along in a stream of unborn realities" (46). Perhaps, Claudine thinks, she should just let herself go and "sink back into the drift of things, into the realm of unfulfilled possibilities" (58).

Musil introduces into this story, as he did in *Young Törless,* the theory of perspectivism in order to express metaphorically the existence of the other pole of the dialectical vision. One can step from the world of reason into "something that is beyond reason, an independent, incomprehensible world of feeling"(50). There is merely a line, a frontier that has to be crossed. If the individual then regards his rational life from the perspective of the other side (with the eyes of the soul, as Törless describes such an experience), he will perceive his daily life in an oddly reversed state of mind. His everyday routine existence will appear as if enclosed in a strange atmosphere and everything that was once familiar will seem totally alien. Now living on this other side, Claudine looks back over the "frontier" at the memory of her husband and her marriage. They look faded and without life, as if existing at a great distance from herself.

Musil describes the little town in such a way that it functions as a geographical metaphor for the Other Realm that lies beyond the frontier of everyday life. The whole town seems to Claudine to be silent, desolate, and empty, as if surrounded by an "utter void"(49). Because of a snow storm, communications with the outer world have broken down and Claudine is unable to write her husband as she had planned. From the point of view of the metaphor of the two worlds, her words are no longer able to cross the frontier, to penetrate into the outer world. Having an affair with a stranger in this town, in this "utter void," could not be considered an act of infidelity against her husband, she decides. Whatever happens here has no relationship whatsoever to the deeper levels of her personal life with her husband. On this other side of the frontier, she and any stranger would exist in a "second life, remote intangible, imaginary" (38) where everything personal is stripped

away. Here one is relieved of the pressure of personality and, therefore, of any feelings of personal guilt. For this is also the realm of the murderer G., where anything and everything that the individual may do is innocent.

The Stranger from the Other Realm

Claudine does meet a stranger who is also staying at her hotel. Anonymous though he may be, she knows that he will be the one who will facilitate the perfection of her love. It is necessary that this man remain a nobody, an anybody, that he not acquire in Claudine's eyes the definite form of a particular personality with a particular history. Indeed, she conceives of her impending affair with the stranger as a union with an animal: "Sodomy, she thought. That is what it would amount to" (46). When this "nobody" looks at her, his gaze seems to be peering out at her from another world. It is with this kind of gaze, she feels, that animals regard human beings, for animals exist totally within that realm beyond the frontiers of personality and rationality. Claudine now seems to understand the way that animals love. And in her sexual fantasies, which are not unlike those of Törless, she imagines herself as an animal being hunted down in the forest, as being caged and beaten, as suffering the most extreme humiliation and degradation.

Although Claudine had already experienced the most violent sexual degradation prior to her second marriage, she had never felt that anything intense or important had happened to her. Deep within Claudine, in an area that no sexual experience could touch, there always continued to exist some "hidden quintessence," an "ultimate integrity" (19) that gave this woman a sense of invulnerability and freedom. She associates this realm with the "soul that stands quietly, unmoved, beside the ravaged body even when it is broken open and disfigured by the infliction of devastating injuries—that stands beside it, in grave and constant awareness and yet averted from it, as beside the body of a stricken beast" (61). The soul is the calm center of her being that remains forever de-

tached, unable to lose itself in any action. This realm she shares with no one but her husband: "That was the inward communion; and what she was about to abandon to this stranger, for him to ravage, was only the surface of her being" (48).

Frustration and Perfection

Two evenings before her departure from home, Claudine, waiting for the stranger's arrival, sits for hours in a small and dark hotel room, which in its claustrophobic atmosphere is strongly reminiscent of the attic room in *Young Törless*. Until this point in their relationship, Claudine and the stranger have exchanged only a few desultory words of conversation. But Claudine has a strong intuition that this man will finally come to her this evening. Carried forward though she is by the pitch of great excitement, Claudine suddenly comes to the peculiar realization that what she is now experiencing is "no longer a sexual desire" (60). This insight is followed by Claudine's rather strange thought that if she gives herself to the stranger, her husband will also be sharing in this act of infidelity: "It is you who do whatever I am doing. . . . We are casting away everything that can be cast away, to hold on to each other all the more tightly, to wrap around us closely what no one can touch" (63). If the "particle of love" within Claudine is able to attain its perfection in her union with the stranger, she feels that the love existing between herself and her husband will become perfect too. To the stranger she will be yielding only her body, and then only in order to achieve a more complete relationship with her husband in a realm far beyond sexuality.

But the stranger does not arrive. Instead, Claudine's love achieves the perfection it has been seeking as she eventually falls asleep quite alone: "on the threshold of dream there was perfection, a great and pure love mantling her in a trembling light" (63). It is as if that "particle of love," which had recently awoken and begun its journey toward perfection, could only achieve final perfection if it were not caught, held fast and dissipated at the final moment by sexual union. Without the stranger's inhibiting phys-

ical presence, therefore, love was able to pass beyond the physical world of the body and into that realm of "ultimate integrity" that lies beneath all sensual experience.

The concept of love that Musil first presents in "The Perfecting of a Love" receives a more complete but also more complex treatment in "The Temptation of Quiet Veronica," the second story in *Unions*. A cursory glance at Rainer Maria Rilke's concept of "great lovers" will help to make Musil's ideas on this subject seem somewhat less obscure. Some of Musil's themes and motifs, such as Claudine's experience of the perfection of love, which was unexpectedly achieved precisely because of the absence of the stranger, and Veronica's conscious rejection of Demeter and Johannes in order to cultivate a state of purest feeling within herself, are ones that Rilke understood and described in his work.

Rilke's prime example of great lovers—a subject he treated in his prose narrative *The Notebooks of Malte Laurids Brigge* (1910) and in *The First Elegy* (1912) of his cycle *Duino Elegies*—are Gaspara Stampa (1523-1554), a noble Italian lady, and Marianna Alcoforado (1640-1723), a Portuguese nun. In the lives of Gaspara Stampa and Marianna Alcoforado, love achieved completion, was "perfected."[7] But the women had to perform the whole task of love themselves. Their male partners, who were bunglers in the fine art of love, eventually became superfluous to its perfection. Rilke (in a letter of 1912) conferred "the Diploma of Proficiency in Love" upon these two women, and asserted that men's knowledge in this area did not pass beyond "an elementary Grammar." Love in the male consumes itself in sexual passion and leaves nothing behind. But because Gaspara and Marianna were deserted by their respective lovers, the intense feelings of these women were able to continue to develop until they finally "outgrew" their particular partners as well as the whole terrestrial world. In this way, their love made a leap into infinity and began a journey toward God. Such love is comparable to a leap into sainthood, Rilke wrote.[8] In the depths of her being, Marianna became like an angel. She was able to turn her outwardly directed feelings back in upon herself and become totally self-sufficient. For Rilke, Marianne becomes the symbol of narcissism perfected. To use Musil's metaphor, these

two women passed beyond dionysian experience and into a state of "contemplatio," a realm of nondionysian mysticism far below or beyond all wordly experience.

The Return from the Void

When Claudine awakens the next morning, she no longer desires the stranger. She has, as it were, already begun her return to daily life from her perfect moment of "contemplatio" and is planning to leave for home and husband on the following day. But now, on her last evening in the hotel, the stranger does come to her room. As Törless attempted to explain the nature of his strange double perception of reality to the assembled company of teachers, so Claudine describes to the stranger how she is able to slip back and forth between two worlds and how strangely transformed each world looks from the perspective of the other. But from his perspective in the everyday world, Claudine's incomprehensible words seem to be no more than the silly chatter of a slightly hysterical woman. Inflated with masculine egoism and pride because he has conquered this unknown woman, the stranger insists that the situation is quite simple: Claudine was attracted to him. Although he admits that he may not be a unique personality, a great artist or a profound philosopher, he can boast of being "a whole man" (66). The stranger's attempts to make himself special in order to explain his irresistible attractiveness are particularly ironic from Claudine's point of view. For as a particular man with a particular history, the stranger could not have conquered her. Claudine surrenders to him only because in her eyes he is no more than an animal.

Having achieved the perfection of love alone the night before, Claudine's infidelity with the stranger on her last evening in town assumes the proportions of nothing more than an ordinary, temporary affair without any deeper meaning or implications. At first she insists that he leave her room. But finally Claudine yields, for she feels that she is giving merely her body to the stranger and, furthermore, not to a particular person but to all men everywhere. He still

remains for her no more than an animal. As she feels her body "swelling up with lust" (67), she retains the strong conviction that at the deepest level of her being she belongs only to her husband. Hence Claudine will now be able to return to her husband and assume a more perfect relationship with him in which the feelings of anxiety and vague discontent so evident in the tea-drinking scene will have been overcome. She has become one with her deepest self; she has achieved the perfect union within. Unlike Musil's typical masculine protagonist, she has not been striving for an ultimate synthesis between reason and emotion, science and mysticism, the masculine and the feminine. She sought, rather, to achieve a state of pure feeling in a realm that excludes alternatives and that, therefore, obviates the individual's need to reconcile and synthesize dialectical perspectives.

Claudine may soon forget her moment of mystical perfection, as Hans Castorp in *The Magic Mountain* quickly forgot the epiphany he experienced in the chapter entitled "Snow." But her feeling of wholeness and unity, the radiance cast from this single moment in eternity, will no doubt continue to exert a strengthening influence upon her everyday life at home.

"The Temptation of Quiet Veronica"

Veronica and Johannes, the two major characters in the second story of *Unions*, once happen to meet at the foot of a staircase during one of their apparently perpetual and aimless wanderings through a dark house. Silently standing there and regarding each other in the twilight, these two figures (Musil remarks) seem to be "no more than a delirious fantasy in a sick person's brain."[9] On first reading, "The Temptation of Quiet Veronica" may well also strike the reader as nothing more than a delirious and quite incomprehensible fantasy in the mind of Robert Musil, and therefore not worth the intensive examination that this work requires in order for it to become even moderately comprehensible. Of all of Musil's

fiction, this story has received the least critical attention. Indeed, critics have positively shunned this work—and for reasons that are readily apparent.

The Stylistic and Thematic Barrier

Because the conversations of the major characters are highly elliptical, they seem at first only to deepen the obscurity of the work rather than to shed any illumination. Even when Veronica and Johannes attempt to explain themselves to each other during their infrequent conversations, the reader is left only with the impression that he has haphazardly overheard bits and pieces of two ever continuing and never fully expressed monologues that exist far removed from daily reality and from patterns of thought and feeling that can be articulated in language. These two protagonists often use rather bizarre metaphors, for nothing less is adequate to express the bizarre feelings that characterize their emotional lives. Not only do Veronica and Johannes have difficulty in comprehending what the other is trying to say, but they often seem unable to understand the meaning of their own words and metaphors. No wonder, then, that their conversations often appear to the reader to verge on the nonsensical, sometimes sounding like the disconnected ravings of mental patients.

Musil makes no great effort to mediate between the esoteric experience and language of his characters and the plight of his sorely pressed reader. He merely presents his characters' obscure conversations as a part of the narrative, which itself is constructed of a series of metaphors just as bizarre and private as those used by Veronica and Johannes themselves. After the characters have given up their always inadequate attempts to render into language at least a partially rational account of their emotions and have plunged back into their own inner worlds, Musil's style as narrator descends (as it were) with his characters and follows along at the level of the protagonists' submerged irrational lives. In its consequent opaqueness and absence of apparent logical progression from event to event, or even from thought to thought, "The Temp-

tation of Quiet Veronica" must be ranked in difficulty not far behind Joyce's *Finnegan's Wake*. In both works, the authors demonstrate little concern with the task of building a bridge from the world of their characters' unconscious to the rational processes of the reader's mind. Musil and Joyce attempt to work as far as possible within the terms of a world of experience existing outside of reason and everyday reality. Joyce's solution to the problem of rendering the workings of the unconscious in its own terms is, however, even more radical than that of Musil. The prose of *Finnegan's Wake* is not merely disconnected, incoherent, and apparently spontaneous; Joyce went to the length of consciously constructing nongrammatical sentences and of fracturing words in order to imitate the "language" of the dream world. Although Musil does observe all the grammatical niceties, his prose, like Joyce's, attempts to convey a mystery that cannot be fully rendered by language in its familiar form. While Joyce attempted to approximate directly a "stream of unconsciousness," Musil presented a stream of consciousness, but one comprised of a series of metaphors all pointing beyond themselves to the mysterious world of the unconscious.

In "The Temptation of Quiet Veronica," the difficulty of Musil's bewildering style is compounded by subject matter of a decidedly repulsive nature, heavily disguised though its presentation may be. Musil, of course, always tended to treat themes and to arrive at moral conclusions that undoubtedly caused discomfort to the average reader of his day. In *Young Törless*, he concluded that self-growth or self-perfection may excuse cruelty toward a "lesser" human being. In "The Perfecting of a Love," he treated a situation in which a highly civilized marriage was able to achieve perfection only after one of its partners attained self-perfection by engaging in an affair with an animallike stranger. In "The Temptation of Quiet Veronica," Musil moves from the theme of homosexuality and adultery to that of a bizarre form of sodomy. Of all of Musil's works, therefore, "The Temptation of Quiet Veronica" in its style and subject matter exists at the furthest remove from both external reality and commonly accepted standards of morality.

The esoteric style and subject matter of "The Temptation of Quiet Veronica" raise the question of what Musil's presuppositions

were concerning the nature of his audience. For whom is he writing this strange story? He is, first of all, addressing his story only to those already convinced, to those who have themselves felt the reality of mystical experience and for whom, consequently, Musil does not have to preface, explicate, and summarize in discursive terms a dimension of the inner life existing apart from everyday reality.

The theme of mysticism is, of course, endemic to the history of German literature. More than seven hundred years before Musil's work Gottfried von Strassburg, in the prologue of his *Tristan*, explicitly informed his audience that his poem was meant only for the privileged few, for those who could understand and sympathize with a state of mystical love that transcends and transgresses all moral codes of daily behavior. Hermann Hesse, in our own day, dedicated his last novel, *The Glass Bead Game* (1943), to the "Journeyers to the East," the East being a metaphor in Hesse's work for that spiritual realm known only to those who have at some point in their lives experienced it themselves. Unlike most other writers, however, Musil does not warn the unwary reader. Because Musil neither warns nor helps prepare the way for his audience, the reader must gird himself initially for a very disconcerting and disorienting experience. On reading this story, he may well feel as if he has been plunged into a chaotic and bottomless world, as if set adrift upon a sea of emotion in which he must himself attempt to find his own equilibrium amid fragmentary conversations, half-expressed thoughts, and dazzling metaphors, all of which seem to follow upon one another without meaningful progression.

Reality Through a Glass Darkly

There are few definitive statements that can be made about the characters, the environment, and the plot. There are four characters: Veronica, aged 28, her very old aunt, who never directly appears in the story, and two men, Johannes and Demeter, also in their late twenties. The three young people are apparently related in some way, possibly as cousins, although the exact nature of their

relationship remains obscure. All four, who belong to the oldest family in the region, live together in a large and gloomy house. Like Claudine and her husband in the tea-drinking scene, Veronica, Johannes, and Demeter also experience life as having come to a standstill. In this house, however, daily existence seems to lack even that delicate if superficial aesthetic delight that Claudine and her husband experience by means of the glittering and highly civilized façade of their lives. It is (to use Musil's metaphor) as if three people were each living in complete isolation in a shadowy dreamlike world at the still bottom of a deep pool of water. They seem to wander about the house in varying states of agonized emotional tension, now and then engaging in elliptical conversations as they glide past each other. Only one action occurs in the story: Johannes leaves in order to commit suicide. Relieved of his physical presence, Veronica, like Claudine, is left free to achieve the ultimate perfection, a union with the deepest level of her being.

The first paragraph at once presents the major theme of the story and creates an atmosphere of total ambiguity. Every suggestion made by the narrator, however vague it may in itself be, is immediately placed into further doubt. The word "perhaps" appears six times in this one paragraph and four of its six sentences begin with this word. Perhaps, the narrator writes, one hears two voices drifting somewhere. But perhaps one doesn't even hear that. Perhaps there exists a point somewhere beyond the confusion of the everyday world to which these voices are striving, there to intermingle in complete union. Perhaps one ought to search for this point. For if one succeeded in finding this point of union, then perhaps the feeling of sickness, confusion, fragmentariness, and weakness would disappear and everything in one's life would arise firm, strong, and clear. Thus, the subject of this work is once again the search for perfection, for union. The impulse for Veronica's search arises out of a desperate yearning for completeness and health, for behind her yearning lies a fear and a premonition: if she is unable to effect a radical change, a kind of recovery, her life will degenerate inexorably into an even deeper condition of illness and meaninglessness.

Several questions arise from a reading of the first paragraph:

What is the nature of this point of union that, if once experienced, would cause all things formerly ugly and bent to become straight and whole? How does Veronica set out to find this point? What has prevented her from achieving it in the past and why does she suddenly begin the search now? The answers to all these questions, as well as a partial explanation for Musil's purposely obscure style, are to be found in an analysis of an experience that had occurred many years before when Veronica was in her teens.

Veronica's response to this experience had been to repress it totally, thereby causing it "to split off" from her daily conscious life. Nevertheless, it continued to exist in her unconscious mind, timelessly fresh, contained in its own shell, ready to burst open when touched upon many years later by the investigations of her conscious mind. Musil does not, however, immediately reveal to the reader the nature of this buried secret. The reader must bear the suspense; he learns the truth only when Veronica herself is able to recapture this experience from the past and allow it to reenact itself upon the screen of her conscious mind. Since Musil does not allow the reader's vision to be wider than that of the protagonist, the narrator's perspective often seems to slide to the side, to slip out of focus, to avoid making a definite observation. In Musil's consciously obscure, vague, and ambiguous style, the reader directly experiences Veronica's own resistances, her own attempts to avoid seeing too clearly, and her almost total ambivalence. She does not want to know the truth and yet she must force herself to remember if she is not to slip into complete despair.

Two Kindred Spirits in Mysticism

Strangely enough, the story begins not with the protagonist, but with Johannes and the description of a severe psychological crisis that he had experienced at some time in the recent past. (Some striking and illuminating parallels can be drawn between his crisis and that of Törless.) Johannes had felt himself to be precariously suspended between an irrational world of the imagination and the world of everday reality. He had made numerous

attempts to pull this incomprehensible Other World, this irrational "it" existing deep within himself into the circumference of everyday reality, but all his mighty efforts had resulted in failure and he had merely become ill with his obsession. Johannes believes that if he could only have gotten this "it" outside of himself and into the external world, he would have become well again, for he then would have called "it" God and worshipped "it," and "it" would in turn have helped and protected him. But this Other World remained within, beyond conscious control and manipulation, lying utterly still, still as the center of a spinning wheel. It was in this strange condition that Johannes had once lived, hovering in a state of unresolved conflict. And even today, after he has given up this obsession, he remains nevertheless certain that his strange intuitions of a world beyond were not the sign of a morbid mental condition, but were rather "premonitions of some wholeness that it was still too soon to apprehend" (71).

It is in their common intuition of an Other Realm that Johannes and Veronica are truly related and can, in turn, be recognized as literary cousins of Törless. Like Törless, who finally declared that he would never again attempt to compare the world of mysticism with that of everyday reality, Johannes too eventually gave up his attempt to wrestle with the inner world and haul "it" out into the everyday world. Finally both young men, utterly exhausted, let the mystical world drop back and rest within its own dimensions—Törless at the end of the novel and Johannes not long before the story begins.

But Veronica does not give up. Her relationship to the Other Realm is quite different from that of Törless and Johannes. She does not want to understand it (as did Törless) or to worship it (as did Johannes): she wants to give herself completely to it, to dissolve totally into it. In terms of Maeterlinck's motto: Veronica has not the slightest desire to bring the treasure to the surface; she wishes only to sink down and take up solitary and permanent residence with it beneath the water. Could she achieve this, she believes it would be an experience analogous to that which Johannes had once called becoming one with God. "The Temptation of Quiet Veronica" describes how she manages to accomplish such a

feat. It is a feat which, as Maeterlinck's motto implies, requires a constant struggle against the laws of nature, which always attempt to pull the individual back to the surface of life, back into everyday reality.

Veronica wonders whether it would be possible to achieve total union with another person. Total mystical union as Veronica conceives of it would presuppose the kind of relationship fundamentally different from that usually existing in daily life. In the ordinary course of love, two bodies may unite completely, but the soul of each lover (Musil asserts) remains separate, aloof, and untouched, always turning away and preparing to leave. It is always the soul that withholds the ultimate commitment in any relationship between two people (100), an insight that Musil had already elaborated in "The Perfecting of a Love." Perhaps if a union of two bodies were resisted, a union of souls might at least become a possibility. For only in a union of souls, in which the joining of bodies is excluded, could a union become so total that (as Veronica says) "nothing is left to stand outside, eavesdropping, estranged" (79). Therefore, it is life and marriage generally, and sexuality specifically, that exercise a continual temptation preventing the union of souls. A most powerful form of this temptation comes to Veronica through Johannes. For now that he has given up his attempts to wrestle with that unknown "it" within himself, he has only one desire: to court Veronica as his wife and lover. In fact, he asks her three times to leave their gloomy house, to go away with him and begin a new life. But she decisively resists this temptaion to participate in a conventional life. She will not marry, as did Claudine, and bury her inner life beneath the edifice of a shared bourgeois existence.

The path to the moment of perfection, which was traveled by Claudine in a rather accidental fashion, is a path upon which Veronica moves in a more conscious and controlled manner. In "The Perfecting of a Love" it is the reader, rather than Claudine, who first becomes aware of the fact that sexual excitement is only the necessary, preliminary step toward Claudine's ultimate perfection, a step upon which she cannot rest but must pass over in order to transform sexual energy into a heightened mystical state. In "The

Temptation of Quiet Veroinca," it is the heroine herself who consciously realizes from the very beginning that she wants only Johannes's soul, only a nonsexual union. She is determined to achieve such a union and nothing less, which means living permanently within that Other Dimension, united only with the soul of another human being. Veronica's attempt foreshadows Ulrich's experiment in living with his sister Agathe. In this relationship Ulrich and Agathe maintain a continual state of heightened mystical intensity, but it constantly runs the risk of collapsing into incestuous sexual union. In her attempt to live only within the Other Dimension, Veronica too is at war with all the impulses of life and nature.

Animals of the Other Realm

Johannes and Veronica both adopt a symbol, that of God and animal, respectively, in order to come to terms with the mystical dimension. While Johannes's concept of nondionysian mysticism can be defined as "contemplatio," Veronica's initial experience of mysticism many years earlier was decidely dionysian. In both states, however, the individual's personality seems to dissolve. Therefore, dissimilar though the symbols chosen by Johannes and Veronica may at first seem, both God and animal represent a dimension of existence beyond the particular ego or character, an impersonal world that is quite "other" than that of daily life.

Johannes's symbol exists within the framework of an old and accepted tradition, in which God and contemplative mysticism have always been closely associated. In the days when he had wanted to become a priest, Johannes had longed to exist within the boundaries of the Other Realm: "By 'God' he meant that *other* feeling, perhaps the feeling of some other dimension in which he would wish to live" (102). Obviously, his attitude toward the Other Realm had had to be one of worship. But since he had been unable to "extract" the mystical element from the Other Realm and project it onto those symbols provided by Catholic theology, a relationship based upon worship had been impossible.

For Musil up to this point, dionysian states have always ex-

isted between one human being and another who was associated in the protagonist's mind with an animal. Unlike Johannes, who experienced difficulty but no fear in his attempt to unite with the dimension he called God, Veronica senses the presence of a danger because her union involves an extreme departure from conventional forms of sexuality. She feels intuitively that the only way in which she could unite with the Other Realm is by sexually uniting with an animal. The metaphor in Claudine's mind—"Sodomy, she [Claudine] thought. That is what it would amount to" (46)— threatens to become a reality in Veronica's life. Veronica's rather obscure and disjointed explanation with regard to the "impersonality" of the Other Realm now becomes clear: "To me it seems no human being could be so impersonal. . . . Only an animal could. . . . Oh, help me! Why does it [the Other Realm] always make me think of an animal . . . ?" (80). This semiarticulated, barely comprehended intuition, however, shocks even Veronica herself, who must reject such a possibility.

In order to reveal Veronica's emotional state, Musil makes use of a technique similar to the one employed in "The Perfecting of a Love". As Claudine's imagination had been gripped, apparently irrationally, by the story of G., the murderer who seemed to commit his sexual crimes while living totally in another dimension, Veronica also becomes fascinated by a story. It is the subject of common gossip that an old woman living in the neighborhood had substituted her two great dogs for the lover who had deserted her many years ago. Veronica, in a fashion reminiscent of Törless's explanation of his own newly formulated law of perspectivism, imagines that a woman could experience these dogs from two quite different points of view. At one moment, the dogs would be asserting themselves, masterfully baring their teeth. They would become sexually demanding creatures who could also transform the woman into an animal—"except for a tiny point in you where you're still yourself" (76). (This "tiny point" is for Veronica, as for Claudine, the soul, that point of ultimate integrity that lies silent and untouched far beneath even the most frenzied of dionysian orgies.) But then in the next moment, the dogs would be totally servile and crouching, mere pets again. Veronica realizes in a mo-

ment of agonizing though inarticulate insight that it is she who is projecting aspects of herself onto these dogs, and that the aroused dogs only mirror her own sexual desire: "So it's not just animals: this thing is yourself and a solitude, it's you and once again you and an empty, hairy room" (76).

Veronica's double perception of the nature of dogs represents only a particular manifestation of a more fundamental duality that pervades all her thoughts and feelings. She also experiences Demeter and Johannes as two quite different kinds of men; and because she unconsciously assimilates both of them into her (as yet) inexplicable obsession with the double nature of animals, Demeter and Johannes reappear in Veronica's mind transformed into two dogs, each of whom is trying in his own way to tempt her into renouncing her special task. Demeter is for Veronica nothing more than a sexually demanding dog, an animal whose desire for physical union exists in direct opposition to her quest for a union of souls. Veronica tells Johannes that in Demeter they both share a common enemy, a statement which recalls Musil's belief that dionysian (sexual) mysticism and contemplative mysticism are mutually exclusive.

Veronica also recalls a specific experience that further explains her perception of Demeter as an animal. She remembers how she had recently been standing at a window of the house watching a rooster copulating in the yard. Demeter had walked up to her and, standing beside her, also began watching the scene outside. In a flash of inspiration, she thought: "Demeter must be like that rooster, living in some terrible enormous emptiness and suddenly leaping forth out of it" (73). Demeter, as a figure in the protagonist's mind, can be recognized in the story as a direct literary descendant both of Basini (the experimental "animal" made to imitate a dog and a pig) and of Claudine's stranger (whom she associates with a he-goat). When Törless, Claudine, and Veronica, respectively, regarded these three figures from a dionysian perspective, all three males seem to be surrounded by an atmosphere of emptiness, solitude, and impersonality existing at the center of a void. And Veronica adds another element to the picture; she keeps thinking of hair. Neither Veronica nor the reader becomes aware

of the reasons for this association until after Veronica has recalled the repressed episode from her early adolescence.

While there exists in the Western tradition an association between sexuality and animality and, in Musil's earlier works, between sexuality and the void, Veronica's association concerning Johannes is both shocking and seemingly paradoxical. She not only connects the animallike Demeter, but also Johannes, the would-be priest, with a dog. The concept of a dog had already manifested itself to Veronica with two faces, as it were, both sexual and servile. The metaphorical concept of a dog with two faces provides a common denominator which enables Veronica to assert the existence of a relationship between extreme spirituality and extreme animality. However there are two steps to Veronica's insight into the animal nature of the priestly temperament. The first step had been taken (at some indefinite time before the story begins) when Demeter hit Johannes in the face. Veronica, who had been a witness to this scene, was impressed not so much by the fact that Johannes turned the other cheek as did Christ. She was startled to see that Johannes simply smiled, that he was capable only of a timid, docile, and friendly smile that arose out of a great fear of physical violence. Recounting this episode to Johannes, she adds: "And then later you told me you were going to become a priest. . . . So it was that I suddenly realized: It isn't Demeter, it's you who are the animal. . . ." (74). In Veronica's imagination, the priestly Johannes seems to embody the attitude of a servile, crouching dog, an attitude analogous in her mind to that of a priest before God. It is a servility that is based upon the renunciation of the human being's individual and unique, if false, personality.

Veronica then takes the final step in the sequence of her associations leading from the theme of priestly servility to that of the void. She tells Johannes: "In a priest there *is* something of an animal! There's that emptiness at the point where other people possess themselves. That meekness—their very clothes reek of it. That empty meekness like a sieve that things may heap up in for an instant—and then it runs empty!" (75). For Veronica, the sexuality of Demeter and the asceticism of Johannes are both rooted in a more fundamental feeling connected with emptiness, solitude,

loneliness, the impersonal, and the void. The animal functions for her as a symbol for both forms of mysticism: the dionysian, which is masterful, and the contemplative, which is servile. As Demeter exists for Veronica like an animal in the middle of a void (as did Basini for Törless and the stranger for Claudine), Johannes is perceived as containing a void, an "empty meekness" within himself that he had "tried to make something of" but had failed.

Veronica has two potential ways of dealing with the mystical dimension of life. Musil writes that she constantly wavers between the dread of one kind of love (the sexual) and a yearning for the other (a union of souls). She readily admits that it would be quite natural to yield to Demeter, in which case (to use Musil's metaphor) she would become like a drop of water being swallowed by a thirsty dog. Since sexual activity would, however, merely dissipate the energies required for entrance into the realm of "contemplatio," she renounces sex. As she tells Johannes: "But suddenly I thought of you, and without having any clear intention I said no to Demeter. . . . There must be a way of doing that thing as you would do it, a good way. . . ." (79). Of course, she does not want Johannes the man any more than she wants Demeter. Veronica is merely drawn to Johannes's previous manner of dealing with mysticism in a nondionysian way. Veronica had once thought that she and Johannes might form a common pilgrimage (as do Ulrich and Agathe in *The Man without Qualities*) in order to look for "it" together in a nondionysian fashion. But Johannes in the meantime has deserted his quest for mystical experience and now wishes merely to marry her.

The Return of the Repressed

Something, however, is hindering Veronica from engaging with the mystical world even as attempted by Johannes in the "good way." It may be recalled that Claudine achieved the perfect moment, the ultimate mystical state of union with the self, only after the sexual energies that had been aroused by the stranger had in turn been left unsatisfied. But it is not possible for Veronica to generate a single burst of sexual energy that could subsequently be

utilized in her quest for the Other Condition. It is because her sexual impulses have been denied direct expression through complete repression that Veronica's every thought and action is laden with continual small and surreptitious discharges of sexual energy. Veronica, the nunlike virgin, seems to swim in a sea of sexuality, which she does not recognize as such. Since she has successfully blocked all direct expression of sexuality, she perceives merely "an empty shape" (72), an empty thought within her of some terrible event that had occurred when she was fourteen years old. This terrible event was nothing less than her first overtly sexual experience which she had immediately repressed from consciousness, and together with this particular memory her overt sexual life in general. Veronica's repression of her sexual life for the past thirteen years is analogous to Claudine's suppression of her promiscuous life subsequent to her second marriage. But just as the past began surreptitiously to obtrude upon Claudine's consciousness, so Veronica, too, now begins to remember.

Before turning to an examination of the repressed episode itself, it is necessary to note, first, how Veronica's present life has become crippled by the years of repression and, second, how a single crucial event experienced at Demeter's side leads to the complete recall of the mysterious past occurrence.

Veronica at once desires and fears to discover this buried secret. Because her emotional life has existed for thirteen years totally separated from her outer life, she now feels as if she is living under a bell-shaped cover made of horn that is becoming ever more opaque. Life seems to be retreating from her; she is unable to experience either intense pleasure or intense suffering. But Veronica now vaguely begins to realize why her existence has become a meaningless blur in which one day mechanically follows upon the next: "some great fear had once prevented [something] from coming to perfection, and since then it had lain within her, hardened and encapsulated, blocking the way for something that might have developed in her" (92).

Veronica's repressed past first manages to intrude, however minimally, into her present life when she and Demeter are watching a rooster copulate. All at once she feels "the empty shape" of

some image inside herself; she is reminded of something else, but is unable to discover what this other thing is. The sight of the copulating animals has, nevertheless, triggered an unconscious association to something in the past that in turn releases a flood of once captive emotions. Veronica wonders whether this flood of emotion is what people call love. It is moving at once in two directions: toward Demeter, who, as his pagan name emphasizes, represents merely a sexual animal, and toward Johannes, the one-time wrestler with a God within.

After a lapse of thirteen years, Veronica suddenly recalls the repressed occurrence in all its detail. The mysterious event arises before her mind's eye "hot, and still alive" (84). When she was fourteen years old, Veronica had owned a large and very hairy St. Bernard dog. She had always felt an enormous attraction toward the hair of this dog, particularly toward the fur in front where the chest muscles rose like two little hills. This hair seemed to form a vast and complex landscape in which she took imaginary walks, strolling this way and that through the woods, fields, and meadows. One day while lying next to the dog, she fell into a half-sleep and experienced a strange sexual fantasy. She imagined that giants must also be like her dog, with mountains, valleys and forests of hair on their chests. What, she secretly thought, if one day the giants were to become angry and fall upon her raging with love. It would be like being overwhelmed by a terrifying earthquake. Tiny blown hairs would begin to fall all over her body. Somewhere a voice would be shrieking in ecstasy and her own breath would become like a multitude of animals engulfing the world. This fantasy left her feeling paralyzed, for she seemed to be turning into an animal herself. When she opened her eyes, the dog appeared to be gazing at her in a peculiar way. Both he and Veronica were in a sexually aroused state. He put out his tongue and caressed her face. Suddenly she was overcome by a profound shock, produced perhaps by a more or less conscious fear that a sexual relationship with her dog might become a real possibility. The metaphor of the raging, hairy giants had merely disguised her sexual attraction toward the dog itself.

Thirteen years later, Veronica is confronted in the form of

Demeter with a situation analogous to that of the sexually aroused dog. But she chooses to pursue the other alternative: she and Johannes, as their biblical names suggest, will attempt to form a union of the most spiritual and exalted kind, one in which the "flood of emotion" that has now begun to surge forward, having been released by her remembrance of the repressed event, will be discharged only in a union of souls.

The Departure

The union of Veronica's soul with the soul of Johannes is being hindered by a final insurmountable obstacle: the presence of his physical body. Veronica makes a tentative suggestion to Johannes as to how their love affair of the soul might be consummated: "perhaps if you were to die. . . ." (81). The total physical extinction of his body would open the way for Veronica's union with his soul. Johannes accepts Veronica's' suggestion almost as a commandment: "I am going away. Certainly—perhaps I shall die" (81). Johannes also seems to understand that the death of the body represents the most direct negation of the (dionysian) animal state and that his death signifies for Veronica the alternative existing at furthest remove from that embodied by the pagan and sensual Demeter. Although Johannnes had already given up the idea of becoming a priest, he now performs a priestly function by negating the instinctual life within himself through suicide, thereby at the same time facilitating Veronica's spiritual marriage with him.

The concept of a spiritual marriage between Veronica and Johannes is, however, finally misleading. Musil writes: "dead people have no souls" (99). More important, the union that Veronica, like Claudine, is seeking does not represent a synthesis of male and female souls on the spiritual level. Ultimately, Johannes's soul as well as his body is of no interest to Veronica. All that is of significance to her is the *intensity of her yearning* for his soul. This intensity, when it reaches its greatest point, will facilitate her union with the deepest aspect of her own soul. Thus Veronica's moment of

perfection represents a process of emotional masturbation culminating in narcissistic spiritual orgasm.

Veronica walks with Johannes to the train station. The liberating flood of her emotions is not, she notes, streaming toward Johannes any longer but rather toward something (metaphorically expressed) in the distance, something floating like an infinitely exalted dome of radiance in the heights above. She seems to be perceiving the approach of the moment of perfection dimly, as if through a web of dreams. If this moment is ever finally to arrive, Johannes must disappear totally, for his living presence is like a dead body whose weight is impeding something within Veronica that is yearning to soar aloft. At this moment when Veronica looks at Johannes, she experiences a powerful and striking impression: "Johannes seemed like a big animal that was lying upon her in exhaustion and which she could not shake off" (93).

The memory of the scene with the St. Bernard dog now returns once again. In fact, the episode with her dog is "replayed," as it were, upon the screen of her consciousness; but Johannes has taken the place of the dog. In her "replay," Veronica also provides the past scene with a conclusion that it did not possess before: the union in the present fantasy reaches its climax. The scene of thirteen years before, as Veronica remembers it, concluded with the dog's putting out his tongue at her. Now, while she is standing with Johannes at the station, Veronica suddenly returns the gesture of the dog: she puts her tongue out at Johannes "almost like a she-animal's reaction when, hard-pressed, she snaps at her pursuer" (93). She experiences the wind blowing down the road as if it were a soft and fragrant animal placing itself upon her with its soft fur covering her completely. The opacity that had veiled her life like a dark mist now appears to be gradually clearing. Everything around her in the outer world seems to be shining "with that queerly vibrant meaning which condenses everyday events into significance" (94).

Veronica begins to sense another person's presence within her bloodstream. She looks intently at Johannes, his hair blowing in the wind and almost touching her. A momentary urge for sexual union with him overwhelms her but quickly passes. Their bodies

remain apart, their eyes closed, "merely allowing it all [the union] to happen secretly, as though they must not know of it" (95). It seems to her as if they are bleeding to death, the blood from one rushing into the veins of the other. Johannes's blood seems to be coursing under her skirts, filling her body. "And so the two of them stood there," Musil writes, "two enormous animals, their backs bowed, outlined against the evening sky" (95).

As was revealed in "The Perfecting of a Love," the energies required to achieve the final state of mystical perfection were redirected sexual energies. Since Veronica's sexual fantasy at the station remains a fantasy, since the energy is redirected rather than discharged, the final step toward perfection now becomes possible.

The Moment of Perfection

As Claudine left her husband by train and eventually achieved her moment of perfection at some geographical distance from him, so Veronica now hopes to achieve her perfection at home by sending Johannes away by train. She knows that Johannes plans not merely to travel to the sea far away, thereby placing geographical distance between them; he intends to go the ultimate distance from her by committing suicide once he reaches the coast. In this knowledge, Veronica feels almost sick with delight as she walks home from the station. She now seems in possession of a new and powerful sense of her own separate and unique existence. Veronica has begun to move steadily along a path toward ultimate union with her deepest self. As she steps through her front door and locks it, Veronica feels that she is standing at the bottom of a deep dark pool of water far away from the everyday world outside. It is a reversal of Törless's implicit attitude toward the world of emotion as expressed by Musil in Maeterlinck's metaphor. Veronica has not attempted to raise it to the rational surface of the everyday world in order to achieve a synthesis of both worlds. She has, rather, now taken up permanent residence at the bottom of the sea within the radiance of the treasure below.

Everything in Veronica's environment on her first night alone

seems to be covered and enveloped by a great light, an over-arching radiance. And when she thinks of Johannes, it is not of him as being dead but simply as being no longer present in the world of the living: "this is what Johannes is like now, he is within this other dimension of reality" (99). Veronica identifies this world of the no-longer-living with the land of dreams: "somewhere there is a totality of feeling where they [dreams] are at home and grow high, arching into a dome" (100-1). This is the world of the awakened soul, a hollow space within the individual that nothing can fill, however much an individual may try to avoid recognizing its existence or to "stuff" it full with trivial worldly experiences. Veronica enters this Other World like a wandering spirit who has finally found its long lost homeland. From her new perspective within the borders of the Other Dimension, the outer world she left behind seems transformed: all things that once existed as separate and unrelated fragments have now assumed symmetry and meaning.

Veronica, now existing within this heightened state, recalls a second past experience that functions in the story as a structural parallel to her memory of the hairy St. Bernard dog. Once when she had been very ill with a high fever, Veronica had talked with angels. During her illness, she had seemed to herself to lose her physical body until she had lain almost transparent upon the bed. She had felt herself to be surrounded by a circle of male angels whose wings rustled and crackled as if from hair standing on end. Whereas Demeter, Johannes, and her aunt had simply assumed that she was suffering from an illness, Veronica had felt only a sense of exultation. Was this, in fact, illness or was it a more profound health? Unfortunately, Veronica's heightened feeling of well-being passed away when her fever passed off. Now with Johannes's departure, she once again experiences a feeling similar to that felt during her illness. But today she has no fever and therefore feels that this heightened state might become permanent.

Sitting alone in her dark bedroom on the night of Johannes's departure, Veronica finally experiences the union of souls. Johannes's image becomes vibrantly alive for her. He seems as close to her as she is to herself, and it is as if she is gazing at herself out of his eyes. Musil describes this relationship as "a proximity less of

the body than of the soul." He continues: "it was like a mysterious spiritual union. At some moments she thought to herself that he was her guardian angel." (107-8). Thus Veronica has managed to achieve the less natural and more difficult of two alternatives. She has rejected sexual union: she did not allow the dog to lie upon her at the age of fourteen nor did she later submit to Demeter. Instead, she induces Johannes into playing the role of her angel, a being no longer physically alive with whom she can spiritually unite and exist forever in a state of constant and permanent union. She believes that he will always be with her; wherever she goes, he will be close to her body, under her skirts. Veronica has not only taken the leading role in this mystical union but has also assimilated the male sexual image: she imagines herself lying exhausted upon Johannes, as the sea must now be lying upon his corpse. Veronica feels she has become like the sea itself.

Veronica is finally aware, however, that her splendid feelings have not really arisen from a union with a man, whether with his body or his soul. Musil writes: "She had begun dimly to realize that it was not Johannes but herself that she experienced with such palpable sensuality" (104). Veronica's moment of ultimate union is more truly, therefore, the moment of ultimate narcissism. Feelings of love that naturally move outward from the psyche in order to be invested in another human being were able, with the contrived absence of Johannes, to be withdrawn from the outer world, taken back, and reinvested in Veronica's own psyche. Although Veronica's existence must now seem to give the impression of being a life of absolute ascetic renunciation, on a more fundamental level the reverse is true. By rejecting Johannes's body, with which she could have experienced at most momentary and temporary physical union, she has chosen a life of permanent sensuality, disguised and transformed though it may be. For it was only upon a basis of total asceticism that Veronica was able to achieve the state of lasting spiritual orgasm in which she now lives. What is Veronica going to do now? Nothing. This state is perfection and thus exists outside of time and all activity. Strange thoughts begin to occur to her: "to love herself and only herself like this" (107). Anything else would be superfluous and meaningless.

The Fall from Paradise

This state of suspended animation and spiritual perfection is not destined to last. The next day a letter arrives from Johannes. It begins: "What are you that I did not kill myself? I am like one who has found his way out into the street. I have got out and cannot go back" (108-9). The warmth, the colors, the taste of earthly life hold him fast. Like Törless who, after being released from the spell of Basini's inner life, declared that life is quite simply life and that things merely happen one after another without any secret design, Johannes's imagination is also gripped by a similar insight: "Everything is outside, quite simple and unrelated, all loosely heaped like a pile of rubble, but it holds me, I am like a post rammed into the ground and taking root again . . . " (109). Veronica realizes fully that he has leaped soberly and somewhat callously away from her and taken refuge in the safety of daily life. She is unable to tear her eyes away from one sentence in the letter: "I have found the way out into the street" (109). In such a statement, Veronica detects a note of derision directed against herself.

Johannes gives up his obsession with Veronica and returns to simple reality. Unlike Törless, who finally realized that Basini himself had nothing to offer and that the seeming complexity of Basini's life was merely a projection of his own problematic and complex psyche, Johannes rejects Veronica for the opposite reason. Her complexity is too much for him; the obscure workings of Veronica's psyche will forever lie beyond his powers of comprehension. It may be that in Musil's opinion, dionysian mysticism (as treated in *Young Törless*) is in itself quite simple, at least for the person in such a state. It only becomes problematic when another individual attempts to comprehend it rationally, that is to say, from a distance. The problems arising from contemplative mysticism, however, are infinitely complex, and it is to this area that Musil will return again and again in *Three Women* and *The Man without Qualities*. Thus, Johannes rejects Veronica because not to do so means being tied to a death-oriented existence. Veronica destroys to some extent everything around her, not least of which is her own life; for only out of the diminution and destruction of physical life can she achieve and maintain her spiritual existence.

Upon receiving the news that Johannes is still alive, Veronica feels as though a heavy cloak were falling over her mind and senses. Her thoughts become confused. She knows that she can never escape into simple reality, and yet her refuge in contemplative mysticism, only recently achieved, is already beginning to crumble. She begins to perceive the outer world intruding upon her in the form of voices, those of Demeter and her aunt. The meaningless and incoherent world is again beginning to assert itself. That heap of unrelated fragments that Johannes had welcomed as representing raw life signifies for Veronica something quite negative, and it is causing her to suffer profoundly as it begins to violate her inner life. At the same time, her inner life, which had seemed so pure and healthy when regarded from the perspective of the mystical state, is now beginning to appear merely diseased. Veronica spends the next few days desperately attempting to remember what that one glorious night of paradise had been like. But by degrees she slowly loses any sense that her life had ever been anything other than imprisonment within an opaque bell jar, devoid of meaning and the feeling of joy. Only occasionally does she recapture a dim memory of "a shadow of pure delight" (112) that had once fallen upon her dreary life.

In the last paragraph of the story, Musil ominously describes how Veronica, once again roaming aimlessly through the dark house, meets Demeter and notices the tip of his beard outlined immeasurably huge against the window-pane. It may be recalled that the outline of a beard was one of Claudine's most powerful impressions of the stranger. By analogic projection of the narrative sequences, it would not be surprising if Veronica now had a purely physical affair with Demeter, just as Claudine after her moment of perfection alone in her bedroom subsequently had an affair with the stranger.

The reader is informed that Johannes, whose role in the structure of "The Temptation of Quiet Veronica" is in many ways analogous to that of Claudine's husband, will eventually be returning to the house. Veronica and Johannes may well continue to live on together as did Claudine and her husband after her return to her bourgeois duties as wife and mother. However, Veronica's

emotional life has been so tortured and twisted and her experience of the Other Realm so intense that it seems unlikely that she will ever be able to find her way back to a shared life with another person in daily reality. Not only is her road back to ordinary reality extremely obsure, Veronica has no desire to find and take it. Whereas Claudine simply boards a train and returns home, Veronica at the end of the story begins an endless drifting, now irrevocably cut off both from daily life *and* the Other World.

The question may now be raised as to whether or not Musil was in essence treating a single relationship in both stories of *Unions*, that is, the relationship between Man and Woman whose prototype could be found in his own marriage. Until more is known about Musil's private life, such an idea can, of course, remain no more than a tempting conjecture for the critic; however, it is striking that these two stories as well as those of *Three Women* deal not only with the perfection of love in general but with obstacles to marriage in particular. If Musil is treating a single relationship, then "The Perfecting of a Love" and "The Temptation of Quiet Veronica" may be regarded as two perspectives on one and the same marriage. From this point of view, the two stories do not differ substantively in their presentation of two different couples, but rather in the depth to which Musil has penetrated the female psyche. In the first story, the true nature of the couple's marriage was disguised by an impressionistic aesthetic patina and the protagonist's search for love took a form not outwardly different from that found in the typical Viennese tale of the short and adulterous affair, the momentary *Seitensprung* of the respectable middle-class citizen while on holiday. (Of the husband, Musil chooses to reveal very little.) Upon the wife's return, life is expected to continue as before; in fact, the relationship between husband and wife will (it is assumed) be happier than it was before. In the second story, however, Musil's view was far less conventional, far more penetrating, and unrelievedly pessimistic. The delightful patina is totally absent and the happy ending has disappeared. Beneath Claudine's realization that "I could be far from you [her husband] and could exist without you" is Veronica's wish that Johannes commit sui-

cide. Beneath Claudine's sexual attraction to the animal nature in man is Veronica's sexual attraction to an animal. If, in its subject matter, "The Perfecting of a Love" finds its nearest literary equivalent in the ordinary novel of romantic love, the closest equivalent for "The Temptation of Quiet Veronica" must be sought in the literature of psychoanalysis.

Regression and the Perfection of Narcissism

Veronica's brief holiday in the mystical realm on the night of Johannes's departure does not mean that she has resolved or forever overcome the pathological condition existing in her daily life. She has only temporarily escaped from it down a path of radical psychological regression. This return to ever earlier stages of psychological development, which occurs in Musil's story in three stages, forms the only narrative progression of the work, a progression that takes place solely within the psyche of the protagonist. The three-step narrative line in "The Temptation of Quiet Veronica" can be regarded as a fictional analogue of some of Freud's theories on neurotic regression and the relationship between narcissism and mysticism.

A psychoanalytic understanding of the story's internal narrative progression may best be facilitated by pursuing the following question: what caused Veronica at the age of 28 to recall from her early adolescence the episode with her St. Bernard dog? Or, more precisely, what was the precipitating psychological factor that initiated the return of this long repressed memory? In quite classic psychoanalytic fashion, the answer is to be found in an apparently trivial event in the present that set off a chain of associations leading backward to Veronica's recollection of a sexual trauma which occurred at a critical stage in her psychological development. Demeter's presence beside her at the window or, rather, the sexual temptation exerted upon her by his physical, animal presence acted as the precipitating agent. The return of the repressed sexual memory (the second step in the narrative) then revealed the specific content of the historical event of thirteen years before. It now

becomes apparent why Veronica so decisively rejects Demeter's advances in the present. The sexual desires which Demeter's pursuit stimulates represent a revival of sexual feelings first aroused in Veronica by her dog. The anxiety produced by this original situation had been so great that it had caused her to repress from that moment on the natural expression of all sexuality along with the memory of the terrifying episode itself. However, as Freud wrote in *Moses and Monotheism*: "What is forgotten is not extinguished but only 'repressed'; its memory-traces are present in all their freshness. . . . They cannot enter into communication with other intellectual processes; they are unconscious—inaccessible to consciousness." The repressed material remains always ready to penetrate into consciousness and the return to consciousness of such memories becomes possible "if the instinctual elements attaching to the repressed receive a special reinforcement." This often occurs for the first time during puberty and again in later life "if at any time in recent experience impressions or experiences occur which resemble the repressed so closely that they are able to awaken it."[10]

The reason for Veronica's fear of sex and her flight from Demeter now become comprehensible. As a 14-year-old girl, she had experienced sex as manifesting itself in either of two states. On the one hand, sex could be something glorious, like finding a treasure beyond counting, like wandering through a wonderful landscape of woods and meadows in which everything is locked in great and potent order. Veronica had associated the hair on the chest of her dog with the hair on the chests of giants. She had then transformed this hair into the landscape through which she was walking in her fantasy. But everything could suddenly explode. There would then be a great earthquake and Veronica, who had been wandering peacefully through this glorious landscape, might all at once be overwhelmed and crushed. Either state is possible, and there is apparently no way to control which state will manifest itself. Moreover, there is yet a third possibility: her experience of radiance and joy would *inevitably* be followed by the experience of herself being destroyed. Veronica thus chose to renounce the treasure and the feeling of order, because to seek it out meant exposing

herself to great risk, the risk of being extinguished as a particular and individual being. When her dog's tongue touched her face, she had felt as if she were no longer Veronica but, rather, an animal too. At this moment, she had been overcome with a feeling of profound fear. Thus when Demeter approaches her thirteen years later, it is as if the dog were again putting out his tongue at her and threatening to annihilate her.[11]

Musil presents a picture of Veronica's psychological state with a series of metaphors rather than with psychological terminology. This study will now, however, shift the focus of its examination from the narrative level to an analysis of certain specific aspects of Veronica's inner life in terms provided by psychoanalytic theory. To what extent is Veronica's rejection of Demeter psychoanalytically comprehensible? Is there an explanation to be found in psychoanalytic thought for Veronica's rather bizarre feeling that Johannes's presence exists within her own body and that she has thereby achieved a spiritual union excluding bodies? And what, finally, is the psychoanalytic meaning of her ultimate union with the deepest aspect of her self which signifies "the perfection of love"?

Veronica's flight from her experience with the St. Bernard dog (by means of forgetting) as well as her present flight from Demeter's advances represent in psychoanalytic theory a defense against genital sexuality. This defense manifests itself through regression to a presexual state, to an early state of libidinal and ego development in which a nonsexual union with Johannes can occur. Freud's theory of regression presupposes that the infantile stages of development are never left totally behind. Earlier fixation points therefore remain available as alternative modes of behavior to which the individual may regress when subjected to external or internal stress that he is unable to overcome.

Freud used the term "secondary narcissism" to designate that state in which the individual's love of himself arises from his introjection of an external object or person followed by the individual's complete identification with him. Musil describes the actual process of psychological introjection moment by moment as Veronica

is waiting at the railway station for Johannes to leave. She finally feels his whole presence within herself. By loving his introjected image, she now also loves herself totally.

Veronica takes the final and ultimate step along the path of psychological regression, a step that leads beyond the secondary narcissism that arose from her love for the introjected Johannes. A psychoanalytical understanding of this final step can most economically be provided by examining Freud's analysis of primary narcissism. (Veronica's primary narcissism does not now exclude the symptoms of secondary narcissism; both forms exist simultaneously.) A regression to primary narcissism presupposes a disintegration of the boundaries of the ego. It represents, therefore, a return to a time in infancy when the ego had not yet been firmly established, to a period before the differentiation of the ego and the id had taken place. At this early stage in the development of the psyche, the ego, such as it is, extends without any sharp boundaries into the unconscious. The individual who has regressed to this point, therefore, no longer feels divided against himself. All endopsychic conflict ceases. At the same time, the ego also seems to extend infinitely outwards. The ego expands until it feels itself to be coextensive with the whole universe. The infant in such a state experiences a feeling of limitless extension and oneness with his world. Veronica's moment of perfection, experienced the evening of Johannes's departure, becomes psychologically comprehensible when regarded in terms of Freud's description of primary narcissism. Like an infant, she too experiences on that evening a sense of totality, of omnipotence and invulnerability. The space between herself and objects around her ceases to be mere emptiness. Instead, a network of relationships now appears to exist between herself and all things. Meaninglessness vanishes and is replaced by a feeling that everything is rich and full of indescribable significance.

The above analysis of primary narcissism also calls to mind Freud's explanation of the mystical impulse and its relationship to Musil's concept of the Other Condition ("der andere Zustand"). Freud regarded mysticism as originating in the infantile state of

primary narcissism. As a working hypothesis, Freud accepted a definition of mysticism (offered by one of his friends) that stressed the "sensation of 'eternity,' a feeling as of something limitless, unbounded—as it were, 'oceanic'."[12] Freud also accepted the assertion (as does Ulrich in *The Man without Qualities*) that mysticism is "a purely subjective fact, not an article of faith; it brings with it no assurance of personal immortality, but it is the source of the religious energy . . . . "[13] Although Freud confessed that he had never been able to discover this feeling within himself, he nevertheless felt able as a psychoanalyst to describe the ideational content usually associated with mysticism, for it is the ideational content experienced by every infant: "it is a feeling of an indissoluble bond, of being one with the external world as a whole."[14] By means of radical psychological regression, says Freud, the mystic temporarily manages to reestablish contact with his infantile life that existed before the ego had become a more or less clearly defined, autonomous entity. In this sense, the mystic is a man without an ego or character. Because the ego of the mystic in a state of primary narcissism has expanded to include not only the id but also the whole external world, the mystic has had of necessity to sacrifice in the process of regression all those unique and peculiar characteristics that accrued to his personality during years of personal experience.

The psychoanalytical explanation of the origin of the mystical impulse also helps to illuminate Johannes's relationship to the Other Realm. We recall that Johannes identified this Other Realm with God. Freud felt that the individual's belief in God fulfilled a need whose origin could be traced back to the period of primary narcissism. In this early stage of psychological development, the child experiences a sense of overwhelming helplessness, of being cast out into an uncanny and threatening world. In the figure of his seemingly omnipotent father, the child takes refuge.[15] When as an adult he again experiences reality as threatening and painful, he may partially regress to that mystical world of "oceanic feeling" when the existence of the father seemed to guarantee the child's safety and well-being. In the adult, however, the figure of the per-

sonal father is projected onto the concept of God, the father of all things.

Musil's concept of the fundamental opposition between Johannes's priestly servility and mystical attitude on the one hand, and Demeter's sexual aggressiveness on the other, can also be interpreted in the light of Freud's analysis of the opposition between "oceanic mysticism" and genital sexuality. Johannes and Demeter are presented in the story as two diametrically opposed types of men. Musil's characterization of Demeter verges, in fact, upon caricature. He represents for Musil simply natural and instinctual life in all its vulgarity and self-assertiveness. Demeter merely becomes what it is natural to be. Johannes's inital development of the priestly temperament, however, is the result of an active negation of all that is natural. Johannes's religious impulse, therefore, represents a denial of sexuality by means of psychological regression to a state of infantile narcissism. Otto Fenichel writes of "religious fanatics who, by such radical denial of their active sexual wishes, try to regain 'peaceful unity with God,' that is, an extreme passive submissiveness, less of a feminine than of an early infantile 'oceanic' nature."[16] Johannes's passivity is, as Veronica perceives, a fundamental aspect of his personality; she experiences a definite sense of disappointment when he does not become a priest, for she considers the priestly relationship to the Other Realm to be one of the few "good ways" of dealing with the mystical state. At the point when Johannes rejected the possibility of becoming a priest, he had already reached and was beginning his return from the furthest point of remove from that alternative represented by Demeter. As his servile attitude toward "the strange condition" passes, he begins to court Veronica. But something of this servile attitude remains. For he is still initially prepared to obey Veronica's command to kill himself, a command which is issued on behalf of the Other Realm and Veronica's need to perfect the mystical state. Johannes's attitude of service has at this point changed very little: instead of subjecting his instinctual life to partial suicide by becoming a priest, he is now prepared to destroy his physical body totally in order to facilitate Veronica's engagement with the mystical realm in "the good way," i.e., in a nondionysian manner.

The Perfection of Narcissism Assessed

In "The Temptation of Quiet Veronica," the mystical experience is given a more intense, sustained, and obscure treatment than in any of Musil's other short stories. Through his choice of vivid and daring metaphors, Musil fully succeeds in expressing the power and the grandeur of that mystical moment which Veronica attempts to extend forever. But Veronica fails in this attempt. And because of her eventual fall back into everyday reality, the mystical experience as seen from "outside" appears as a temptation and a danger. From the perspective of everyday reality, the mystical state represents a temptation to forsake the world and enter into a condition of psychological hibernation so total and absolute that it seems not unlike catatonic schizophrenia.

The negative and critical judgments and terminology provided by psychiatry, however, have no validity within the boundaries of the Other Realm. Nor do such negative judgments impede the wish to return to the Other Realm by those who have once entered it but have since fallen back into everyday reality. When Veronica returns to reality, she continues to yearn for the Other Realm. She does not consider it a danger or a temptation; for when she was in that heightened state she felt totally happy and healthy, and when she was not in it she felt completely wretched and weak. But Musil concluded "The Temptation of Quiet Veronica" from the perspective of everyday reality, not from that of Veronica's heightened state. Therefore, Musil's own final evaluation of Veronica's mystical experience is implicitly negative.

A comparison of Musil's concept of the Other Realm and Freud's reductive explanation of mysticism immediately raises the question of their differing evaluation of this state. For Freud, the primary narcissism of the mystic represents a regression from mature forms of sexuality to infantile ones, a regression arising from an overwhelming fear of adult sexuality. From his perspective as physician and psychologist, Freud's condemnation in this regard is immediate and unambivalent. Man's primary allegiance must be to the reality principle and the secondary processes, i.e., to those attributes and abilities that Ulrich in *The Man without Qualities*

subsumes under the symbol of the first tree of his life. Man must ally himself with the ego and its constant struggles to reconcile the differing and conflicting demands of the psychic apparatus as a whole. Since psychological growth presupposes a constant struggle to master new and higher stages of development, man must surrender the easy satisfaction of infantile pleasures, accept the difficult path of maturation, and acknowledge reality, however painful it may be. As a therapist, however, Freud also recognized that man's psyche remains closely bound to the pleasure-principle, the instinctual needs, and the sources of immediate gratification. Neurosis is caused by man's inability to outgrow the child within him and to take up the struggle implicit in the process of psychological development. To retreat, as did Veronica, means that the ego has been defeated in battle and has opted for the neurotic defense mechanism of regression. But there is a further price to pay. Because the ego has escaped anxiety at a higher level, it will sooner or later have to experience the anxiety appropriate to the lower stage to which it has regressed. Regression does not therefore represent a solution but only a temporary and specious reduction of conflict. In Veronica's case, the anxiety appropriate to mysticism (i.e., primary narcissism) is the so-called "separation anxiety," a condition from which Veronica suffers in the days immediately after her loss of the perfect moment when she no longer feels that mystical sense of unity with all things.

Musil reaches his ultimately negative evaluation of Veronica's pursuit of mysticism only by working through two mutually exclusive perspectives. This approach is consistent with his tendency to experience life in terms of various alternatives. Although Musil's ultimate aim may well have been a synthesis of all perspectives, from which would then emerge the single true perspective, in practice he continually finds himself confronted by two perspectives and therefore by two possible ways of reaching an evaluation.

Regarding the mystical state from the first of Musil's perspectives, i.e., considering it totally from within its own boundaries, the Other Condition cannot be evaluated at all. Where no standard of comparison exists because of the absence of any external point of reference, the possibility of judgment also ceases. Therefore, Mu-

sil's description of the mystical moment as experienced by Veronica after Johannes's departure is totally positive, although in a
special sense. Veronica, Musil writes, was then living within the
light of the awakened soul, "her thoughts were able to reach the
idea of a haleness [Gesundheit] that was tremendous as mountain
air, a state in which she might master all her emotions with the
utmost ease" (103). This state is positive simply because of the
absence of any and all negativity. All things are "right." Or, because neither the negative nor the false exist in this state, perhaps
it is more correct to say that everything merely "is." Thus it is only
through the absence of judgment that the Other Dimension signifies total happiness.

In "The Temptation of Quiet Veronica," it is not merely the
existence of a second perspective opposed to that of mysticism
which is significant, but rather the fact that the second perspective
follows the first in time. Mysticism is finally revealed to be an
impossibility because whereas the mystical state can only exist outside of time, man's psychic life cannot for long (except in psycho-
sis) escape from the effects of time. To suspend time would mean
to suspend the natural tendency of the psyche to develop, to unfold
itself in time. The mystical impulse and that of psychological development are in direct conflict, as Freud was well aware. It was
therefore Musil's recognition of the effects of the passage of time
upon the psyche that finally forced him to condemn Veronica's
mystical experience as an "impossibility."

By way of making this idea more comprehensible, the action
in Maeterlinck's metaphor of the diver, which takes place in a
completely physical world, may be reinterpreted in psychological
terms. The diver on the surface is able to see the mystical treasure
glimmering below; he may with great effort even be able to reach
it at the bottom of the sea and remain there with it a few moments.
But in time he will inevitably be drawn back into the upper world,
back to the surface. Our last vision of Veronica is one of her swim-
ming alone on the surface, as it were. She has sacrificed all human
contact in order to achieve the moment of mystical perfection.
Now she has neither the treasure nor contact with human society.
Thus the physical body will, quite aside from the intentions of the

mind, draw the individual back. Nature itself opposes the mystical impulse.

Johannes returns not only to the surface but apparently also to everyday life. His desire to die on behalf of Veronica passes when he discovers life out there "in the street"—colors, foods, warmth, texture, sounds. When Johannes returns to the house from his trip, he will be a changed person, as was Claudine when she returned from her trip. Although he experienced the power of the mystical world, he has also felt and assimilated the life that Demeter knows, the immediacy of all the senses. Johannes thus emerges in this story as the most complex and interesting character: he alone, in his struggle with the Other Realm, progresses (as did Törless) to a state of higher self-awareness based upon a recognition of the most extreme and polar aspects of life. Johannes did struggle, whereas Demeter was always at one with his animal self and will remain forever as a caricature of life at its lowest level. As for Veronica, it is clear that she had only wanted to surrender herself to the mystical realm from the very beginning and as quickly and completely as possible.

Musil's final evaluation of Veronica's mystical state is not far removed from Freud's condemnation of primary narcissism. But while Freud, as a never ceasing champion of the claims of reason, always tended to evaluate phenomena from the single perspective of the ego and its requirements, Musil seems to have been forced against his own will into adopting a rather similar position. From the point of view of the ego and rationality, Musil thus admits that Veronica's feelings must be regarded as a "disease, and full of impossibilities" (103). He further describes the Other Condition metaphorically as a world with "walls painted by fever and delusions, and between those walls the words spoken by the sane and healthy have no resonance, but fall to the ground, meaningless" (108). Concerning one of Veronica's previous illnesses, when she seemed to be existing in another world of absolute perfection, Musil wrote: "And at that time it seemed to her she had achieved everything in the world. But it was only a fever, and when it passed off she realized that it must be so" (106). On the evening of Johannes's departure, Veronica recalls this earlier episode and perceives

that there is now once again "a touch of that bygone illness in the sensual feelings she had about herself" (106). Thus for Musil time effects a correction, a revaluation of the belief that the perfect moment was finally perfect. It was perfect only in itself; from outside itself, however, the total perfection of this sensual moment is perceived as an illness, as a form of infantile eroticism.

Musil's condemnation of mysticism as experienced by Veronica should not be interpreted as meaning that Musil is at this point condemning mysticism *per se*, as did Freud. The conclusion of "The Temptation of Quiet Veronica" should not lead to such a generalization. Musil has not abandoned mysticism on behalf of the world of everyday reality. In fact, if man were able to live permanently in the mystical moment (and without the sacrifice of his sanity) Musil would have been able to affirm mysticism. At this point in his career, Musil apparently still believed that the problematic aspect of mysticism did not necessarily lie in the nature of mysticism itself. Rather, the problematic aspect arises because there is something wrong with man's *relationship* to the mystical realm. He believed, further, that the faulty relationship existing between mysticism and everyday reality had to be diagnosed, that is to say, described in literature and then repaired in life. Until this occurs, man will be condemned to oscillate within a fatal either/or alternative. The choice will continue to be *either* the madness and neurosis of, for instance, the killer G. ("The Perfecting of a Love"), Moosbrugger (*The Man without Qualities*), and Veronica *or* the meaninglessness and boredom of everyday reality devoid of significance; *either* a sense of emotional wholeness and unity at the price of psychopathology *or* sanity at the price of spiritual fragmentation and a feeling of emptiness and emotional bankruptcy. Both extremes will always remain equally negative as long as they remain totally disconnected alternatives.

In his next collection of short stories, *Three Women*, Musil pursues the possibility of effecting a synthesis between both alternatives in the hope that the negative elements on both sides of the reason-mysticism equation will cancel each other out, leaving behind only the positive aspects. And in *The Man without Qualities*, the protagonist once again makes a descent into the mystical realm

as did Veronica. In his last experiment in mysticism, however, Musil introduced a new element. As if in the hope of avoiding the pathology of the single individual in the mystical realm, Musil provides Ulrich with another point of human contact outside himself. The joint pilgrimage to the sources of the mystical impulse that Veronica and Johannes did not take is made hand in hand by Ulrich and his sister Agathe.

Since the "action" of "The Temptation of Quiet Veronica" is quite literally the process by which the individual overcomes repression, Musil's story of the overcoming of repression provides a striking analogue to one psychoanalytic theory of art. According to this theory, art overcomes repression. Therefore, both the writer of fiction as well as the reader are liberated (to a greater or lesser extent) from the tyranny of the ego and are able to return (at least temporarily) to an earlier stage of psychological development, to a period prior to the repression of infantile pleasures. Literature, regarded as substitute gratification and wish fulfilment, thus tends to undo repression and leads toward the utopia of total narcissism. However, in Freud's view, the phenomenon of literature is more closely related to the infantile, the sexual, and the dreamlike than to the secondary processes, characterized by reason, logic, and the scientific attitude. Literature essentially represents for Freud a temporary escape from the pain and frustrations of civilization, a form of infantile self-indulgence in which the sorely pressed individual takes refuge when the burdens of renunciation and repression become too great. It was for this reason that Freud, as a physician and moralist, had an ambivalent if not negative attitude toward literature throughout his life. For Freud, psychoanalytic therapy, not art, is the preferred means of finally overcoming repression, because therapy requires constant analytic probing by the conscious mind in order to recall the repressed material. Freud's moral condemnation of art in this regard aside, Musil's "The Temptation of Quiet Veronica" stands as a classic example of a description in literature of the process of overcoming repression.

IV ✤

Three Mysterious Women: "Grigia," "The Lady from Portugal," "Tonka"

IN *THREE WOMEN,* a collection of three short stories first published in 1924, Musil returned (contrary to what the title of this work may suggest) to the narrative perspective of the masculine protagonist. As was the case with young Törless, so, too, Homo in "Grigia," Ketten in "The Lady from Portugal," and the unnamed young scientist in "Tonka" are forced first to recognize and then to come to terms with an irrational dimension in life that unexpectedly confronts them, a mystical dimension whose presence and power threatens to destroy the ordered and rational existences they have known for years. In *Unions,* this irrational dimension was explored from within, so to speak, for the narrative perspective rested within the feminine psyches of Claudine and Veronica; the influence of Musil's own rational and analytic temperament was correspondingly reduced to a minimum in these two stories. But in *Three Women,* the women whose lives embody the mystical dimension are viewed totally from outside, from the rational and analytic perspectives of the three masculine protagonists. Musil has, within the framework of these three further studies of mysticism, articulated his own masculine perspective. While Musil attempted to explore the mystical state as profoundly as possible and within its own terms in *Unions,* he sought in *Three Women* to achieve a balance, to discover some kind of stable and creative relationship between the masculine and the feminine psyches, between the rational and the mystical ways of experiencing life. The search for such a balance between these two extreme perspectives was a constant personal preoccupation in Musil's own life, and all three stories can be viewed on one level as more or less

disguised autobiographical studies. Musil, like his protagonists, was always attempting to find "the right way of living."

Two of the three stories can actually be traced back to autobiographical detail. "Grigia," which appeared in 1921, was based directly upon a personal experience. In 1915 Musil left his wife in order to serve in the Austrian army at the Italian front. Homo, the protagonist of "Grigia," leaves his wife in order to become part of an engineering (rather than military) expedition in Italy.

"Tonka," published in 1922, is about a love affair which resembles one Musil recorded in his diaries as early as 1902. In his early manhood he had a love affair with an uneducated girl that began before the conclusion of his university education and continued through his years in Stuttgart where he was working on his invention. The life of the young scientist in "Tonka" forms an almost exact parallel to this episode in Musil's own life. "The Lady from Portugal," which was written last and appeared in 1923, is a striking exception not only to the other two stories but to all of Musil's major fiction as well.

Whereas the action of "Grigia" and "Tonka" takes place in modern Europe, the setting of "The Lady from Portugal" is Europe in the Middle Ages. Both "Grigia" and "Tonka" draw upon love affairs in the author's past for their subject matter, that is, upon a sequence of events that had already ended when Musil began to write about them and which he could, therefore, regard with some objectivity. In "The Lady from Portugal," the perfection and stability of a marriage itself receives its most extensive treatment in all of Musil's work. This may well have required the façade of a long past age in order to allow Musil the freedom to deal with problems that continued to demand solution in his own daily life. Thus, it is only on the surface that this story appears to be the most objective and impersonal of all his works. These unusual circumstances may help to account for the fact that "The Lady from Portugal" is artistically the most perfect of all of Musil's fiction, for it was here that Musil's life-long quest to discover a balance between the rational and the mystical realm was finally achieved. In this sense, "The Lady from Portugal" provides the axis around which all of Musil's smaller and larger works revolve.

And it was for this reason that, although he wrote this story last, he gave it the central position when he published the collection of *Three Women*. The degree of artistic success that he achieved in "The Lady from Portugal" unfortunately eluded him in all his later literary efforts.

"Grigia"

The very first sentence of "Grigia" sounds an ominous note of doom that continues to swell throughout the story until its conclusion, the inevitable collapse of a man who dies because he has lost the will to live: "There is a time in life when everything perceptibly slows down, as though one's life were hesitating to go on or trying to change its course."[1] The second and final sentence of the first paragraph continues: "It may be that at this time one is more liable to disaster" (115). "The Lady from Portugal" and "Tonka" also tell the story of men who meet disaster; but it is precisely because of this disaster that they manage not only to survive but to achieve an eventual broadening and deepening of their inner lives. For Homo, the protagonist of "Grigia," however, the disaster is fatal.

The Crisis of Middle Age

Homo is ripe for disaster, for his life is not merely slowing down, it has come to a stop. On the threshold of middle life, he is a successful scientist and family man. Yet there now seems to be a certain aimlessness about his life, a lack of passionate commitment to any particular person or idea. Because his wife and child have left him to spend the summer at a spa, he is now alone and able to reflect upon and evaluate his life to date. His marriage is no longer what it once was and he cannot understand why this should be so. He also seems to feel vaguely dissatisfied with himself without

being able to comprehend any reason for his discontent. Is something missing from his life, something of which he is only now becoming aware? Like Gustav von Aschenbach in "Death in Venice," he sets off for the South, possibly in an unconscious search for psychological resurrection. This kind of crisis in the life of a middle-aged man has been extensively examined by C.G. Jung. The following presentation of Jung's analysis of this problem may serve as a convenient framework for an understanding of the development and significance of Homo's mental breakdown.

C.G. Jung devoted an important part of his psychoanalytic work to that transitional period in middle age when many men awaken one day to an overwhelming feeling of emptiness and a lack of meaning in their daily lives. Such men may have gained recognition in their professional lives and have succeeded well as husbands, fathers, and citizens. From the perspective of their acquaintances, they seem to have achieved good and useful lives. Jung's investigations revealed, however, that these men have often had to pay a price for their success, a price that first manifests itself in those middle years that ought to be filled with the contented enjoyment of the fruits of early struggle overcome. What, then, is the psychological price of success? In order to succeed in the competitive outer world, such men have been compelled to concentrate all their intellectual and emotional energies upon one aspect of their personality, i.e., upon the development of social, intellectual, scientific, and practical skills. The danger of such concentration— particularly in Western culture—is that the individual comes to identify himself too closely and too exclusively with his profession. He becomes his persona, a term that Jung defined as a mask that one exhibits to the outer world, a mask designed to create a favorable impression so that one will be more readily accepted by society. But because the persona is not identical with the whole psyche, such an identification means that the rest of the personality has been and is continuously being denied. The instinctual, unconscious, irrational side of human nature suffers from years of repression as a result, and this causes an imbalance in the psyche that finally makes itself known. At the beginning of middle age, therefore, there is an increased risk of mental breakdown.

The crisis often makes its appearance after some profoundly disturbing experience, e.g., an illness or a significant change in the individual's interpersonal relationships. He then feels compelled to leave the ordinary and the usual paths of external reality, to ignore the demands of daily life, and to turn his back upon his previously assumed responsibilities toward family and society. The need to find a new way of living arises with great urgency and sweeps aside as mere trivialities all other considerations. The second half of life is then devoted to a process of initiation into an inner reality that transcends the boundaries and limitations of empirical reality. At this time of life, the individual's sense of his own meaning and significance is seen to lie precisely in those ignored and neglected aspects of the psyche that had been repressed for so many years on behalf of his need to control and manipulate the outer world. The persona becomes deflated, and this deflation then allows the stunted sides of man's nature to grow. The typical middle-aged patient, Jung stated, arrived at his office with problems that fell outside the scope and theory of Freudian analysis. For such cases are not concerned with problems of sexual maladjustment. The focus of Jungian therapy is to help the patient make a creative choice, for he does have alternatives: he may either stoically resign himself to bourgeois boredom or he may explore a new dimension within himself that is nearer to the religious than to the scientific impulse.

The reversal of the individual's direction of interest from the outer to the inner world represents, for Jung, a perfectly understandable urge toward a more complete development of the personality. Jung presupposes, however, that the very occurrence of such a crisis of middle age is indicative of a "higher" type of man who possesses a Faustian urge toward self-expression or, rather, toward the expression of all aspects of the self. This process of the expansion of the personality to include the "darker" aspects of the psyche is a necessary step in what Jung termed "the process of individuation." Jungian psychotherapy is itself primarily an individuation process. In this regard, Jung asserted that man possesses a mystical or religious function, the expression of which is as necessary for mental health and for the continuing development of

the individuation process as is the expression of the sexual instincts in Freudian theory. In fact, Jung argued that the extreme form of life based primarily upon reason might actually lead to an outbreak of the religious impulse in middle age. Jung's concept of this process of reversal from a rational and superficial existence to one which recognizes and includes the mystical depths of human existence is given analogous treatment by Nietzsche in *The Birth of Tragedy*. Nietzsche, however, expressed the dialectical reversal from reason in cultural and historical rather than in primarily psychological terms. He analyzed the imminent reversal from a rational and Socratic toward a more mystical, dionysian culture which, he believed, was destined to occur in Germany under the aegis of Wagnerian music, a music of the future that represented a new synthesis of the apollonian and the long repressed dionysian impulses in European culture. But why was such a reversal in German culture destined to occur?

In his early work, Nietzsche believed that Western culture was unfortunately dominated by the Socratic man, i.e., that type of man who related to life primarily and one-sidedly through the application of conscious processes, through reason and the scientific attitude. Such an approach demoted the irrational, the mystical, and the religious to the realm of the primitive and nonsensical. Socratic consciousness measures and subdues nature and presupposes that suffering is meaningless and can therefore only brutalize man. The scientific man (as Nietzsche analyzed him) believes (erroneously) that intelligence can penetrate into the irrational dimensions of life and can there introduce corrections to what he perceives to be flaws in life and nature. But Nietzsche predicted that the "higher" type of man would sooner or later arrive at the limits of science and then be forced to gaze into the mystical depths.[2] Intuitive and aesthetic perception would then no longer be ridiculed but welcomed as a means to salvation. Europe as a whole would soon recognize the poverty of the rational temperament and would undergo a dialectical reversal. That is why Europe today (to return to Jung, who was very conscious of continuing Nietzsche's analysis on this subject) is seeking to find a way out of its present schizophrenic state in which the inner (irrational) man has been

allowed to atrophy while the outer (scientific) man has become inflated to a pathological degree. As evidence for Europe's urgent need for cultural change, Jung cites the West's ever increasing interest in the East and in the more highly mystical religions.[3]

A fictional analogue to the analyses of Jung and Nietzsche may be found in "Grigia"—but only up to a point. It should first be noted that, if Musil knew little of Freud's work, he knew even less about the psychology of C.G. Jung. Therefore Jung's psycho-analytic theories, which have been abstracted and presented above as a prologue to the analysis of "Grigia" in this chapter, should not be regarded as having consciously informed Musil's writing of this short story. The Jungian perspective that follows is offered as merely one of many possible ways of viewing "Grigia." Musil and Jung did, of course, live and develop in the same cultural atmosphere, and the many preoccupations, theories, and evaluations that they shared arose out of a passionate concern with the same political, artistic, and intellectual tradition, a tradition which reached its intellectual culmination in the work of Nietzsche. Both Musil and Jung not only admired Nietzsche's psychological and cultural analyses, they absorbed them totally into their own thought.[4]

There is a point, however, at which Musil's fictional analogue to the theories of Nietzsche and Jung ends. Where do their psychological hypotheses and cultural criticism diverge? Both Nietzsche (in *The Birth of Tragedy*) and Jung emphasized the positive and creative aspects of the dialectical reversal of reason to mysticism and regarded it as the beginning of salvation. But Musil revealed that what for one man might be a creative challenge to reach ever higher stages of development could function for another as a temptation to destruction. What was it, we may therefore ask in advance, that Nietzsche and Jung assumed would be present in the character of a particular man or culture that would make renewal a possibility? What was it that Homo lacked?

A reconstruction of Homo's life before he leaves for Italy reveals an apparently quite ordinary existence unmarked by any unusual experience or striking features. He is a successful geologist, husband, and father of a small boy. On evaluating his past life, he

mentions only the fact that with the birth of his son his marriage appeared to have become in some way less intense. He continues to love his wife as before, but the existence of "the boy had earlier killed the other-worldly" aspect of their relationship. (This strange sentiment may well reflect Musil's own belief that he, as a small boy, had been an intruder in his family.) The preoccupations and responsibilities of the bourgeois husband and father continued to grow through the years. He now appears to consider himself to be fairly happy and fulfilled in his role as *pater familias*. But like Claudine, Homo is also filled with a feeling of vague discontent, an awareness that through the years his life has lost something extremely important. When his wife and son leave for a spa, Homo finds himself alone for the first time since he was married. Thus "Grigia" begins with the breaking of the family unit as "The Perfecting of a Love" began with Claudine's departure from her husband and *Young Törless* with Törless's separation from his parents. As Törless perceived the absence of a "self" within, so Homo experiences at this point in his life "a sort of self-dissolution." Both thereby become vulnerable to an irrational dimension in life from which most individuals are protected by membership in a family or social unit of some kind. Homo sets off by train, as did Claudine, and begins his journey into an Other World. Unlike Claudine, however, he never returns.

A Landscape of the Soul

Homo receives a letter inviting him to join, as its geologist, a company that is about to reopen old Venetian gold mines in the mountains of Northern Italy. He accepts and sets off almost immediately. Like Claudine, he is traveling in Spring and the snows in the mountains are melting. Both Homo and his environment are undergoing a process of loosening and dissolution in preparation for a transformation. The countryside into which the expedition takes him is described as being quite fantastic and mysterious. It is a half-way world located between North and South. The landscape is filled with such oddities as a prehistoric lake-village built on piles

and set in the middle of fairy-tale-like mountains filled with great lumps of rock crystal and amethyst. This world is located 5,000 feet above sea level, and everything that happens at this height is "no longer part of reality, but a play floating in the air" (123). For the protagonist, it is a world apart from daily reality, and the moral standards of home can no longer be used to direct and evaluate his experience here. This hermetically sealed world becomes the appropriate setting for Homo's seduction into the Other Realm, as was the remote attic room for Törless's sexual experiences with Basini, and the isolated little town for Claudine's seduction by the stranger. Communications with the outer world become superfluous. As Claudine was unable to send her husband letters, so Homo no longer bothers sending letters to his wife.

Musil's descriptions of the landscape, the people, and their activities in "Grigia" are very different in degree and kind from the descriptions in "The Temptation of Quiet Veronica." Because Veronica's interest is directed almost exclusively toward her inner life, everything in the outer world seems vague, insubstantial, and abstract. Musil's descriptions in "Grigia," however, are filled to bursting with the exact observation of colorful details. The following quotation is typical of the style of this short story and also indicates Musil's radical departure here from the narrative stream of subjective emotional states in *Unions:* "All white and mauve, green and brown, these were the meadows around him. He was no phantom. A fairy-tale world of ancient larches, feathery with new green, spread over an emerald slope. Under the moss there might be living crystals, mauve and white" (123). With such exotic, colorful details, Musil strives to evoke a world at once pastoral and magical, "an enchanted world ordained for him alone" (125), a world that "was brighter and more highly spiced than any life he had led before" (123). This essentially objective and masculine perspective, as opposed to the feminine perspective of *Unions,* is continued in "The Lady from Portugal" and "Tonka."

The relationship between the five men of the company and the female inhabitants of the region seems in its strangeness to match the physical landscape of the area, and Musil's description of the countryside prepares the reader for the relationship between Homo

and the woman named Grigia. The five men are received like gods, for they are regarded by the women as the bringers of great blessings to their backward mountain life. They are a never ending source of food, tools, and money. Here a man is everywhere met with love simply because he is there. A man is not scrutinized and judged to determine whether he is worthy of love. His character is irrelevant; it is not recognized. His ideas about life are also of no importance. Whether a man is stupid or intelligent, ugly or handsome, weak or strong—all such considerations do not exist for these women.

One day Homo hears about an event which had occurred fifteen years before his arrival. The story concerns the relationship between some of the women of this area and a man who, like Homo, comes from outside. Many of the men of the region had, upon marrying, immediately left their wives in order to seek work in America. Years had often passed before they returned home again with the money they had earned abroad. One day a man had arrived from America, claiming wife and house. After the money ran out, he left and at some distance away claimed another woman as his wife. After this had occurred several times, he was revealed to all as a swindler, who had worked with the real husbands in America and had cunningly gathered detailed information about the wives and homes they had left behind. Significantly, the various women who had been fooled were not particularly outraged when the truth was revealed. In fact, they would have been glad to have the swindler back. The underlying idea that men are interchangeable grips Homo's imagination. Nevertheless, primitive behavior of this kind which presupposes an extreme degree of impersonality in human relationship eludes Homo's sophisticated modern comprehension. Perhaps it is because these women seem to lack a specific personality, which is so much a part of Western man's concept of himself, that they seem to Homo not to exist totally in the here and now. He notices, for example, that they all wear kerchiefs that suggest "bygone centuries" and possess a strange gaze that seems to have begun at some distant point in prehistoric time. This gaze seems to have continued to exist throughout the ages and still shines dimly through into the present.

In the perspective of this gaze, Homo meditates, perhaps all men are the same.

In the midst of this landscape and this life, Homo begins involuntarily to experience strange epiphanies. In certain heightened moments, he perceives the external world as manifesting itself in inexplicable aesthetic patterns. Such experiences had never occurred to him in his earlier life as geologist, husband, and father. The first time this happens is when his gaze falls upon the wallpaper of his bedroom. The paper has an indescribably bewildering pattern, which strikes him as being at once ordinary and extremely strange. Staring at that pattern Homo himself "seemed to turn into a mere tangle of rising and falling tendrils that would grow within a couple of seconds from nothingness to their full size and then as rapidly disappear into themselves again" (116). Shortly thereafter, he notices little red, blue, and pink villas standing vividly among the trees "like scattered cubes inanimately manifesting to every eye some strange morphological law of which they themselves knew nothing" (117). Homo also perceives that the horses in the meadow stand in certain patterns "as if it were done according to some secretly agreed aesthetic principle" (126). What is this strange order, this inexplicable pattern that pervades nature and that man is sometimes able to glimpse? The narrator answers: this is the way "God had ordered things, wholly as a wonder" (124). Homo wants to cut himself totally loose from the order imposed by man's rational mind and to drift upon this newly discovered tide of nature.

A Messenger from Nature

Homo names his peasant mistress "Grigia," the gray one, after the name which she herself had given to her cow. In so doing, Homo makes a specific connection between this woman and the animal world, which is typical of Musil's masculine protagonist. But Grigia is further associated in Homo's mind with nature in general, both in a positive and negative fashion. On the one hand, her real name, Lene Maria Lenzi, has a sound that suggests amethyst crystals and flowers to him. On the other hand, Homo finds

Grigia to be "as naturally lovely as a slender little poisonous mush-
room" (130); she also reminds him of a scarab, a beetle that as a
religious ornament was inscribed with quotations from the Egyp-
tian *Book of the Dead* and was buried in tombs with mummies.
Grigia talks a "magical language" (133) that reduces their rational
communication to a minimum. Most of the time Homo seems
quite unable to fathom what she is saying. Her chance remarks
appear to him to be filled with mysterious meaning that does not
permit translation into the language of everyday life. Homo has a
certain fear of Grigia, a feeling that he likens to the "residual dread
of Nature" (131) which all men have. Musil writes of nature: "she
is earthy, edgy, poisonous, and inhuman at all points where man
does not impose his will upon her. Probably it was just this that
fascinated him in this peasant woman" (131). When Homo becomes Grigia's lover, he accepts the situation passively, as if something had simply happened to him; their affair is something into
which he has drifted rather than something which he has himself
voluntarily instigated.

Homo's "inexhaustible amazement that she [Grigia] did so
much resemble a woman" (131) reveals that for him she represents
not a particular woman in a particular time and place but rather
something of vast and undefinable importance. Jung's theories on
the anima provide an illuminating parallel. Jung defines the anima
as the unconscious and latent feminine side of the male that com-
plements his conscious masculinity.[5] "She" also represents the collective image of woman that exists in the unconscious of every
male psyche. The anima may reveal herself in a man's feelings and
moods, in his love of nature, in his receptiveness to mystical experience, and in his relationship to the unconscious in general. As a
symbolic image, the anima may appear in dreams or the individual
may project this inner image of woman into the outer world—a
possibility that becomes a reality in "Grigia." A man does not
decide to make such a projection onto a particular woman; it happens to him and he is unaware of his part in the process. In fact, it
is precisely the most unconscious and latent elements of the psyche
that are continually projected into the outer world, and the meet-

ing of the individual with his anima projection represents an important stage in what Jung terms the process of individuation.

The European male in particular tends to repress the feminine aspects of his nature. He demotes and devalues the anima and strives not to recognize its existence. If the individual develops only his masculine traits such as reason, intelligence, and the analytic skills, the repressed feminine aspects accumulate in his unconscious. This means that European man makes the acquaintance of his contra-sexual nature usually in the form of its projection. The more scientific and rational the persona, as in Homo's case, the more archaic and powerful will be the anima projection. Jung wrote that "if the persona is intellectual, the anima will certainly be sentimental."[6] Jolande Jacobi, in her definitive study of Jung's psychology, summarizes this inverse relationship in the following way: "Therefore in principle an abstract scientist's anima will be primitive, emotional, and romantic." [7] Thus it is, Jung believed, that men of high intelligence often become ensnared by the most crude and unsophisticated of women—women not unlike Grigia.

The anima may appear in two ways: either as a good and noble goddesslike figure or as a *femme fatale,* a prostitute, witch, Greek Siren, or tempting nymph who lures men from their homes and families. In either form, she is often associated with the earth and nature as is Grigia. The anima may also be symbolized by an animal, such as a cow, a cat, or a tiger. Jung notes that "something strangely meaningful clings to her, a secret knowledge or hidden wisdom."[8] Since it is the negative aspect of the anima that dominates in "Grigia," the chief danger in Jungian terms is that Homo will succumb to the fascinating and dangerous influence of this archetype of the collective unconscious. A Siberian tale, quoted by a Jungian analyst, illustrates the dangerous aspect of the anima and its parallels to "Grigia" are clear:

> One day a lonely hunter sees a beautiful woman emerging from the deep forest on the other side of the river. She waves at him and sings:

Oh, come lonely hunter in the stillness of dusk. Come, come! I
miss you, I miss you!
Now I will embrace you, embrace you!
Come, come! My nest is near, my nest is near!
Come, come, lonely hunter, now in the stillness of the dusk!

He throws off his clothes and swims across the river, but suddenly she flies away in the form of an owl, laughing mockingly at
him. When he tries to swim back to find his clothes, he drowns in
the river.[9]

A woman who seems rather vague, dreamy, and mysterious is
a figure who particularly attracts the anima projections of men.
For around such a woman a man is able to weave all kinds of
fantastic images with little hindrance from reality. (An extreme
literary example of this process may be found in the relationship
between the poetic dreamer Nathanael and the beautiful mechanical doll Olimpia in E.T.A. Hoffmann's novella, "The Sandman.")
Although Grigia does not actively tempt Homo as did the beautiful woman in the fairy tale, he does succumb to her influence.
Homo, unlike Johannes, is unable to break the spell of his fascination with this woman, escape from her, and return to ordinary life.

A retrospective Jungian interpretation of *Unions,* in which the
protagonists are women, sheds a different light on those texts than
did the Freudian approach. Jung terms the contra-sexual element
in the woman the animus; "he" may (like the anima) take either a
positive or negative form and may manifest himself on any of four
levels of development. When projected in his negative form, he
functions to lure a woman away from the real world, specifically
from her marriage. He personifies woman's fantasies of escape
from all familial and social responsibilities. On the first and most
primitive level of manifestation, he is the personification of mere
physicality, of brute sexuality. Here the animus may appear in
dreams or be projected into outer reality as an animal—as a dog, a
bull, a lion, or as any sexually powerful beast. Such a primitive
manifestation is particularly likely if, as in Claudine's case where
the stranger is associated with a he-goat, the animus in the uncon-

scious is highly undifferentiated due to years of non-recognition as
a result of repression. In "The Temptation of Quiet Veronica," the
animus appears in two forms: Demeter embodies the lowest and
Johannes the highest of its aspects. At the most advanced stage of
animus development, the projected animus functions, as did Johannes, as a mediator between woman and the religious dimension
in her psyche. As M.-L. von Franz writes, she "can find her way to
an intensified spiritual attitude to life"[10] through him and thus provide her life with new meaning and significance.

In the Hand of God

Homo has a strong intuition that behind the fairy-tale-like
appearance of the Italian mountain landscape there lies something
hidden, something that he is awaiting with great yearning. (Upon
Claudine's leaving her spouse, her senses, too, seem to lean forward in yearning for some unknown possibility.) Homo is overcome by the conviction that he is soon to lie dead in this landscape,
for "his old life had lost all strength; it was like a butterfly growing
feebler as autumn draws on" (134). The landscape as well as the
events he witnesses suggest the omnipresence of death. He sees an
old peasant waving his scythe like death in person and he watches
the slaughter of a pig, a scene which makes a great impression
upon him. To his eye, the leaves of the vineyard and woods seem
interlaced as in graveyard wreaths. Homo feels as if released from
a desire to live as well as from a fear of dying. In such a state,
Musil writes, one seems to be passively wallowing in God's hand:
"one may lie obliquely, or almost upright like a saint ascending to
heaven in a green cloud. Those were bridal days and ascension
days" (136). The obviously religious connotations of Musil's metaphor describing Homo's saintlike passivity in the presence of the
Other Realm recalls Veronica's saintlike renunciation of daily life
and her drifting away into a mystical dimension. Both Veronica
and Homo are, on a secular level, saints of the inner life and both
eventually ascend into the mystical realm, never to return to the
everyday world.

Homo's surrendering himself to "drift on his own tide" (124) is reinforced by an epiphany that he has one day while walking alone through a forest. It is an experience that he considers to be religious in nature; he sinks upon one knee and spreads out his arms. At that moment Homo feels as if he is being lifted out of his own embrace and he seems to hear his wife's voice. Suddenly he feels as if his body is being recast into the mould of her body. He experiences a total spiritual reunion with his wife, who is at some physical distance from him. (The parallel to Veronica's reunion with the supposedly dead Johannes is striking). We may assume that Homo's union with his wife at a distance is far more complete than had been any previous union achieved in her presence. Musil adds: "He was not a man inclined to religious belief, but at this moment he was illuminated within" (125). For the first time in his life he knows love "as a heavenly sacrament" (125). It seems to Homo that destiny has brought him to this enchanted world which was meant for him alone.

The protagonist's experience of total union with the beloved (Claudine with her husband, Veronica with Johannes, Homo with his wife) becomes possible only with the physical absence of the partner. Spiritual love-at-a-distance and sexual union with the beloved are mutually exclusive. Moreover, where the possibility of spiritual union with the beloved exists, it seems to arise initially out of a desire for sexual union with someone else, a third person. In fact, the precondition for spiritual "reunion" is the radical separation of the spiritual or emotional impulse from the purely instinctual one, each being directed toward a different individual. As we have repeatedly seen, the sexual objects of Musil's protagonists do not appear in merely human guise, but generally take on the characteristics of an animal such as a goat, a dog, or a cow. Although the object of the spiritual impulse does not undergo a correspondingly great process of intensification and simplification (for instance, into a Madonnalike or goddesslike figure worthy of worship), the reunion is experienced as the ideal relationship. Such a love is felt by the protagonist as a "heavenly sacrament" that exists outside of time in "eternity" (125). Homo wonders how, when he dies, he will be able to take his wife along to the other side. The

division in the male psyche between the sacred and the profane, the eternal and the worldly, to which psychoanalysis has given some attention, reaches a most subtle culmination in Musil's work in general; it is also a theme which has had a long history in German literature, stretching from the medieval epics to the novels of Hermann Hesse.

Given the exclusivity of the impulses of love and sexuality as well as their causally interconnected nature, the further Homo's physical relationship with Grigia progresses, the more profound the mystical relationship with his wife is able to become. Of this corresponding relationship, Musil wrote: "When he kissed it [Grigia's mouth] he never knew whether he loved this woman or whether a miracle was being worked upon him and Grigia was only part of a mission linking him ever more closely with his beloved [his wife] in eternity" (134). Homo does not feel that his love for his wife is diminishing because of his affair with Grigia: it is growing stronger, being ever renewed. What does a momentary sexual affair with Grigia mean when compared to Homo's being together with his wife for all eternity? Nothing. It is from this perspective that the following rather obscure remark made by Claudine in "The Perfecting of a Love" becomes comprehensible in retrospect. Upon opening the bolt on her bedroom door in order to allow the stranger to enter, Claudine thinks of herself and her husband: "We are casting away everything that can be cast away, to hold on to each other all the more tightly, to wrap around us closely what no one can touch" (63). Then for an instant, cast up into her waking mind, comes the thought: "This man [the goatlike stranger] will triumph over us. But what is triumph?" (63). The stranger will merely triumph sexually, which is of no importance, whereas Claudine will become reunited with her husband forever. The mystical union of husband and wife will triumph and this belief explains Claudine's interpretation of adultery with the stranger: "It is you [her husband] who do whatever I am doing" (63).

At the same time that Homo's sexual affair is approaching its culmination, he also seems to be moving ever further from daily sensual reality and into a realm of total spirituality. Thus, Homo's psyche undergoes a paradoxical reversal: the sexual experience

causes an internal psychological change in which the claims of physical life are eventually denied, become superfluous, and fade into insignificance. The mystical world, in which the reunion with his wife takes place, has no connection with reality, provides no help with or direction for dealing with the problems of daily living. It is a self-contained world that claims the individual's complete allegiance. Musil writes of Homo's spiritual love for his wife: "It was weightless and free of all earthly attachment in that strange and wonderful way known only to one who has had to reckon up with his life and who henceforth may wait only for death" (135). Death is the inevitable culmination of such a reunion. Approaching "the other side," Homo experiences, as did Veronica, a feeling of complete health: "at this time something within him rose up and was straight, like a lame man who suddenly throws away his crutches and walks on his own" (135). This state is not the health of life but the perfection of a mystical realm bordering upon death, in which struggle and despair have disappeared because all the problems of living as a particular individual have been left behind.

Into the Grave of Eternity

Grigia wants to sever her relationship with Homo because her husband is apparently becoming suspicious. Nevertheless, Homo forces her into one last meeting. They retreat into the solitude of a dark mine shaft. In "The Perfecting of a Love," the frightening thought once came to Claudine that she might one day find herself abandoned in a prison of inner solitude so total that she could only compare it to "a passage leading underground" (32), a tunnel that would lead her to "a vast, unfamiliar, unwanted reality" (33). Such psychological solipsism is a form of death from which Claudine escapes. Homo, however, literally enacts that which remained a metaphor in Claudine's life. He unites with Grigia one final time in the kind of dark passage described by Claudine, and Grigia seems to trickle through him like soft, dry earth. But Grigia's husband, Musil writes, is standing outside and in an act of revenge rolls a

large stone over the entrance to the mine, an act which suggests the sealing of the crucified Christ in his tomb.

Homo watches Grigia's reaction of panic with an attitude of detached interest. He notes that she squeaks like a pig and rocks senselessly like a crazed horse. Such frantic behavior, Homo realizes, is quite in accord with nature: it is natural to want to live and to fear death. But Homo wants nothing at all. He merely recognizes his destiny, which is to continue to drift until he crosses over "to the other side," into the realm of eternity and death. In a very short time, Homo totally forgets about Grigia's existence, as Veronica ceased to care about Johannes once he departed for the coast. Eventually Grigia finds a crevice through which she slips into the outer world. The reader's last impression of her is not of an anima figure, certainly not of a *femme fatale*. She is merely a frightened woman who wants above all to live. Like Johannes, Grigia escapes back into life, leaving Homo alone. He feels betrayed by Grigia, as did Veronica when Johannes found his "way out into the street." Unlike Veronica, however, Homo at this point needs no one and nothing because his wife is now within him in a permanent spiritual union beyond the flesh. Grigia may and does return to a relationship with a husband of flesh and blood.

The reader is informed that Homo could probably also have escaped, but that he had no wish to do so. Like Veronica, who at the end of the story stands imprisoned behind the door of her dark house, Homo sits imprisoned by his own lack of volition behind a narrow crevice in the dark cave. But unlike Veronica, who soon falls out of the perfect moment and into an ever deepening despair because she knows that Johannes will be returning, Homo appears to feel no anxiety or depression. In "The Temptation of Quiet Veronica," the spiritual union was destroyed because Johannes did not die. In "Grigia" however, Homo knows that the spiritual union will not be destroyed, for he himself will die and thereby preserve it. Whereas Veronica was dependent upon another person's committing suicide, Homo is completely in control: he can achieve what he wants by committing suicide himself. In this sense, he has succeeded in going on a permanent holiday in mysticism, a holiday that will reach its culmination at the moment of his death.

Homo's psychological development may be summarized in a fashion analogous to the "narrative sequence" that Jung perceived as occurring in the individuation process, a process in which the individual compensates for overdeveloped consciousness by drawing upon the depths of his unconscious. The first step (successfully completed by Homo) requires the individuation and the realization of hidden aspects of the personality—a process usually accomplished through their projection into the outer world. The anima figure, a personification of the unconscious, is able when projected to function as a mediator between the conscious and the unconscious. But although Homo's experience of the feminine and irrational element in his psyche, as manifested by Grigia as an anima figure, broadened and deepened his previously imbalanced personality, Homo failed from the Jungian perspective to conclude the second and crucial step of individuation. The second step is governed by what Jung termed "the transcendent function," the purpose of which is to integrate and unite all the opposing aspects of the personality which have become conscious to the individual in their projected form. It is only after such integration takes place that the ultimate goal of psychological wholeness is reached. Jung defined such wholeness as "the self" and distinguished it from "the ego." Whereas the ego is the center of the conscious mind alone, the self is the center of the totality of the ego and the unconscious and represents, therefore, a synthesis of ego and unconscious. It is this new center of the personality, the self rather than the ego, toward which Jung's therapy strives and which Nietzsche's concept of the Superman presupposes.

Although Homo's ego (to use the term in the Jungian sense) underwent a process of dissolution that began with his separation from his family, there never followed a stage of psychological development in which the newly uncovered irrational elements of Homo's personality became integrated into his conscious experience. When projected, the anima may be used to construct a bridge from the ego to the self. But this bridge was never constructed because Homo's ego dissolved. And as Jolande Jacobi argues concerning the successful completion of the individuation process: "no essential values of the conscious personality, that is, the ego, must

be impaired, for if this happens, there is no one left to do the integrating. For unconscious compensation is only effective when it co-operates with an integrated consciousness."[11] Jung's concept of the individuation process assumes that the psyche naturally strives for the goal of complete integration. Although this may in fact be generally true, Homo had no such desire. The three cases of Claudine, Veronica, and Homo represent three stages of progessively greater disintegration of the ego. Under the initial stimulation of an erotic impulse, the egos of these three protagonists begin to dissolve. At the point of the ego's near extinction, the psyche achieves a state of totally nondionysian mysticism. Such a state may be perfection in itself, but it is a death-oriented state. Only Claudine manages to return to everyday life. Veronica returns to an existence halfway between life and death. Homo alone achieves the ultimate perfection of death, unchallenged by the passage of time.

In *The Man without Qualities*, every activity from the most trivial to the most cerebral is colored by the doom-laden advent of the First World War, an event which Musil connects with the chaos of dionysian mysticism. In "Grigia," Musil specifically associates the boredom and sensuality of the men on the mining expedition with the violence of the war that was about to fall upon Europe like "a knife slashing down out of the sky, a destroying angel, angelic madness" (129). With the words "destroying angel," Musil intimates a connection between religion and war, mysticism being the common denominator of both. From one point of view, Homo, the mining engineer, is just another member of this heterogeneous group of men who form what Musil calls "that standard psychic unit that is Europe" (129). The choice which Homo, like Europe, can make at this period in time is a choice between two forms of mysticism, as formulated by Homo himself in the middle of the story: "Homo murmured to himself: ' . . . Kill, and yet feel the presence of God? . . . Feel the presence of God and yet kill?' " (130). Unlike the other men on the expedition, he places himself in the hand of God. The rest of Europe, however, plunges on into the other alternative, the First World War. Homo took the road of contemplative mysticism and self-extinction, disguised though it

may have been under the veneer of a superficial dionysian affair with a peasant woman. Europe chose the opposite road of dionysian war and murder, an alternative that was often disguised under a pretentious façade of pseudo-mystical rhetoric.

"The Lady from Portugal"

The second story in the trilogy *Three Women* is set (as was the first story, "Grigia" in a geographical area that is intentionally vague, in a region situated between North and South and in a world at once specifically medieval and yet enveloped in the timelessness of the fairy tale. Generations earlier, the Ketten family had come from the North and stopped, as did Homo, on the threshold of the South near the Brenner pass in Italy. It is in such an ambiguous geographical setting that Musil treats once again the conflict between reason and mysticism. And it is because of the way in which the present Herr von Ketten eventually resolves this duality (which, as in "Grigia," Musil treats as an internal psychological conflict between the male and female principles) that he manages to escape the destiny of all the previous heads of his family. Generation after generation, all of them had died before reaching their sixtieth birthday. Each one of them had been cut down by death as soon as he had completed a great task. Ketten also accomplishes a great task, by which and through which his life becomes defined. Like his ancestors, he, too, suffers a "death," but is then, as if by a miracle, reborn and restored to life with his family and the others for whom he is responsible.

The Wolf and His Moonlady

Because of the importance to this story of the conflict within Ketten of the male and female principles as Musil understood them, Musil goes to great pains to describe husband and wife in

terms that are not only at once both concrete and symbolic, but also at first antagonistic. Throughout the story, Musil compares Ketten's life and nature to that of a wolf, a ferocious beast of prey who pursues his goal inexorably and without deviation. If Ketten can get what he wants by honest means, he does so; but, if not, he uses methods both violent and cunning. He is alert, cruel, and aggressive. Ketten is also compared with the landscape surrounding his family seat. The castle stands on a sheer and lonely cliff. Five hundred feet below a torrent of water rages so loudly that no sound can penetrate from the outer world into the castle; nor can any sound from the castle reach the outer world. The patterns in which the woods rise and fall on the mountainsides bestow an air of savagery and violence upon the landscape. The atmosphere surrounding the stunted trees and ragged cliffs is chilly and the countryside is described as being inhabited by stags, wild boars, wolves, dragons, and perhaps even the unicorn. Eagles soar in the clouds above, and demons and spirits seem to lurk in the upper air. After his courtship in Portugal, a land of beauty described in terms of the gentle blue waves of the sea, Ketten brings his wife home to his castle. Although she had assumed that the landscape would be in some way similar to the nature of her husband, what she sees as she rides up to the castle for the first time is something "unimaginably hideous."[12] Her first impulse is to flee. But she forces herself to remain by assuming that the castle and the landscape have a beauty of their own, "like a man's ways, to which one had to become accustomed" (146).

Ketten, for his part, perceives his lady from Portugal as being more than merely a very beautiful woman from the South. She is an unceasing mystery to him, an enchantment that can never be dispelled: "Embracing the woman, might he not suddenly be brought up short by the force of some magical resistance?" (151). On one occasion, when she is standing on the steps waiting to mount her horse, she seems to Ketten as if she were about to step into the saddle and ride off into an Other World. Amid the continuing violence of Ketten's life, she blooms silently as a rose; she is also compared to a pearl necklace that could easily be crushed but which nevertheless continues to exist in the everyday world,

absolutely invulnerable. Eventually a legend arises among the people that Ketten has sold his soul to the Devil, who now lives in his castle disguised as a beautiful woman. It is significant that husband and wife rarely seem to talk to each other. And yet, everything that is meaningful in Ketten's life is in some way connected with his lady's existence, an uncanny existence that cannot be expressed discursively in language or comprehended by reason. Ketten's intense love for his "moonlady" reflects a deep and secret yearning of his soul. Compared with this feeling, he takes no joy in increasing his worldly possessions and in expanding his household.

Ketten's wife, the lady from Portugal, is a close literary relation of Homo's mistress, Grigia. From a Jungian perspective, both women represent the anima figure, Grigia a lower stage of its development and the Portugese lady a higher one. The first stage, which was examined in the previous story, is often represented by an Eve, a woman who expresses only the instinctual and biological needs of man. The second stage is represented by a figure like Faust's Helen, who embodies not only the sexual but also the aesthetic elements of man's nature.[13] The Portugese lady may be regarded as embodying this higher aspect. The way in which the anima figure first manifests itself in "Grigia" is different from the way it is introduced in "The Lady from Portugal," and this difference determines the utter dissimilarity of atmospheres pervading the two works. Homo rides into Grigia's world, into the world of the anima, and his attitude toward her causes the story to be enveloped by a sentimental and romantically pastoral mood. But in "The Lady from Portugal," it is the woman who rides into the man's world; the story therefore takes place in a violent, masculine, and almost primeval setting.

The Temptation of the Warrior

When Ketten brings his bride home after a year-long courtship in Portugal, he is eighteen years old. He spends the next twelve years almost without interruption in a war with the Bishop of Trent, a war that the Ketten family has been waging on and off

for generations. Musil indicates the presence of ambivalence in Ketten's sense of identity by the fact that he bears two names, the German "von Ketten" (North) and the Italian "delle Catene" (South). The narrator comments, further, that Ketten himself did not know whether he revealed his true self during the one-year period of his graceful courtship in the South, throughout which he had behaved in accordance with the rules of feminine society, or only in all the other years of incessant and brutal warfare. Because his existence as a human being is defined by his role in the external world as leader of the army against the Bishop's forces, he must resist the temptations of his wife's world. Ketten must play the role of man, as understood in his society. For in the world of medieval northern Italy, life is war and the man who kills survives. It is Ketten's dilemma that he must fight and murder while at the same time feeling drawn toward another alien and ambiguous world whose human expression appears in his gentle and silent wife. Her very being seems always to be "luring him on into some Other Realm" (146). This is the world of religious feeling; it is the realm of God, as both Johannes and Homo designated it. But it is also a realm that negates all those virtues and vices required by a war lord in order to achieve victory over his enemies.

Musil describes Ketten's attitude toward these two worlds of being in terms of the sun and the moon: "To command is a thing of clarity; such a life is day-bright, solid to the touch, and the thrust of a spear under an iron collar that has slipped is as simple as pointing one's finger at something and being able to say: This is *this*. But the other thing is as alien as the moon" (152). Out of this other soft and ambiguous world no commands are given and none are received, for it is sufficient unto itself. Sometimes in the evenings when Ketten is sitting at the campfire, half-dreaming and in a state of total physical exhaustion, this Other World seems to creep out of the shadows toward him and threatens to undo his manly strength and determination. The same question that Homo had asked himself expresses in a most lucid and dramatic fashion the dilemma of Ketten's life: "Kill, and yet feel the presence of God? . . . Feel the presence of God and yet kill?" (130).

Ketten resists the temptation and manages to remain keen,

alert, and cruel, happy in the knowledge that he is still able to "cause others to die without that other thing" (152), i.e., the mystical realm, intruding to paralyze all activity. While there never seemed to be a point in Homo's life where he considered the possibility of resisting the temptation of the mystical realm, the thought never occurs to Ketten that he could ever surrender to the Bishop and yield to this alien world. Ketten is filled with "the happiness of not yielding, and this was the very soul of his soul" (152). Homo's family will survive without him. Ketten, however, must defend his wife, sons, and subjects by waging aggressive war. There is no alternative for him: Ketten must repress the same impulse in which Homo, having once discovered it, indulged himself to the point where life became irrelevant to him.

It is clear—to continue the comparison between "Grigia" and "The Lady from Portugal"—that the relationship of the protagonist to mysticism is different in both stories. The duality in "Grigia" was that between two forms of mysticism: Homo's love-at-a-distance for his wife (contemplative mysticism) and his attraction to the exotic Grigia (dionysian mysticism). The glory of Homo's one moment of eternal "reunion" with his wife caused the sexual attraction for Grigia to fade by comparison into insignificance, although their relationship continued to drift on. The final struggle was one between Homo's passive drifting off into death and his instinctual desire to live. Because of the intensity and purity of the mystical "reunion" with his wife, Homo relinquished his life almost with an air of indifference. In "The Lady from Portugal," however, the initial conflict is between Ketten's everyday duties to the world as a man and his attraction to the mystical realm in general, for both dionysian and contemplative mysticism are present in one woman. From a Jungian point of view, Ketten has married his anima: Madonnalike wife and exotic temptress are one. It is obvious, then, that neither "Grigia" nor "The Lady from Portugal" can be regarded as merely describing a superficial conflict between man and woman. Neither Grigia nor the lady are simple, external, active female temptresses, to whom the male protagonist must succumb or from whom he must flee. It is true that Homo succumbs. And in "The Lady from Portugal," Ketten is

always in flight. In the twelve years of war, Ketten in fact never
spends more then twelve hours at home: "Doubtless he feared to
stay at home longer, just as a tired man dare not sit down" (149).
But the conflict is essentially endopsychic. Both Homo and Ketten
are dealing with an impulse from within themselves that manifests
itself externally in the form of a particular woman. The unconscious nature of this psychological dynamic explains why Homo
felt such an irrational attraction for Grigia as well as why Ketten
chose to marry such an exotic woman from the South. Both
women are able to accommodate the projection of the protagonist's repressed feminine soul, a repression that had been required
on behalf of the pursuit of extremely masculine professions: that of
scientist and soldier.

Victory and Decline

The Bishop falls ill and dies, and the cathedral chapter, being
without its leader, decides to sue for peace. A war that has lasted
for four generations comes to an end. After having spent almost
every waking moment of his life and every ounce of his strength in
the violent pursuit of a specific goal, Ketten suddenly finds himself
with nothing to do but to manage his estates, a task that his wife
had discharged adequately enough during the twelve years of his
absence. (A striking parallel exists here between Ketten's life and
that of the author. It will be recalled that Musil suddenly lost his
job in 1922 due to cutbacks in government expenditures, thus ending a twelve-year period of steady employment that had begun
with his marriage. This was a traumatic experience for Musil who,
at 42, was twelve years older than the 30-year-old Ketten, but it
finally permitted him to devote himself entirely to his creative
work as a writer. Ketten, too, now faces a traumatic turning point
in his life.) A man who has been defined and supported mainly by
his profession as a soldier is now expected to return to a life of
tranquility and passivity. The prospect for his declining years is a
life of boredom and meaninglessness, circumscribed by the duties
of the farmer—"no goal," as the narrator comments, "for a great

lord" (154). Then, while traveling home, Ketten is stung by a fly, whereupon he falls into deep and protracted illness. Ketten, who had won his war with the Bishop and who had survived hundreds of dangerous engagements on the battle field as well as numerous wounds from the enemy, is defeated by a fly. Or, more precisely, the success of the fly's attack is merely an external sign of the fact that Ketten's life, now without its high goal, has fallen into a state of total vulnerability. He no longer possesses a reason to fight and to survive.

Ketten's fever continues to linger on. While his wife chalks secret signs on his door and bedposts, learned doctors are called from distant places. But nothing helps. Ketten becomes ever more isolated in his suffering. This man, who had once stood squarely in the middle of wordly events, now feels that the world is steadily receding from him. For days and even weeks, he is only vaguely aware of what is happening around him. Previously, he had never remained very long in the presence of his wife, because "if he had ever remained longer, he would have had to be truly as he was" (151)—an oblique statement which implicitly, though only tentatively, suggests that his deepest impulse is to surrender as did Homo. Cared for by his wife, he will now be forced into confronting whatever his true nature might really be, for the persona of the soldier, the professional disguise, will gradually be burned away by the fever.

Jung once stated that a significant number of his patients were not suffering from any clinically definable neurosis, but rather from the aimlessness and senselessness of their daily existence.[14] It is at such periods in the individual's life that he tends to fall either mentally or physically ill. However, such illness can be regarded as the first stage of a process in which the individual moves toward greater psychological health: illness may indeed be the transitional stage through which the individual passes as he outgrows the first half of his psychic development and enters the second half. Ketten's illness functions in precisely this fashion. While the individual's prime task in the first half of his life is concerned with his adaptation to the demands of the external environment, his task in the second half is, as Jacobi writes, directed toward "the so-called

'initiation into the inner reality,' a deeper self-knowledge and knowledge of humanity, a 'turning back' (*reflectio*) to the traits of one's nature that have hitherto remained unconscious or become so."[15] The following observation made by another Jungian analyst, M.-L. von Franz, is relevant to the diagnosis not only of Ketten's illness but also of the "higher" function of this illness in contributing towards his psychic development: "The actual process of individuation—the conscious coming-to-terms with one's own inner center (psychic nucleus) or Self—generally begins with a wounding of the personality and the suffering that accompanies it."[16]

M.-L. von Franz also draws attention to one theme which persistently occurs in the fairy tales of different cultures and is also directly related to the subject of Musil's story, namely, the suffering of the individual psyche at the beginning of the individuation process: "Beneath the surface a person is suffering from a deadly boredom that makes everything seem meaningless and empty. Many myths and fairy tales symbolically describe this initial stage in the process of individuation by telling of a king who has fallen ill or grown old."[17] Jung in his psychotherapy often made much reference to the quests of heroes in fairy tales in order to illuminate the state of a patient's psyche. In "The Lady from Portugal," Musil may well have presented an aesthetic version of his own inner psychic condition which, because of its high degree of objectification, appears to the reader as a self-contained, sophisticated exercise in the fairy tale genre. The symbolic manner in which Musil was able to capture the inner life of the individual by the aesthetic means of a fairy-tale-like story is illuminated by Jung's explanation of the origin and function of all fairy tales. In Jung's thought, fairy tales represent an aesthetic formulation of various developmental stages of the psyche of a race or culture as a whole, and the literature of Jungian psychology refers to a number of fairy tales which are analagous to the one that Musil wrote.

During the course of his illness, Ketten eventually feels that he has died and is surprised that dying was so peaceful. At the same time, he also feels that he is standing somewhere at the periphery of life, as though he might be able to come back to life again. What it is that will make it possible for him to return to life

is not yet clear. However, Ketten believes that only part of his being has gone on ahead into death, and that his bones have been left behind on the bed. Ketten sees his wife bending over him and he looks directly into her face. At this point halfway between life and death, Ketten experiences the equivalent of Veronica's and Homo's mystical moment of "reunion." In a vision, he sees himself and his wife arise together out of his dead body and walk quietly into the distance. The Ketten resting in bed as well as the Ketten walking with his wife in the distance seem to be cradled in some gigantic and benevolent hand: "Doubtless that was God" (156), he thinks. Veronica's and Homo's respective mystical moments differ in a significant manner from that of Ketten: their experience is one of "melting," of "flowing" into the beloved, of a union so total that the personalities dissolve. In Ketten's ephiphany, on the other hand, he and his wife appear and remain as two separate and independent individuals, existing side by side in total equality. This ephiphany proves to be prophetic of the couple's happy fate after Ketten has overcome his crisis.

Time continues to pass without any significant change occurring in Ketten's condition until the day on which a fearful thought suddenly grips his mind. He realizes that if he is going to return to life, he must gather together all of his will-power now. If he is not to die completely, he must exert his will upon the course of events in daily reality; he must will an action (as Veronica felt she had to recall a repressed memory in order to prevent herself from degenerating into insanity). As is consonant with Ketten's behavior before his illness, he kills. The first stage of his recovery is indicated by his ordering the killing of a wolf. Why it is that he chooses specifically a wolf as his victim requires further elaboration. During Ketten's absence in the field, his wife had adopted a wolf. She was particularly attracted to the wolf because it reminded her of her husband. (This relationship between a woman and an animal is reminiscent of that between Veronica and her dog, although the sexual aspect of the attraction is not overtly mentioned by Musil in the case of the Portugese lady except indirectly and ironically when she once wonders whether her two sons are really hers, for they remind her of two young wolves rather than of two children.)

It may be recalled that throughout the story the narrator has often compared Ketten's behavior with that of a wolf. It is clear that Ketten, his wife, and Musil's reader cannot help but be quite conscious of the parallel between the man and the wolf. Without informing his wife, Ketten, who is still too weak to carry out the action himself, orders a serving man to kill the beast. What Ketten has done is to destroy the usurper; for in his feverish mind, the wolf seemed more like the vigorous Ketten he once had been than this man now victimized and broken by suffering and illness. By means of this violent action, Ketten has begun the process of recovering his old identity. When the Portuguese lady learns what her husband has done, her blood seems at first to freeze in her veins. But she accepts and in fact welcomes his act of violence, for in this decision she, too, recognizes the return of the vigorous man she had married twelve years before. She goes to his bedside, "and for the first time he looked her straight in the eyes again" (157). His shame has passed and he is now able to gaze at his wife, feeling himself to be truly her husband.

The Little Cat from the World Beyond[18]

An interpretation of the complex function of the little cat in this story presents many difficulties. The following analysis will be informed by two perspectives: first, the transformation of the cat into human being and, second, the cat's life and death as a secular analogue to the religious drama of the sacrifice of the scapegoat.

Although he has willed an action by having the wolf killed, Ketten is unable by his own powers to reach the second stage of recovery, and it seems to him that only some miracle from outside can now alter his situation for the better. The bearer of the miracle arrives one day quite unexpectedly and unannounced at the gate of the castle. A more inauspicious beginning for a miracle can hardly be imagined. It is a small cat who arrives, but it is a rather strange cat. This cat insists upon entering the castle through the front gate as human beings do and not by climbing over the wall cat-fashion. The cat also strikes everyone as possessing a slightly sadder and more meditative air than is appropriate for a mere kitten. It also

seems to lack something, and "this absence of whatever would have made it into an ordinary kitten—was like a second presence, a hovering double, perhaps, or a faint halo surrounding it" (162). It is the absence of something in cat-nature that makes the kitten more than an animal and relates it to human beings. In the context of Musil's psychology, to be a human being means (among other things) to lack to a greater or lesser extent something in or of animal nature; man is the only animal who has lost his instincts. What takes the place of this absence in man and in this particular cat? The unnatural psychological vacuum, caused by the absence of instinctual nature, becomes "filled" with illness and suffering.

Musil's story of the humanization and eventual spiritualization of the cat by means of illness represents an artistic climax in the history of an idea that has received analogous formulations in German romanticism, Christianity, philosophy, and psychoanalysis. Although an examination of the evolution of this idea lies beyond the scope of this study, a few examples may be cited which assert the heightening effect of physical and mental suffering. Novalis believed that through illness the human being achieved a higher plane of existence because a life of disease and suffering promoted "a higher synthesis";[19] for this reason, he welcomed the arrival of pain.[20] Drawing a connection between disease and God, Grillparzer wrote in a poem: "Illness, you are a gift of God/ Let us therefore praise Him."[21] Heine, implying an opposition between animal health and a religious depth of feeling, wrote: "In Christianity man attains to self-consciousness of the spirit through pain. Illness spiritualizes, even animals are spiritualized."[22] Nietzsche, following this tradition, believed that illness could function as a stimulus toward achieving a higher form of human existence and thus felt gratitude toward his own illnesses for the part they had played in the stimulation of his spiritual growth.[23] (Nietzsche's concept of creative illness and its corollary, "the great health," has already been examined in connection with *Young Törless*.) Thus, of the mutually exclusive concepts of man as a healthy animal and man as a sick but spiritualized being, the latter has generally re-

ceived positive evaluation in Christianity, romanticism, and on occasion in Nietzsche's philosophy.

With the advent of psychoanalysis, however, the unequivocal evaluation of these alternatives became more hesitant, for spiritualization through suffering was regarded as being founded on neurosis. As Freud notes: "It is easy, as we can see, for a barbarian to be healthy; for a civilized man the task is hard."[24] Civilized man should strive for health and not for illness; but as modern life becomes ever more complex, the sufferings and consequent neuroses imposed by an ever greater need for the renunciation of instinctual pleasures will become ever greater too. The creation of civilization and civilized man by means of the sublimation of repressed animal drives (sexual and aggressive) may well be a magnificent development in the history of the human race; but the devastating price to be paid in man's psychological health is becoming ever more apparent too. Freud could not, however, recommend that sublimation be undone and that man return to a primitive state of animal well-being. The tragic nature of the two alternatives facing man seemed to Freud to constitute an irresolvable dilemma. More as an observation than an evaluation, Freud concluded: "the possibility of neurosis . . . is in a sense a human prerogative."[25] Nietzsche's heroic "undetermined man" of the nineteenth century, freed from instinct, has thus become Freud's neurotic man of the twentieth.

Musil's position in the history of this problem may now be indicated. In a spirit nearer to the romantics and Nietzsche than to Freud, Musil treated the process of psychological heightening through suffering, but chose to do so in the context of medieval Europe. Because he set the story in a religious world, the metaphors provided by Christian theology became available to him. And as the work of C.G. Jung has revealed, religious metaphors give dramatic and objective expression to profound psychological truths and processes that are the same in every age.

The cat in "The Lady from Portugal" becomes sick and, like Ketten, grows ever weaker. After three days, its vomiting and filth have become so unbearable that Ketten, with feelings of great

guilt, has the cat forcibly removed to a peasant's house outside the castle walls. But the cat returns and continues its physical decline. The cat's intense and sustained suffering seems to be transforming it into a human being. Heine's statement is particularly relevant here: "I believe that by suffering even animals could be made human."[26] Ketten has the distinct feeling that his "illness and its deathly gentleness had been transformed into that little animal's body and so were no longer merely within him" (162). He believes that his own destiny is "being vicariously accomplished in this little cat already half released from earthly bonds" (164). As Ketten killed the wolf, his wife now orders that the cat be taken away and destroyed. With the death of the cat and its illness, Ketten's illness passes and he returns to life.

It is the Portuguese lady who, not surprisingly, has the first intuition into the meaning of the "miracle," into the significance of the cat's appearance, illness, and death. She says to Ketten: "If God could become man, then He can also become a kitten" (168). She intuitively recognizes the intrinsically religious nature of the cat's last passion and her insight receives further confirmation from the narrator, who stresses the religious connotations of the cat's sickness: he terms the cat's suffering "its martyrdom" (163) and describes its struggles as a trial of strength between the cat's "imperceptible halo and the dreadful filth" (163). In reality—if one may distinguish between the characters' reactions and the objective world from which their reactions arose—this final episode merely tells of a somewhat odd-looking kitten, who happens to catch a disease and finally dies in an extremely wretched manner. The religious significance is projected upon the cat by Ketten and his wife.

Jung's psychology offers some illuminating insights into why, how, and for what purpose such projections occur. The presupposition for Jung's theories about the religious impulse is his belief, as noted above, that its expresssion is as important for the psychic health of the individual as are the equally natural expressions of sexual and aggressive urges. By means of ritual and drama, religions have given external form in action and verbal formulae to certain profound psychological needs. Fordham explains dogma as

being "the product of conscious thought working on and refining the raw material of the unconscious."²⁷ Thus, dogma and ritual may be regarded as crystallized forms of original mystical experiences that take place prior to and are more profound than their eventual expression in orthodox religious terms. Jung identified the fundamental forms that the external religious drama takes in the West: organized religion expresses "the living process of the unconscious in the form of the drama of repentance, sacrifice, and redemption."²⁸ In "The Lady from Portugal," Musil has presented a story whose central mystery is closely related to a religious drama: the sacrifice of the scapegoat which brings salvation to the sick in mind and body.

While Ketten is a foe of the Church, the Bishop—so Ketten's chaplain tells him—is able to pray to God, and this must prove of ultimate disadvantage to Ketten's interests. It is a decided irony, therefore, that when the Bishop becomes ill he dies, while Ketten is saved by the kind of sacrifice and redemption that is at the heart of Christian theology. Ketten's situation, in this regard, is analogous to the relationship between the individual and the Church in the modern world as analyzed by Jung. Although modern man may possess a religious impulse that is in no way inferior to the drive experienced by his medieval brothers, he is no longer able to return to the Church and to find in the Christian drama of Christ's suffering and self-sacrifice for man a satisfactory expression of the "living processes of the unconscious." In place of the search for God, the modern individual is in search of that mysterious entity "the whole man," which represents the culmination of the individuation process. Jung expressed this historical change as follows: "There is no deity in the [modern] mandala, nor is there any submission or reconciliation to a deity. The place of the deity seems to be taken by the wholeness of man."²⁹ The problem that the contemporary Church faces arises from the fact that modern man is no longer able to feel the presence of God within its walls. Musil once noted in his diaries that the Church was the "ruin of the Other Condition (*des andern Zustandes*)."³⁰ Today's unfortunate situation has occurred for two reasons, Jung asserted: first, the Church's creed and ritual have become so elaborate and obscure that they have degen-

erated into mere formalities and, second, the Church (as in Musil's "The Lady from Portugal") reveals a face to the believer that little distinguishes it from any secular power bent upon increasing its political power and extending its ownership of land. Ultimately, it is the Bishop who appears as the warrior and Ketten who undergoes a profound religious transformation. In this sense, Ketten is really a representative of modern man who continues to undergo profound psychological transformation but who no longer interprets them in the context of metaphors provided by Christian theology. Jung believed that his own "process of individuation" provided man with a new series of metaphors for the expression of spiritual experience in the modern world.

A few observations may now be offered by way of summarizing the function of the animal and animal metaphors in Musil's fiction up to this point. First, characters are often "debased" and identified with animals: Basini behaves like a pig, Claudine's stranger is compared to a goat, Demeter is associated with a dog, and Grigia is identified with a cow. The function of such metaphors is clear: certain human beings are thereby reduced to the animal level or, more specifically, they are transformed into sexual objects. Such characters function in the narrative as projections of the protagonist in a state of dionysian mysticism, the major examples of which are found in "The Temptation of Quiet Veronica" and "Grigia." The thought once occurred to Veronica that an animal would be like the Other Dimension. Not only does she compare the sensual Demeter with a dog but the priestlike Johannes as well. And just as Johannes seems to have lost the instincts of the lower animals so too has the cat in "The Lady from Portugal." Both Johannes and the cat are associated with animals, but in their aura of impersonality (which is present in all animals) and in the absence of animal instincts, they become in the minds of Veronica and the Kettens, respectively, the bearers of a projected religious impulse. It is the martyred cat alone of all the other animals (dogs, pigs, cows) mentioned above who brings salvation: the cat is the bearer of the miracle whereby Ketten, who feels that he has already died, achieves a resurrection of the body. In "Grigia" Homo's religious impulse remained merely at the level of a profound feeling. In

"The Lady from Portugal," Ketten's religious feelings are given symbolic expression in the drama of the sufferings and death of the little cat.

It should be noted also that although such religious terms as "spiritual," "resurrection," and "salvation" have been used in this analysis of the function of the cat in "The Lady from Portugal"— for the story is set during an age of faith—Musil's narrative never transcends the secular plane of existence. As is also the case in Jung's writings, religious experience provides metaphors for psychological occurrences. But whereas Jung analyzes these psychological processes from within, Musil merely indicates from outside what may be occurring within the psyche of the protagonist. The act of psychologizing is left to the reader.

The Climb into Manhood

At some indefinite point during Ketten's illness a young Portuguese knight, a childhood friend of Ketten's wife, had arrived at the castle for an extended visit. In front of this radiantly healthy young man, Ketten "lay in the grass like a dog, filled with shame" (157). As the days passed, suspicions arose in Ketten's mind that his wife and her friend were deceiving him. But he was unable, because of his debilitated state, either to investigate his suspicions or to take any immediate and decisive action, as he would have done in times long gone by when he had been the great and forceful warrior. Suffering had now become his new occupation. After his illness passes, however, Ketten firmly decides that if his wife does not send the knight away, he will kill him in spite of all the rules of hospitality. Nevertheless, although Ketten finally makes a decision, he finds himself unable to act upon it and to carry out the kind of task that he had previously found to be so easy to accomplish. For now, after his illness, fighting and killing strike him as being a "senseless, alien mode of action" (165). This revaluation and striking reversal of his former style of life provide the most graphic indication of the change that illness and suffering have wrought upon his psyche. On the other hand, it is not in Ketten's

nature to continue to suffer his suspicions quietly. Moreover, although he is over his physical illness because of the miracle of the cat, he has not yet recovered his self. The miracle of the cat was a passive occurrence: Ketten had merely watched and believed that the cat had taken on his illness. Therefore, although Ketten was cured of his physical illness, he is not yet a whole man. He knows intuitively that "he would never be wholly well again if he did not wrench himself free of all this" (165). The Portuguese knight provides the pretext for a second act of will that completes Ketten's final stage of recovery just as the murder of the wolf signified the first step in his return to health.

Ketten recalls that he had once consulted a soothsaying woman who had made him the following prophecy: "You will be cured only when you accomplish a task" (161). Suddenly a thought comes to him. As a boy, he had always wanted to climb the cliff on top of which the castle was built. The accomplishment of this feat will be the task, the "trial by ordeal," through which Ketten will regain himself. It is a suicidal task, he knows, for no human being can scale such a sheer and high cliff. Nevertheless, he begins to climb at nightfall and as he climbs he feels that it is not he but the little cat from "the world beyond" who is returning to the castle in this fashion. As the cat had entered the castle as a human being, a human being is now entering the castle like a cat. Sweat pours from his body and waves of heat flash through his limbs. By means of this supreme physical exertion combined with the risk of sudden death, he has duplicated to a great extent the situation on the field of battle. Ketten recaptures and reenters his body and his earlier spirit by accomplishing the task: "it was strange to feel how in this struggle with death strength and health came flowing back into his limbs" (166). He reaches the castle and "with his strength his ferocity had also returned" (166). With dagger at his side, he climbs through the window and into the bedroom of the young knight. But the bed is empty. He immediately goes to his wife's bedroom and is overjoyed to find that the knight is not there either. A servant tells Ketten that the knight had ridden away at the rising of the moon. Considering the Portuguese lady's identification with

the moon, we may safely interpret this remark as meaning that Ketten's wife herself had sent him away. In this regard, the Portuguese lady would be following the pattern set by the two earlier Musil women, who also eventually either reject or leave men associated solely with vitality and sexuality: Claudine leaves the stranger and returns to her husband and Veronica rejects Demeter utterly. The Portuguese lady is startled by Ketten's entry and sits up in bed "as though in her dreams she had been waiting for this" (167). She knows that her husband has finally returned to her after twelve years of battle and many months of illness.

In "Grigia" and "The Lady from Portugal," Musil has presented women who exert a profound effect upon the life of the male protagonist. Whether as a particular, although somewhat strange woman (if Musil's narrative is read on a literal level) or whether as the feminine element within the male psyche (if the narrative is "internalized" for the purposes of psychological interpretation), she functions to lure the protagonist toward the "other side." The temptation of the protagonist in "Grigia" leads to his death, although the preconditions for his disintegration were already present within himself before he met his peasant mistress. (Grigia was herself no more directly responsible for Homo's death than Tadzio was for the collapse and death of Gustav von Aschenbach in "Death in Venice.") The Portuguese lady also tempts the protagonist to experience another dimension—either of life in general or one existing within his own psyche: it is a world of gentleness, patience, suffering, passivity, and intuition.

The fact that Homo dies and Ketten is reborn reflects the differing relationship of the protagonist to the mystical realm in the two stories. It would have been conveniently symmetrical to be able to argue that while Grigia represents a mysticism that destroys, the lady from Portugal is a force that saves. But such an interpretation places too great a significance upon the women as characters; the essential difference in these two stories is one that exists between the two male protagonists. It should also be pointed out that the Portuguese lady does not save Ketten: at most she is able to chalk magic signs on his door. She can but nurse him; only

something that seems to transcend the human altogether, only "a miracle" followed by the exertion of Ketten's own mental and physical powers is able to save him. But as a representative of that other aspect of life, which Ketten as a warrior had had to repress, the lady from Portugal introduces her husband to and nurses him through that realm in which miracles occur, a realm where scientific thought and rational proof bow before intuition and faith. Unlike Homo, Ketten passes through this Other World, makes contact with its deepest level near the point of death, and emerges beyond it. Thus Ketten's relationship to his wife and to the Other Realm as represented by the cat finally serves only to enlarge his personality, to widen and deepen his understanding of life.

Musil has on occasion been misinterpreted as suggesting that psychological perfection is to be found in the hermaphroditic ideal. But as Veronica's perfect mystical moment could not be sustained in time and was eventually destroyed, so the hermaphroditic balance, if it occurs, also passes. For Musil always returns to reality, to "possible possibilities." Ketten may well experience the mystical world of his wife, a feminine dimension within himself, in such an intense fashion that the ferocious wolf within him almost dies. But he eventually returns into his old self. In this regard, Musil and Jung are in agreement. Fordham wrote: "A man, for instance, by accepting and learning to know his anima, may become more receptive, or he may develop his intuition or his feeling, but he cannot possess himself of those qualities."[30] Feminine qualities may be present in him in the form of compassion, mercy, sensitivity, and so forth, but they will remain in a sense only worthy accretions, additions to his fundamental self that are necessary to produce a more balanced life. Ketten remains essentially what he was before, tempered by the opposite way of life without undergoing a total conversion to it. Ketten began as the ferocious wolf, became a climbing cat who had come back from the dead, and ends not as half-wolf, half-cat, but as a wolf again. But although he aggressively defends what is his, he is no longer "cruel as a knife." He is glad, therefore, that the Portuguese knight has escaped and that he will not need to kill him. In Ketten we now recognize neither a

very worldly wolf nor an otherworldly cat, but a balanced human being—a rather rare phenomenon in Musil's fiction.

"Tonka"

"Tonka," the last of the stories in the collection *Three Women,* elaborates the same themes treated in "Grigia" and "The Lady from Portugal" while also adumbrating some of the central philosophical and psychological issues to be explored by Musil in *The Man without Qualities.* The unnamed protagonist, a young scientist, first meets Tonka during the year of his obligatory military service. As in earlier works, "Tonka," too, reveals Musil's preoccupation with those situations in which the normal and habitual patterns of an individual's life have been suddenly disrupted. In this story, compulsory military service functions as one of those events which, like attendance at boarding school or an extended trip away from home and family, throw the protagonist into a world of new relationships. It is at such times that the individual becomes particularly vulnerable.

In the first two stories of the trilogy, the women encountered by the respective protagonists in an alien environment are also themselves surrounded by a correspondingly enigmatic aura. Similarly, whenever the young scientist recalls his initial meeting with Tonka, it seems to him to have occurred in the midst of a fairy-tale-like atmosphere, the same kind of mysterious atmosphere that enveloped the lives of Grigia and the lady from Portugal. As was also the case in the earlier two stories, "Tonka" describes the difficult relationship of a highly worldly man with an extremely mysterious and other-worldly woman. In "Tonka," however, the rational component of the male mind has been presented in its fullest intellectual development; consciousness and the laws of logic become the ultimate guide in the young scientist's behavior toward Tonka. Although the protagonist's reason is eventually victorious over the temptation toward mysticism, the conflict between reason and

mysticism reaches its most profound and tragic culmination in this final story of Musil's collection.

The "Free Spirit" and the Snowflake

The young scientist in "Tonka" could claim direct descent from the "free spirit," Nietzsche's new model of man, whom the philosopher in his middle period considered to be the most appropriate and only adequate form of life for creative survival in the coming age. Since the young scientist may also be regarded as a precursor of Ulrich, an extensive analysis of this new form of life will be reserved for the next chapter, The Rise and Fall of a Rational Man, in which Ulrich's experiment in "scientific living" is examined. However, the protagonist of "Tonka" may be briefly described here as a man who, like Ulrich, goes through life overburdened by his ideas. He would like to abolish the emotional aspects of life as far as is possible; he professes an aversion to poetry and intuition and rejects the ideals of compassion and simplicity. It is his conviction that the achievement of the scientific ideal in daily existence must be built upon a foundation of intellectual power and emotional asceticism. Until the scientific ideal achieves its goal of giving rational meaning to life, man must recognize that Western civilization is passing through an interim period and that he must, therefore, be as tough and austere as if he were embarked upon a long expedition toward the frontiers of a new world. Musil characterizes the young scientist's relationship to his time with the following metaphor: "He flew, he was between the ages; he was somewhere in midair."[32]

The protagonist's life bears certain similarities to that of Homo or, rather, to that of Homo as he probably once was as a young engineer. Unlike the middle-aged Homo, however, the protagonist's scientific way of life has not yet been tested over the course of years. (In Ulrich's life the reader actually experiences the breakdown and ultimate failure of the scientific way of life.) The young scientist gains strength and confidence from the mere exercise of his intellect upon his new invention. He survives because of

the strength of his rational mind. But the victory of his intellect over irrationality is paid for with Tonka's unhappiness and ultimate despair. Tonka becomes, like Faust's Gretchen, merely an episode in the protagonist's quest for ever greater significance and meaning in life.

The protagonist conceives of Tonka at once as a being who bears some kind of inverse but cryptic correspondence to his own existence. In her life, he seems to experience everything that he is not; and Tonka, it might be added, who also recognizes the differences between them, does not want to become like him but wishes merely to remain in his presence: "she was Nature adjusting itself to Mind, not wanting to become Mind"(192). She is also described—as are so many of Musil's women—as being rather like an animal, a dog, for instance, who finds its happiness in the company of the highly complex society of man. In spite of the influence of the highly sophisticated protagonist, who now and again attempts to overcome Tonka's naivité by enlightening her through hectoring lectures as to the ways of the world, "she remains pure and unspoiled, like Nature herself" (191). While the protagonist is imbued with a particularly strong ambition to succeed in his scientific profession, Tonka has no desire to ascend in the world. Without the slightest thought of her own future, she merely follows the young scientist to a large city in Germany where he continues to work on his invention. Tonka seems merely "to be"; she strikes the protagonist as being so simple and so transparently the same that when he looks at her, he sometimes thinks he must be seeing an hallucination rather than a human being. Is such a being real or imaginary, he wonders. Is she good or evil? Sometimes the protagonist believes that Tonka possesses a goodness that is completely inexplicable, a kind of goodness that a dog might have. When contemplating Tonka at other times, he feels simply that his mind has reached the edge of some intellectual and moral frontier which it is unable to pass beyond.

It is in the use and function of language in daily communication that the difference between the protagonist and Tonka becomes most readily apparent, and this difference in turn reflects a more abstract distinction in Musil's story between the young scien-

tist as mind and Tonka as nature. While the young scientist admits that nothing has ever happened to him that he was unable to examine from various points of view and then express in precisely the right words, Tonka is almost totally inarticulate. (It may be recalled that verbal communication between Homo and Grigia was also minimal and that even Ketten and the Portuguese lady refrained from speaking to each other about their innermost lives.)

Tonka is able to understand the world only through her emotions, and when she is once asked to express her feelings in words, she admits: "I can't say it"(176). She declares quite simply that she would rather sing. Other people, the narrator remarks, express their desires, believe in the validity and necessity of what they are saying, and thus end by getting whatever it is they want. Without the shield and weapon of language, Tonka is always the victim. Does Tonka's inability arise from stupidity? No. She merely does not speak the language of everyday life, but rather a "language of the totality of things"(178). Not only is she unable to talk, she is also unable to cry. How can one define something that neither speaks nor weeps? In her world, Tonka is great, the protagonist believes, as he himself is in his own world. She lives under the protection of the moon, a symbol also closely associated with the lady from Portugal. She is described as "a snowflake falling all alone in the midst of a summer's day"(219). With this metaphor, Musil strikingly captures Tonka's situation in the modern world of men: she is out of season, as vulnerable and alone as a single snowflake soon to be destroyed by the sun; she is as beautiful and mysterious and unexpected as a snowflake in summer falling from a purer realm. Thus Tonka's characteristics form the most perfect complement to the young scientist's intelligence, articulateness, ambition, and instinct to survive.

The Temptation

After having lived with her lover for several years, Tonka realizes one day that she is pregnant. When the young scientist (characteristically) counts back to the day that conception must

have occurred, he discovers that he had been away on that date. Tonka claims, however, that by the time she had noticed her pregnancy, it was already too late to be able to calculate the date of conception with any degree of accuracy. The protagonist's suspicions will not be soothed by such a vague appeal; he is a scientist and so will accept nothing less from life than quite unambiguous answers. He begins to question her constantly, to analyze the situation from various points of view, and to attempt to catch her in contradictions. Now that Tonka knows that he distrusts her, she is totally unable to talk to him. Her answer to all his cross-examinations is alway the same: "Send me away if you won't believe me"(206).

As Törless experienced the world sometimes with the "eyes of reason" and sometimes "with those other eyes," so the protagonist now sees Tonka's every action in a double perspective. Her silence merely increases the ambiguity of the situation. What looks like stubborness could be innocence, what seems like guilty remorse could be merely Tonka's fear of his anger; what appears like cunning might be merely her sorrow at his distrust. In an atmosphere of such suspicion, even the protagonist realizes that the clearest signs of faithfulness can become instantly transformed into the most unmistakable signs of faithlessness. He now begins to revaluate their past life together so that what had once seemed positive becomes negative. Thus the protagonist recalls the way Tonka had simply attached herself to him; he wonders whether that might not have been a sign of her absolute indifference. Since it must have been clear to Tonka from the very beginning that he would never marry her, would it not have been natural for Tonka to have rebelled at her situation? Instead of that, however, she had merely obeyed him like a servile dog who follows its master's orders. Perhaps, then, she might have just as easily obeyed some other man when ordered. It is clear that no amount of investigation and cross-examination will ever resolve the protagonist's double perspective, a situation which is analogous to Törless's inability to find a point of synthesis between the perspectives of reason and mysticism. But the protagonist's ability to present all the circumstantial evidence needed to prove Tonka's guilt does not thereby seem to decrease in

any degree the validity of her claim to innocence. Moreover, Tonka is unable to engage in medical or philosophical argument in order to dispose of his suspicions. She is able to vouch for herself only "with the truth of her whole being" (206). Thus, an abyss yawns between the scientific perspective that demands objective verification by empirical evidence and a realm of truth beyond reason that demands nothing more or less than simple faith.

Tonka's pregnancy, if the young scientist accepts her claim, exists as a direct attack upon his way of life as an enlightened man of the modern world. The difficulty could be resolved if Tonka would only admit that she had been unfaithful, for mere infidelity is a situation with which he might eventually have been able to deal both intellectually and emotionally. But Tonka now seems to him to be existing "in a world that does not know the concept 'truth'. Tonka was now living in the deep world of fairy-tale" (197). Sometimes it seems to the young scientist that Tonka is living in an earlier world totally removed from the criterion of reason, in a fairy-tale like world of the immaculate conception and the Virgin Mary. In such an earlier age, Tonka would have become famous throughout the land. She would have been recognized as a miracle upon earth and people would have traveled from great distances to pay her homage. And he also wonders, in moments when he begins to doubt his own rational arguments, whether what is now happening to Tonka may not have a significance more profound than any that might be provided by the framework of scientific truth. Compared to the world of faith, what are mere scientific truths? Insignificant fragments of a superficial reality that remain without meaning because they exist in a world without passion. On occasion, in a half dreamlike condition, when he is no longer laboring on his invention, the young scientist experiences a presentiment that perhaps scientific work is not his true life. (Ketten, too, experienced similar moments when he used to sit alone by the camp fire in the evening after a day of battle with the enemy.) Perhaps there is a world of greater meaning beyond empirical truth. But if miracles can still occur even in the scientific age, then the world should be different too, the protagonist observes. For then Tonka would exist within the context of a world-view that could accept

her situation. And if this were so, then the protagonist would be able to commit himself fully and do battle for her. In fact, even in the context of the present scientific age, he sometimes perceives that "he was already beginning to surrender" (219) to Tonka's mysterious Other World.

There are several ways in which the protagonist experiences as a temptation Tonka's assertion that she has been faithful to him. Tonka has contracted a disease in connection with her pregnancy which the doctors believe may have come from the father of the child. The irrational fantasy immediately assails the protagonist that if he were to accept Tonka's belief that he is the father, then he would in the same instant become diseased too. Thus, on one level of his being, to reject Tonka means to retain his health. Second, he also feels that he will never be able to utter the words "I believe you" (219) to her, because it is precisely this not believing that "kept him immune and safely anchored to the earth" (218). Thus, to reject Tonka also means that he will be able to retain his tie to reality, if not to sanity itself. As a man of the "earth," he must not allow himself to become "moon-struck" by Tonka's inexplicable condition. Third, the protagonist becomes convinced that in some obscure fashion his belief in Tonka stands opposed to the completion of his invention and therefore to success in his scientific career. Faith in Tonka is opposed to the certainty of success in the scientific world, and Musil strikingly expresses this opposition in a scientific formulation involving percentages. Of the young scientist's faith in Tonka, Musil writes: "The question [is] whether he would force himself to believe in Tonka against the niney-nine per cent probability that she had been unfaithful to him and that he was simply a fool" (211). Of the certainty of his scientific success, the young scientist's colleagues maintain: "The probability of it already amounted to ninety-nine per cent!" (211). Although the young scientist is finally unable to say that he totally disbelieves Tonka, he is also unable to assert that he does believe her; he remains paralyzed between two perspectives. Sometimes the protagonist wishes that Tonka would simply die so that this intolerable situation would be resolved once and for all.

Death and Renewal

One day Tonka leaves for the hospital in which she is shortly
to die, still without having heard the protagonist affirm his faith in
her fidelity to him. Until the very end, he remains distant, uncommitted, and unable to overcome his rational deduction that Tonka
must have yielded to the seductions of a nameless stranger. Not
until she is dead is he able to give himself totally to her, as he had
never been able to do while she was still living. After hearing of
Tonka's death, he experiences an ineffable moment reminiscent of
similar moments found in the two preceding stories where Musil
treated the themes of religious mysticism and love-at-a-distance.
Homo, thinking of his absent wife, had suddenly been overwhelmed with something like a "profound religious feeling" (124),
a mystical moment; he had experienced a "Reunion. He was taking her with him for all eternity" (125). When thinking of the now
deceased Tonka, the protagonist likewise experiences an apparently inexplicable religious impulse: "But I shall be with you like
God Himself" (220). For Johannes in "The Temptation of Quiet
Veronica," the mystical realm was the eternal realm of God and to
merge totally with it was to merge with God. It is only in the
mystical dimension that Tonka and the protagonist can become
united as equals without (as Veronica had once said) there being
anything "left to stand outside, eavesdropping, estranged" (79).
Veronica's reunion and mingling of herself with Johannes, which
occurred at the railway station after his departure, foreshadows in
a strikingly similar manner the experience that now overwhelms
the young scientist: "Tonka! Tonka! He felt her from the ground
under his feet to the crown of his head, and the whole of her life"
(222). But for him this moment lasts only for an instant.

The conclusion of "Tonka" thus represents a continuation of
Musil's treatment of the conflict between the highly rational male
and the mystical realm toward which he is tempted by woman. In
Musil's ordering of the stories, however, "Tonka" also reveals a
regression in the author's resolution of the conflict. The common
denominator for a comparison of all three stories can be found in
the final relationship between the protagonist and the three myste-

rious women in terms of who lives and who dies. In the first story, the cowlike Grigia lives and Homo dies. In the third story, the rebirth of the protagonist is facilitated by the death of the doglike Tonka. Both of these conclusions represent a less mature resolution of conflict than in the second story, "The Lady from Portugal." In this work, a cat dies and it is the death of an animal, rather than of an animallike woman, that facilitates Ketten's resurrection to life. Both man and woman then continue to live on together. Thus "Grigia" and "Tonka" express the two extreme alternatives to the resolution of the conflict: Homo surrenders completely to the mystical impulse and dies, while the young scientist, by choosing to follow not the irrational star of Tonka but rather the star of his scientific invention, is able to survive. In "Tonka," the protagonist's "healthy urge to live" (203), his certain feeling that a highly successful life will be his destiny, is guaranteed by his own confidence in the power of his rational mind. It may also be added that both of the masculine survivors (as opposed to Homo) actively affirm life by completing a difficult masculine task, respectively, climbing a cliff and completing an invention.

The conclusion of "Tonka" is strongly reminiscent of the conclusion of *Young Törless*. Both protagonists eventually manage to escape from their fascination with the mystical realm, and after a period of intense emotional strain bordering on illness, they are able to find their way back into daily existence, into a cool and sober morning of life that seems to promise their ultimate success. (Analogous conclusions can also be found in other works of Musil: Claudine leaves her goatlike lover to return to the everyday banalities of her marriage; Johannes overcomes his fascination with Veronica by escaping "into the street"; Ketten surmounts his illness and returns to his wife and children; and Ulrich eventually breaks off his relationship with Agathe and escapes into the daily life of Europe at war.) Both Törless and the young scientist find themselves standing alone, able to dedicate their reassembled energies to the further expansion of their intellectual and emotional lives. Törless and the young scientist feel changed by their experiences, respectively, of Basini and Tonka, but not fundamentally transformed. They have merely grown.

Musil's summary of the young scientist's interpretation of his experience with Tonka strikingly recalls the conclusions that Törless eventually drew many years later, after he had left the school: "From that time on much came to his mind that made him a little better than most people, because there was a small warm shadow that had fallen across his brilliant life. That was no help to Tonka now. But it was a help to him" (222). And at that moment he, who had felt that his previous life with Tonka had lain under a great dark shadow, was able to feel only "the cheer and comfort of the light" (222). Like Törless, he now knows that there is a dimension in life that is darker, richer, and more significant than his rational mind had at first imagined. He has encountered it and has been enriched by it. But like Ketten, the young scientist will continue onward in his own essentially masculine role. The hermaphroditic synthesis is not Musil's ideal. Musil stresses, rather, the protagonist's renewal on a higher plane of his own masculine being; his masculinity is now merely tempered by a knowledge of the feminine other side of life. In the most ideal circumstances, the polarity of masculine and feminine will exist in the never resolved but continuing conflict of the kind of marriage achieved by the Kettens.

Jung also believed that the fundamental problems of life can never be completely resolved, for they reflect a polarity inherent in the nature of all things. Thus, an intense conflict in the individual between the polarities of reason and mysticism, of male and female principles, can result at very best in a raising of consciousness; such thesis and antithesis can never be resolved in a comforting synthesis. In the face of such failure, however, the impulse to live will normally reassert its sway in the individual and move him "above" the irreconcilable conflict. As Jung wrote: "What, on a lower level, had led to the wildest conflicts and to panicky outbursts of emotions, from the higher level of personality now looked like a storm in a valley seen from the mountain top. This does not mean that the storm is robbed of its reality, but instead of being in it one is now above it."[33] In the context of the Nietzschean framework used to interpret Törless's ascent from emotional chaos and intellectual despair to a pinnacle of cool reflectivity, the young scientist in "Tonka" has also achieved—not Nietzsche's poetic syn-

thesis of the Superman—but rather his state of "the great health." Ketten, too, gained "the great health," which is always the result of a lonely process of self-growth. He went further, however, and placed his newly-won personal health at the service of his relationship with another human being, his wife. He thereby achieved a marriage of "great health," a concept which is totally alien to Nietzsche's thought.

The Question of the Absurd: Kierkegaard

Is Musil in "Tonka" once again treating the theme of the masculine protagonist's conflict between the world of everyday reason and that of the irrational as represented by woman? Or has he in this last story pushed the dichotomy to its furthest possible point? If the latter interpretation is correct, then Musil's paradigmatic dualism reappears in "Tonka" not as a struggle merely between masculine reason and a feminine irrational world but as the conflict between human reason as such with the absurd, that is to say, with a sphere of experience which not merely transcends reason but contradicts it. "Tonka" has recently been analyzed in a most compelling fashion primarily from the perspective of a struggle within the protagonist between the claims of the rational and those of the absurd.[34] The concept of the absurd has received its fullest philosophical expression in Kierkegaard's *Fear and Trembling* and it is this work, therefore, that provides the best point of departure for an examination of the question of the absurd in "Tonka." However, if "Tonka" is regarded primarily in the context of the Kierkegaardian absurd, the philosophical and intellectual implications of this story must of necessity dominate, although they do not thereby necessarily deny the psychological aspects of the protagonist's conflict.

Such a philosophical approach, however, does not give a complete picture of the character of the young scientist because it deemphasizes his life in its merely human dimension. It will be argued in this and the following sections that the philosophical theme of the absurd masks a psychological and ethical problem:

the fact of Tonka's pregnancy is not presented by Musil as an example of the the absurd, that is to say, of an aberration in the natural and rational order of events. It is, rather, used to illustrate a psychological problem, a defect in the young scientist's character which prevents him from participating fully and permanently in any human relationship. While the moral and psychological implications of the typical masculine protagonist's conduct toward other people is not totally ignored in Musil's work as a whole, such questions are usually of secondary importance. However, because of the existence of an intense personal relationship between the protagonist and Tonka, ethical questions do arise in this final story of the trilogy which cannot be ignored. The application of moral and ethical considerations in a discussion of "Tonka" does not superimpose an alien framework upon Musil's story. For even the narrator of "Tonka" experiences an ambivalence (unexpected in Musil's work) between the claims of ethical behavior and the demands of a lonely dedication to truth.

The following analysis will begin with an exploration of Kierkegaard's concept of the absurd and its application to "Tonka." The purpose of such an analysis is to reveal how an understanding of the young scientist's behavior is expanded if not viewed solely through the perspective of Kierkegaard's nineteenth-century theological framework. The analysis will then pass on to a consideration of a more contemporary concept of the absurd as formulated in the twentieth century thought of Albert Camus. It will be argued that Camus's analysis of the absurd provides a more useful framework for an understanding of Musil's world-view in general than that offered by Kierkegaard's thought, but nevertheless one which is also of limited value since Musil's primary concern in "Tonka" is not, finally, with the absurd in any form.

In *Fear and Trembling*, Kierkegaard deals with the conflict between the ethical and the religious modes of being. Abraham is commanded by God to commit the most unethical and irrational act imaginable to a father: the murder of his only son. But because the command to sacrifice the son comes from God, Abraham feels released from his ethical duty of nurturing and protecting his child.

However absurd the command of God may appear to the rational mind of man, the believer must be prepared to leap over ethical and rational objections and into a state of complete faith in and acceptance of God's will. Johannes de Silentio, the narrator, writes of Abraham at this moment of transition from the universally accepted code of morality to the individual's lonely confrontation with God: "he left one thing behind, took one thing with him: he left his earthly understanding behind and took faith with him."[35] Beneath Abraham's conflict in *The Old Testament* lies hidden a similar conflict which is at the heart of Christian faith. In fact, one critic has asserted that "whatever Johannes says about Abraham is to be understood obliquely of the Christian believer."[36] It is in man's relationship to Christ that the absurdity of faith achieves its most lucid and agonizing expression. Christ made claims that cannot only not be objectively certified or investigated but that violate every rational probability and human expectation: God came into the world as a particular human being at a particular point in history, suffered at the hands of evil men, and died in total humiliation. The test of Christian faith is based upon man's acceptance of the absurdity of the Incarnation. A related test of man's absolute trust and faith in the irrational ways of God is provided by the doctrine of the Immaculate Conception.

The concept of the absurd receives three different expressions in the three cases mentioned above. In the first instance, Abraham's God orders an action which, from the viewpoint of the community, is unethical and irrational. In an analogous situation, Christ makes the absurd claim of his Incarnation, for which he demands the assent of the Jewish community. The individual may choose to believe or not, may take "the leap" or remain on this side of the religious mode of being. Only in the last example does the problem of the absurd pass beyond the question of obedience based on faith; here the problem of the absurd, presented in its most radical form, assumes the undeniable physiological reality of a pregnancy. It is, therefore, in Johannes de Silentio's remarks concerning the Immaculate Conception that the relevance of Kierkegaard's concept of the absurd to Musil's "Tonka" emerges.

Not to believe in the possibility of the Immaculate Conception means of necessity to pass a negative moral judgment upon the Virgin Mary (and by analogy upon Tonka). Rather than believing that Tonka has become a second Virgin Mary, thereby contravening the rational order of natural events, the young scientist inevitably makes the negative moral judgment that Tonka has been unfaithful to him. A comparison of *Fear and Trembling* with "Tonka" in regard to the concept of the Immaculate Conception raises more than the question of faith, however; it brings into focus an important moral and ethical issue: should not the young scientist have leaped over the objections made by his reason as did Abraham, as does the Christian in his belief in the purity of the Virgin Mary? For is not the alternative to belief a sterile rationalism that both destroys Tonka's happiness and existence and condemns the protagonist to total emotional impoverishment?

What was possible for Abraham in the ancient world of *The Old Testament*, however, is not merely impossible for the young scientist, it is also (Musil strongly implies) undesirable in the modern world. Even so religious a spirit as Johannes de Silentio, writing in the 1840s, finds the leap of faith into the absurd to be an impossibility for himself. What separates Abraham from Kierkegaard's Johannes and from Musil's young scientist is a long tradition of rational and scientific thought which has produced an attitude of mind that can neither be denied nor leaped over. Johannes realizes with sorrow that the obstacle lies within himself: "I have no faith at all, I am by nature a shrewd pate, and every such person always has difficulty in making movements of faith."[37] Shortly thereafter he admits once again: "I am unable to make the movements of faith, I cannot shut my eyes and plunge confidently into the absurd, for me that is an impossibility."[38] God once spoke directly to Abraham, but today the heavens are silent. If this silence exists for Johannes, a man who fervently desires faith, how much more must it be the case for Musil's young scientist who "was a fanatical disciple of the cool, soberly fantastical, world-encompassing spirit of modern technology," a man who "was in favour of doing away with the emotions" (188-89). The spiritual

landscape of the modern world is totally different from that inhabited by Abraham in the Book of Genesis.

In Musil's world, a man of faith would appear as but one
example, as one variation of the silly sentimentalist or weak-
minded romantic. Today the absurd remains merely absurd.
Therefore, the Kierkegaardian leap can no longer be considered as
a desirable spiritual exercise and test, for the absurd in the modern
world does not provide a point of departure for the discovery of a
life endowed with translogical significance. In a world without
God, faith represents not a courageous leap beyond the universally
comprehensible ethical codes of a particular community, a leap
which culminates in a lonely and absolute relationship of the individual with his creator. Acceptance of the absurd in the twentieth
century represents, rather, a form of "philosophical suicide,"[39] as
Albert Camus termed it. The young scientist is unable to make the
leap for the same reason that led Camus in *The Myth of Sisyphus* to
reject Kierkegaard's praise of Abraham's leap into irrational faith.
On the question of the individual's relationship to the absurd, Musil's spiritual landscape is, therefore, closer to that of Camus than it
is to that of Kierkegaard.

A Question of the Absurd: Camus

In *The Myth of Sisyphus*, Camus analyzes the situation of
modern man, who discovers himself to be shipwrecked in an absurd universe. Camus condemns the various ways by which modern man has taken flight from the discomforting recognition of his
present-day situation, and he indicates the intellectual price that
man must pay for any flight from reality into a metaphysical illusion of order and stability. Camus attacks Kierkegaard's concept
of the leap into faith and places such a response in the tradition of
"humiliated thought,"[40] a tradition which constantly points out the
severe limitations and defects of rationalism. Camus objects to this
tradition because it demands that intelligence sacrifice itself and
bow down before the absurd. Thus "god is maintained only

through the negation of human reason."[41] Reason may well have its limits, Camus writes, but "if I recognize the limits of reason, I do not therefore negate it, recognizing its relative powers. I merely want to remain in this middle path where intelligence can remain clear."[42] Camus finds that Kierkegaard does not respect the equilibrium that ought to exist between reason, on the one hand, and the feeling of the absurd on the other. Because Kierkegaard wants to be "cured" of this tormenting duality of life, he negates his reason and leaps into the absurd.

It should be added that Camus committed two serious errors in his interpretation of Kierkegaard's *Fear and Trembling*. First of all, he ignored the subtlety and range of Kierkegaard's response to the absurd by failing to distinguish between Kierkegaard himself, the narrator Johannes de Silentio, and Abraham, and thus between their differing responses. Second, and more important, Camus erroneously assumed that Kierkegaard's Christian eventually passes beyond daily struggle and conflict when he takes flight from the world by leaping into the absurd. Kierkegaard asserts the opposite: when the Christian gives up the finite through his faith in the absurd, he does not forever lose the finite but gains it back again "every inch."[43] The Christian does not retreat into a monastery, but continues to live in the everyday finite world, discharging his responsibilities and burdened by the same worries that plague everyman in daily life. There will always be a discontinuity between reason and faith, secular culture and Christianity. This dichotomy will remain absolute, forever incapable of being reduced. To leap into faith will not reduce the offense to reason caused by the absurdity of faith.

Kierkegaard's objection to the Christianity of the Church of Denmark was that its members strove to ignore the objective uncertainty of Christ's absurd claims and thus retreated into a weak-minded subjectivism that reduced the act of faith to an easily attainable state. Such ease represents the absence of faith, for it signifies the absence of passion and struggle. But the true Christian must hang perpetually suspended in mid-air, as it were, grasping with one hand the pole of reason and with the other that of faith. This state of suspension will not cause the poles of reason and faith

to move nearer to each other; the more firmly the individual grasps one pole, the more violently will the other move in the opposite direction. Grasping both poles with equal strength, the Christian becomes spiritually crucified ever anew. The continuing test of his faith consists in his resisting the temptation to let go of one pole and swing free upon the other, living henceforth either by reason or by faith alone.

It is Kierkegaard's emphasis upon suffering, conflict, and passion that Camus totally fails to appreciate. Camus's lack of understanding in this regard arises from his *a priori* assumption that God does not exist, an assumption that invalidates any leap beyond the secular world, whereas the fact of God's existence is the *a priori* assumption at the heart of Kierkegaard's thought. Although Kierkegaard and Camus differ radically in their metaphysical presuppositions, the psychological state that Kierkegaard advocates for the Christian is analogous to the one that Camus advocates for the existential hero in the twentieth century. For Camus, existential man must assume a position midway between the absurd and the rational: he must forever maintain an equilibrium between his nostalgia for irrational unity, on the one hand, and his rational perception of the existence of an unjust, incoherent, and incomprehensible world, on the other.

It may well be that Camus considered Kierkegaard's manner of retaining the dimension of passion and conflict in his thought while at the same time positing the existence of a higher spiritual order to be merely theological sleight of hand.   From such a point of view, Kierkegaard's psychological need for struggle, even for self-torture, rose beyond that which was necessitated by the logic of his theological argument. His argument exhorted man to leap into faith and therefore to leave the world behind. But Kierkegaard's emotional need for passionate struggle led to an ancillary assertion that posited a double motion in the act of faith. First, the Christian leaps beyond the rational limitations and ethical standards of daily life. Thus in his lonely encounter with God, the individual leaves the finite world behind. Second, at the moment of absolute faith, the finite everyday world is returned to him. The very way in which Kierkegaard formulated this assertion laid the

foundation for his further self-torture: the man of faith could achieve everything, both God and the world, as did Abraham. Kierkegaard and Johannes, however, because their faith was insufficient, could achieve neither God nor the everyday world. They were thereby condemned to "infinite resignation,"[44] to existing outside the grace of God as well as outside the joys of communal and family life.

Kierkegaard's passionate, spiritually crucified Christian (whether or not Kierkegaard's analysis may represent an emotional or intellectual sleight of hand trick) disappears in the context of Camus's spiritual landscape devoid of God. Camus's world-view rests upon the ashes of Kierkegaard's theology in the sense that Camus retains the psychological imperative of heroic struggle while rejecting Kierkegaard's metaphysical premise. It is at this point that we may indicate how the landscape of Musil's fiction at once differs from the world of Kierkegaard's analysis of Abraham, the Incarnation, and Immaculate Conception and begins to resemble the more bleak world of Camus. Musil's young scientist resembles Johannes de Silentio, the typically modern "shrewd pate" who must fail rather than the mythical Abraham who succeeds. But Kierkegaard's and Camus's differing evaluation of the failure of the "shrewd pate" reveals a profound change in the evaluation of reason in the nineteenth and twentieth centuries. Johannes suffers from a sense of inadequacy and guilt in his recognition that he is unable to deny his reason and make the leap of faith, as did Abraham. Camus, on the other hand, in essence urges such a failure, for to leap into the absurd in a Godless world is to commit "philosophical suicide." Such an act is never even remotely a possibility for the young scientist, Musil's prototype of modern rational man in a world without God.

Although Musil's protagonist does not experience the absurd in Kierkegaardian terms, in which the absurd can be transformed into a creative religious experience that transcends the limitations of arid rationality, he does, as a man of Camus's twentieth century, experience moments of the absurd. But a comparison of these moments, when regarded in the context of Musil's *Weltanschauug* as a whole, reveals that Musil's concept of the absurd is comparable to

that of Camus only up to a point. As in Camus's fiction, moments occur to the Musil protagonist when everything in the world seems to fall apart into meaningless details and a jumble of fragments, when the "ceiling" and the "floor" of existence fall away, leaving him floating freely in a world of impersonal forces and upon fields of surging energy. People and events then suddenly appear grotesque, silly, paradoxical, and life seems empty, strange, unintelligible. These moments occur when man regards the world through his reason and finds that all his expectations, needs, and presuppositions are met with total frustration. Camus asserts that the world is not absurd in and of itself. The feeling of absurdity arises only when reason confronts the irrationality of the world: "The absurd is born of this confrontation between the human need and the unreasonable silence of the world."[45] Thus the absurd depends as much upon man and his expectations as upon the world. But it is only up to this point that Camus's analysis of the absurd is illuminating in a consideration of Musil's work. Although the absurd forms an extreme pole to reason in the *Weltanschauung* of Camus, the extreme pole to reason in Musil's work is that of mysticism. It is in the perspective of mysticism, of intense emotional states, that the fragmented and meaningless world revealed to man's rational mind becomes whole, significant, and ordered. Musil is, therefore, not an existentialist in Camus's strict definition of the term, for into Musil's *Weltanschauung* is built the possibility of an escape from nihilism into a radiant world of joy and meaning.

The differences in regard to reason, mysticism, and the absurd in the work of Kierkegaard, Camus, and Musil can, nevertheless, be interpreted from a single unifying perspective in that the individual is given a series of ever possible existential choices. Beneath every existential choice lies a moral evaluation regarding the place of reason, mysticism, and the absurd in modern life. Because Camus is concerned with finding a way of living in the full knowledge of the absurd without veiling it either behind a total rationalism or a total irrationalism, he would reject the choices made both by Kierkegaard and by Musil as revealing nostalgia for an essentially religious experience of spiritual unification. It is for

this reason that Abraham's leap into the presence of God as well as Musil's back-door escape into mystical states could serve as excellent illustrations of Camus's definition of philosophical suicide, however much Ulrich may plead that reason is not negated in his experiment in mysticism. This form of philosophical suicide has already been examined in the context of Claudine's, Veronica's, and Homo's lives. It will be further analyzed in connection with Ulrich's second experiment. In "Tonka," however, Musil has presented a case of the opposite extreme: the young scientist escapes from life into the world of reason—an extreme solution which Camus would also have condemned. The young scientist believes—as one can assume that the young Homo did before him and the young Ulrich will after him—that reason, science, and modern technology can provide a foundation for meaning and structure in the modern world. For the young scientist, reason seems to promise the way to future happiness. Whereas Camus advocates a position between extremes, Musil's characters either embody one extreme or vacillate back and forth between two extremes. Thus, in *Three Women*, Homo illustrates the one extreme of total flight into mysticism while the young scientist escapes into rationality; Ketten alone appears to achieve a balance between the two by the end of the story. In Camus's world, man must accept the fact that life is an endless struggle which can never be overcome. But Musil's work is directed toward the possibility of an eventual synthesis of extremes. The absurd, unlike the mystical, cannot by definition be synthesized with any perspective. Thus Camus's heroic pessimism stands in direct opposition to Musil's utopian hopes.

A Life Without Dialogue

Of all of Musil's works, not one is situated as much within the confines of the everyday world of conflict and suffering as is "Tonka." The scenes of "action" in Musil's other fiction tend to verge upon or actually take place in a heightened world of the fantastical and the mystical; or, where this is not the case, Musil writes of a protagonist who, quite aloof from the cares of daily life, occupies

himself with problems which he can only formulate by using a highly abstract and intellectual terminology.   Although both fantastical and intellectual elements appear in "Tonka" (as was also the case in *Young Törless*), they are set against the background of a rather depressing daily reality.   In this story, the protagonist lives in a large and quite unpleasant city, is alienated from his family, suffers from great poverty, and is racked with jealousy. The young scientist is vulnerable to the everyday world in two senses: first, like Rilke's Malte Laurids Brigge, he feels himself to be standing at the edge of an abyss of poverty.   It should be added, however, that Malte feels himself to be much more fundamentally threatened than does the young scientist; for despite the reality of his poverty, the young scientist (unlike Malte) never really identifies himself with the poor and the outcasts nor imagines that they are beckoning to him to join their ranks, however seedier the restaurants become to which he takes Tonka and however shabbier his once fine clothes begin to look.   Second, the young scientist has taken upon himself the responsibility of caring for another human being, and it is this second aspect of his life that will be examined in the present section.

The emphasis of the following approach to "Tonka," which centers upon a (negative) critical appraisal of the protagonist's human relationships rather than upon a (positive) admiring explication of his ideas, should not be construed as implying that Musil's abstract philosophical expression of highly personal problems must be regarded as merely an intellectual disguise that the critic must peel away in order to discover the story's hidden psychological truth. Semiphilosophical or pseudophilosophical formulation constitutes a major aspect of Musil's fiction and cannot be "psychologized away." Yet, an objection might be made that to place emphasis upon human interrelationships (as will be done here) not only reverses the prevailing critical interpretation of this story but it also reverses the direction in which Musil's literary sensibility habitually sought expression.   Musil's tendency in his major fiction was, admittedly, always to press for more abstract and generalized formulations of personal conflict.   This process of transformation into ever more abstract formulation and summary, which

reflects the author's desire to comprehend personal problems in intellectual and general rather than in psychological terms, forms the central axis of those works that are essentially concerned with the behavior and attitudes of the male protagonists, beginning with *Young Törless*, continuing in "Tonka," and culminating in Ulrich's first experiment in *The Man without Qualities*. Nevertheless, the critic of "Tonka" may take advantage of the rare opportunity presented by this story to examine Musil's central preoccupations from a rather different perspective than that afforded by his other works into which the external world, with its network of human relationships, scarcely seems to intrude. He may thus with profit look behind the intellectual façade constructed by the brilliantly articulated ideas of this typical masculine protagonist.

The young scientist's all but total abandonment of Tonka may be evaluated in terms of two quite different perspectives, both of which issue from two opposing moral codes: the Judeo-Christian morality of love for all men and compassion for the weak and the Nietzschean morality of the solitary hero's dedication to a self-imposed task without regard for the human consequences. Although the positive Nietzschean evaluation of the young scientist's behavior quite explicitly and consciously dominates the conclusion of "Tonka," Musil's sympathy for the young woman is equally clear throughout the story. Unlike the author's disturbingly dispassionate appraisal of Törless's cruelty toward Basini, Musil's recognition of Tonka as the unfortunate and totally innocent victim of a "free spirit's" quest for knowledge does reveal a newly acquired degree of compassion on his part. The following analysis will offer a negative critique of the young scientist's treatment of Tonka while the next section will justify his abandonment of Tonka within the framework of Nietzsche's critique of woman and his morality of the masculine task.

The young scientist faces a test, the terms of which involve not the acceptance of the absurd but rather the acceptance of a human being. The absurdity of Tonka's pregnancy is never presented by Musil as a fact—as was the case in Kierkegaard's discussion of the Virgin Mary; its absurd nature remains no more than an ironic observation which is never given serious consideration as a possi-

bility occuring in the contemporary world. If the question of the absurd is put aside, it becomes evident that the young scientist rejects Tonka's pregnancy not primarily because of the risk to his reason that acceptance of the absurd might entail; rather, by disavowing even the possibility of his paternity, he is revealing a far greater fear—that of risking his egoistic autonomy. For the fundamental difficulty inherent in the young scientist's life is not the fear that he might commit philosophical suicide by taking a leap into faith, but the fact that he is unable to give of himself emotionally and to accept responsibility for another human being. In order to diminish the greater risk, the young scientist constructs a dichotomy in his mind between Tonka and his invention, between a human relationship and his commitment to the world of science and technology. By refusing to consider that he might be the child's father as well as by dwelling upon Tonka's possible infidelity, he is, in effect, paving the way toward a complete withdrawal of his emotional energies from her so that he can redirect them toward his scientific labors. But even if Tonka had been unfaithful, is her infidelity sufficient justification for the protagonist's abandonment of her? Comparing the deeper love Homo feels for his wife with the brief affair in which he indulged with Grigia, Homo comments: "no one will sacrifice eternity for the sake of a quarter of an hour's frivolity" (125).

Had the young scientist loved Tonka, her infidelity with a stranger would have seemed irrelevant, a mere quarter of an hour's frivolity. The protagonist chooses, however, to use the possibility of Tonka's unfaithfulness as a pretext to abandon her. He chooses himself. Regarded from this perspective, the basic problem of "Tonka" appears in the character of the young scientist: it is to be found in his "defective dialogue" with Tonka (to use a concept from Buber's philosophy) which arises out of his narcissism (to use a term from Freudian psychology). Thus an understanding of the protagonist's relationship to Tonka must begin with the recognition that his rejection of her arises not because his reason is too strong but because his love is too weak.

The young scientist's relationship to Tonka is marked by inequality from the very beginning, both on the social and intellec-

tual level. Their relationship begins as an affair typical of the time, in which a young man of education and social position takes a poor servant girl from his own house as a mistress. But instead of remaining a brief affair, the little experiment in sexuality turns into a long drawn-out agony which the young scientist is unable to break off at the appropriate moment, as was no doubt customary in such cases. As the dominant partner, it is for him to dissolve the affair, for a girl like Tonka was simply expected to wait for a word from him—and she does. Her situation of utter passivity and dependence precludes the possibility of a meaningful relationship between the two of them.

Their affair represents the inverse of the "I-Thou" relationship as advocated by Buber, that is to say, a relationship based upon a full sharing of all aspects of life, i.e., one in which two people are fulfilled in a state of reciprocity. Whoever is not acquainted with the "I-Thou" relationship or "the equality of all lovers," Buber writes, "does not know love."[46] For Buber there can be no solitary "I" in and of itself but only the "I" existing and known in two basic ways. If the relationship is not that of "I-Thou," it then exists on the "I-It" level, the level without love. The "I" existing on this lower level deals with people and daily reality only indirectly through reason, abstraction, and concepts; it strives to replace direct experience with the "acquisition of information."[47] Such an approach to reality reaches its culmination in the attitude of the scientist toward the world: he sorts, calculates, orders. The "I-It" relationship, lacking the immediacy, spontaneity, and unpredictability implicit in lived relationships, directs a man toward the mastery and exploitation of others rather than toward a sharing and growing in mutual trust. Buber writes: "without It a human being cannot live. But whoever lives only with that is no human."[48] The "I" that exists apart from the web of interpersonal relationships, as does Musil's young scientist, soon becomes a pale abstraction of a human being. It should be added that Buber did not believe that the life of dialogue was a privilege for special people such as the highly intelligent. It is a possibility that exists for all men. There are merely those who give themselves and those who withhold themselves.   And those who give themselves are

able to bridge both social and intellectual inequalities, as the young scientist and Tonka were unable to do.

The young scientist's detachment from Tonka is further reflected by a corresponding absence in him of any relationship to the social world in general. Musil writes: "He stood in the hollow space under the cascade of it [the noise of daily life]— untouched by even a splash, but utterly cut off" (201). For Buber the "I-Thou" dialogue between two individuals must exist within a social context. Thus he conceived of a community as a living "We," as an aggregate of "I's" and "Thou's" united by a number of common concerns. The young scientist reveals not the slightest interest in the common concerns of the community and he is, in this sense too, a typical Musil protagonist. He is imprisoned in his own monologue—assuming, of course, that he possesses even a relationship with himself, which sometimes seems doubtful.

How does Tonka herself regard her relationship to the young scientist in the light of her pregnancy? Unlike Kleist's Marquise von O . . . , Tonka never thinks of her pregnancy as an inexplicable, absurd event and thus is never forced to the point where she must, so to say, commit "philosophical suicide" and accept the irrationality of her own immaculate conception.[49] Whether or not she is telling the truth is something that neither the young scientist nor the reader will ever be able to know with absolute certainty. A doubt will always remain. But the young scientist continues to look for evidence: he finds, for instance, that Tonka had marked in her calendar a large red exclamation point on the day of her supposed conception, whereas all the other pages are covered merely with everyday domestic notations. Most of the time, the protagonist has an absolute "conviction of Tonka's infidelity" (203) and can feel only pity for her: "Poor Tonka, she has had to pay so dearly for a single passing aberration!"(215). However, there is one quite simple and rational explanation for her pregnancy; the child is his and Tonka is telling the truth. Tonka noticed her pregnancy only when it was no longer possible to establish the day of conception with any certainty. For Tonka, therefore, the breakdown in his relationship to her is caused not by the absurdity of her pregnancy at all, but simply by the fact that he obviously no longer loves her.

Since he does not love her, all other considerations are irrelevant for her. Tonka does not argue with him, she does not defend herself or attack his lack of faith in her. She becomes silent not because she has been visited by a pregnancy that is absurd and thus beyond the limits of language; she is silent because "he mistrusted her" (199). It is his lack of love that defines Tonka and her condition: "Nothing could be interpreted on its own merits alone, one thing depended on the other, one had to trust or mistrust the whole of it, love it or take it for deceit and delusion. If one was to understand Tonka, one had to respond to her in one definite way; one had, as it were, to call out to her, telling her who she was. What she was, depended almost entirely on him" (207-8). Buber also believed that the individual must be affirmed and confirmed by another. An animal has no need to be confirmed, for it is what it is without any question. But man must discover what he is through his confirmation in dialogue with another human being. From this point of view, Tonka eventually becomes in reality what she was in the young scientist's eyes: an apparently fickle servant girl who betrayed him and had to suffer the consequences. Tonka begins to fade away and there is nothing left for her to do but die.

The Freudian Defense

An examination of how the young scientist's relationship to Tonka is defective leads inevitably to a consideration of why his feelings for her are so ambivalent, so filled with conflict and personal suffering. A significant and rather peculiar turning point in his emotional relationship toward Tonka occurs at her death. While she is dying, he affects an attitude of coldness, of almost cruel indifference toward her. (At one point, he admits to the wish that she might die.) But immediately after her death, he is overwhelmed with a feeling of profound love for Tonka: "He felt her, from the ground under his feet to the crown of his head, and the whole of her life" (222). What has changed? Tonka as a physical presence has disappeared, the body has died. It may be recalled that Veronica experienced a similar moment when Johannes left

her to commit suicide. And Homo's mystical moment of total love for his wife occurred only when she was far away from him. Thus, it is the physical body that is the last obstacle to the fullest development of the feeling of love. This situation has been pointed out before, but a psychological explanation has not yet been undertaken. Such an implicitly negative evaluation of the physical body in general is intensified in Musil's work by the male protagonist's often expressed disgust for the female body in particular. This tendency reaches its culmination in *The Man without Qualities* where Ulrich obsessively notes all the small, numerous, and repulsive physiological details of the various women in his circle.   Can any reason be found to explain such decided disgust for the female body?

Musil was preoccupied with the theme of mother-son incest throughout his life. As early as 1905, he treated this theme in sketches for "Tonka" and for what was to become *The Man without Qualities*.[50] In *Young Törless*, the development and resolution of the protagonist's emotional confusions are framed, so to say, by the presence of his mother, who appears at the very beginning and the very end of the novel. More significant, however, is her unwelcome appearance in Törless's mind during the scene in which he cannot help associating her with the prostitute Božena. When the sexual ambiguities are (more or less) resolved at the end of the novel, Frau Törless appears more as a physical body, that is, more as a woman like other women, and less as the virginal creature of Törless's childlike imagination. The last sentence in the novel emphasizes Törless's new perception of his mother as having a body: "And, drawing a deep breath, he considered the faint whiff of scent that rose from his mother's corseted waist" (173). At the end of his career, Musil pursued the theme of incest in the relationship between Ulrich and his sister Agathe. But as psychoanalysis has pointed out, brother-sister incest may be regarded as a façade: "When there are several children in the family, the Oedipus complex expands and becomes a family complex. As the children grow up, a little boy may take his sister as his love object, who then replaces his 'faithless' mother."[51] To return to a consideration of "Tonka," however, a work which occurs at the midpoint of Musil's

career, it is clear that this story represents a continuation and development of the mother-son relationship first presented in *Young Törless*. But "Tonka" is also the only work in which Musil allows himself to treat this difficult relationship over an extended period of time. This theme will now be briefly examined in the context of psychoanalytic thought.

The fear of incest typically causes the masculine psyche to generate a double image of woman: the adored and noble virgin, on the one hand, and the common and ultimately rejected whore, on the other. Such a division in the mind of the male reveals the operation of a mechanism of defense against incestuous instinctual impulses. The instinctual life is isolated from the rest of the personality and projected upon a "lower woman." Fenichel explains as follows:

> Very frequent is the assignment of love and hate, originally pertaining to one and the same person, to different objects. Persons who have elevated this mechanism to a predominant character trait finally come to separate all persons and all things into completely antithetical categories. Another example is the isolation of tenderness and sensuality, so that sensuality is experienced only toward objects with whom there is no emotional relationship. Under present cultural conditions prostitution gives men a good opportunity for such isolation.[52]

Thus, the young scientist will never be able to achieve that kind of emotional relationship with Tonka which she desires. Such a marked isolation of tenderness and sensuality was also clearly evident in Homo's relationship to his wife and to Grigia. Musil even "projected" this essentially masculine dynamic into the feminine psyches of Claudine and Veronica, who experience a similar division between, respectively, the refined husband and the goat-like stranger and between the priestlike Johannes and the doglike Demeter. This division most frequently manifests itself in the male psyche in terms of class structure.   As Fenichel writes, the social position of parents may influence the form of an Oedipus complex:

"Most children unconsciously equate "socially low" and "instinctual, uninhibited" [as opposed to] "socially high" and "sublimated, inhibited." If a person from a well-to-do home feels especially attracted to those of a lower social level, analysis frequently reveals not only a longing for reassurance against humiliation . . . but also a longing for the prohibited sensuality.[53]

Both Božena and Tonka as well as Grigia come from the lowest social class.

"Tonka" is a "replay" and further development of the conflict in Törless's mind between the warring images of his mother and Božena. In the later story, however, Törless has grown up, so to say, into the young scientist, while Božena, "the ageing and degraded prostitute" (37), has in turn become younger, the naive and innocent girl that Božena had been before she entered domestic service. What becomes reality for the young scientist remains in the subjunctive for Törless: "Had Božena been pure and beautiful and had he been capable of love at that time, he would perhaps have sunk his teeth in her flesh" (36). Reversing Törless's rejection of Božena—"Leave me out of it" (37), he had told Beineberg—the young scientist makes Tonka his mistress. Thus, the scientist takes that path which Törless only contemplated, the path that leads through a gate "out of the world of those calm and irreproachable beings [Törless's parents]" (41) and into a realm of sensuality. Whereas Törless only thinks of "stepping out of his privileged position and going among common people—among them? no, lower than them!" (36)—the young scientist does so upon the arm of Tonka and together they sink into the lowest level of poverty and social degradation.

The parallels existing between *Young Törless* and "Tonka" touch upon more than the mother-prostitute dichotomy. Both works also reproduce in fiction the same triangular family configuration of father, mother, and lover which existed in the household of the young Musil. In *Young Törless,* this configuration was transposed to the Beineberg household, where a certain "cousin" Karl used to pursue Beineberg's mother, a situation that foreshadows "uncle" Hyacinth's displacement of the father in the young scien-

tist's household. This triangle is described to the boys by Božena, who had once been in service with the Beineberg family as Tonka had once served the family of the young scientist. Upon Törless's hearing this bit of scandal, Musil notes: "Beineberg's mother turned into his own" (38). In Musil's mind, Frau Törless obviously represented a transformation of Musil's own mother, for his father had also been unambiguously displaced by an "uncle" Reiter, who one day moved in with the Musil family and remained for forty years. It is evident that the young Musil, when writing *Young Törless* in 1905-1906, was still unable to deal directly with the relationship between his mother and Reiter. He therefore projected it into the Beineberg family while at the same time allowing a faint reverberation of this problem to sound in Törless's mind. Fifteen years had to pass before he could treat the theme directly in the context of the protagonist's own life.

The young scientist's attitude toward his "uncle" Hyacinth is, not surprisingly, one of disdain and loathing grounded in sexual jealousy. (The presence of this father-substitute also serves as a psychologically convenient figure for the son's psychic conflict: the son can direct his hatred toward the sexual father-substitute, while continuing to admire and love his displaced father.) Regarded in this context, the agony which the protagonist had once experienced many years before as a very young boy watching his mother and Hyacinth in a dark railway car becomes readily comprehensible. In the bright light of the following morning, the boy realizes that this scene had been quite innocent and totally without sexual implications. Fenichel's comments concerning such scenes are illuminating:

> Instead of a primal scene all kinds of primal-scene substitutes may have been experienced: observations of animals, of nude adults, and even of scenes that objectively are entirely nonsexual but that are subjectively experienced as sexual. The effectiveness of such scenes is greater if other objectively harmless experiences readily facilitate a transference of what has been witnessed to the parents.[54]

Hyacinth has assumed the position that the young protagonist would like to have occupied and, like Hamlet, he feels deep sorrow for his father and decides to challenge his mother in the morning with her infidelity. The continued existence within the young scientist (even years after the childhood scene in the train) of unconscious feelings of competition with his "uncle" may partially account for his desire to cultivate a way of life totally opposite to that of Hyacinth, thereby attempting to minimize the sexual parallels existing between them. Because he regards Hyacinth as sentimental, self-indulgent, and "soft," he is forced into becoming rational, courageous, and ascetic.

The more mature young scientist fully realizes what the young Törless only began to suspect: that his mother is not the pristine and exalted figure of his childhood dreams, for she has betrayed him with another man, Hyacinth. By the end of *Young Törless*, the mother has also begun to cross the line in Törless's mind and to approach the image of Božena. Tonka is unable however, to cross the line, in the opposite direction, i.e., to pass from being a Božena into becoming a pristine and noble figure within the protagonist's mind. Tonka remains a Božena and so is eventually rejected by the young scientist. The division of the emotional life of the male which is implicit here is commented upon by Musil in *Young Törless*. There, passion is seen as a form of "hatred," as "a panic-stricken flight" (36), while the feeling of love is reserved for the virginal mother figure who is "like a star, beyond the reach of all desire, in some cloudless distance, clear and without depths . . . ." (39).

The most extreme form of this division between the tender and the sexual, in which the sexual impulse becomes blended with feelings of anger and contempt, is found in the figure of Moosbrugger, the mass-murderer of prostitutes in *The Man without Qualities*. Despite his horrible crimes, Moosbrugger can be regarded as but a more radical embodiment of that same problem that distresses so many of Musil's masculine protagonists. To paraphrase a sentence from Freud's paper "Contributions to the Psychology of Love" in Volume Four of the *Collected Papers*: such men cannot sexually

desire where they tenderly love, and they cannot tenderly love where they sexually desire. Only in the realm of the young scientist's dreams is Tonka able to make the transition from sexuality to love and thus begin to approach the kind of exalted fantasy that Törless had had of his mother: "there is a realm where she [Tonka] is grand, noble, and good, where she is not a little shop-girl, but his equal, deserving of great destiny" (221). Tonka ascends into this realm only temporarily in the young scientist's dreams at night, but by means of her death she ascends and remains there forever. The dead Tonka now lives in the realm of Homo's absent wife, the same mystical world in which Ulrich places Agathe, only to have his sister degenerate in his mind into a Božena, a sexual being, and thus one who must also be ultimately rejected. The young scientist's emotional frigidity does not arise merely as a reaction to the sentimentalities of Hyacinth's nature and to Hyacinth's love for his mother, which is quite genuine. His disdain for Hyacinth is only an isolated aspect of his rejection of the emotional life in general. From a psychoanalytic perspective, his overemphasis upon the development of the rational faculties functions as a defense against oedipal feelings. In retrospect, it can also be said that Törless's aim in attempting to express his dionysian fantasies in the context of reason and language was due less to a desire for intellectual comprehension than to a need to escape from the threatening power of sex by taking flight into a world of rational order. In a psychoanalytic perspective, mathematics becomes the supreme defense against oedipal wishes. As Veronica retreated into a mystical state of total submersion in the self, the young scientist retreats into a world of science and technology. They both take an essentially narcissistic flight into two opposing extreme states in order to escape from the same danger: involvement in the sexual life of another human being and, more fundamentally, the reanimation of their own psychopathological sexual impulses.

The type of man so common in Musil's work, who appears to be cold, abstract, and emotionless often withdraws from the instinctual world into the isolated and isolating world of words and

ideas which serve him as a form of protection against feeling. In the name of preserving the purity of the idea from its corruption by the emotions, he may desperately attempt to disconnect every idea from any emotional contact. Such a man may well develop his powers of logic to an extreme, for the life of logic depends to a great extent upon its isolation from the rest of life. Although such a life may be justified in the name of man's search for objectivity, the extreme isolation of reason from feeling is regarded in psychoanalytic theory as directed fundamentally toward defense.   Musil first described this tendency in Törless, developed it in the young scientist, and allowed it to reach its full, if not grotesque, fruition in Ulrich's first experiment. Fenichel writes of one such neurotic patient who, because he could never feel at ease in any situation, hated his profession, his friends, and life in general. He "loved his only hobby: mathematics. For him it was the field in which there were no emotions."[55] The obvious appropriateness of this quotation as a partial description of the mathematician Ulrich requires no comment.

What happens to the individual when "the pleasure principle" has undergone prolonged repression in the name of objectivity may be gauged by the fact of Ulrich's nervous breakdown. In "Tonka", however, Musil's evaluation of the life of science and logic is not yet as negative as it is to become in *The Man without Qualities*. Although Musil presents enough of a psychological context in "Tonka" for the reader to be able to reach a negative moral judgment of the young scientist's behavior toward Tonka, the protagonist regards his own life with Tonka and release from her in an unambiguously positive light. The concluding section of this analysis of "Tonka" will examine the protagonist's intellectual and scientific temperament from a positive perspective.   In this light, the young scientist appears not as a man suffering from a defective interpersonal relationship arising from a psychopathological condition. He emerges rather as a hero of cognition who has renounced the ordinary joys of communal life for an ascetic and lonely existence selflessly dedicated to intellectual exploration at the outermost boundaries of the human mind and spirit.

The Masculine Task

The common denominator between Kierkegaard's *Fear and Trembling* and Musil's "Tonka" is to be found in the theme of the conflict between a man's dedication to his work and the difficulties that ensue in his relationship to a woman because of his divided loyalties. The commitment of his intellectual and emotional energies to his self-imposed intellectual task exists (so he interprets his situation) in an inverse relationship to his emotional commitment to a woman. While this theme is both central and obvious in all the stories of *Three Women*, it remains latent in *Fear and Trembling*. Writing in the context of a theological explication of a biblical passage, Kierkegaard "cleansed" his own text of all personal allusions, relegating the biographical references to his diaries. But while he was examining the problem of Abraham's relationship to Isaac, Kierkegaard was also coming to terms with his relationship to Regina Olsen. As Kierkegaard placed Abraham's test of faith within the context of a task that God had placed upon Abraham, so Kierkegaard in *Fear and Trembling* was simultaneously dealing with his own task of achieving the religious mode of life as had Abraham in *The Old Testament*. As Abraham was forced to sacrifice Isaac, so Kierkegaard believed that his renunciation of Regina was in accord with the will of God. The complexities of Kierkegaard's feelings toward Regina Olsen are detailed in Walter Lowrie's definitive two-volume study of Kierkegaard's life.[56]

What follows here should not be interpreted as an attempt to reduce theology to psychology; for it is, admittedly, in Kierkegaard's objectification of his personal crisis through the theological explication of the Abraham-Isaac story that his genius has made a unique contribution to Western intellectual history. It is, however, on the level of biography that a comparison of the conflicts in the commitments of the young scientist and Kierkegaard yield illuminating insights. Although in one case we are dealing with a character in a work of modern fiction and in the other with a theologian who once lived, the major conflict in their lives is the same: both men were invested with an absolute devotion to their professions. After much inner struggle, they finally rejected personal relation-

ships with women. Eventually, they interpreted this renunciation as having contributed not only toward the success of their tasks but also toward the enrichment of their inner lives.

The choices made by Kierkegaard and the young scientist reveal the operation of a process which psychoanalysis has termed "the sublimation of Eros." Kierkegaard described his task as the lonely spiritual encounter of the individual with God. In the perspective of the Kierkegaardian religious mode of life, marriage is relegated to the ethical sphere, to the world of social relationships and of moral and ethical obligations. The relationship even to a single woman was for Kierkegaard a way of life nearer to that of the vulgar crowd than to the realm of God. Kierkegaard further believed that isolation alone guarantees the integrity of the personal life. To choose Regina, therefore, would mean not only to withhold full commitment to God but to deny and inhibit the growth of the self. It was in this manner that Kierkegaard justified the breaking of his engagement to Regina Olsen in August 1841. While Kierkegaard made a decisive break in his relationship to Regina, the young scientist is unable to confront Tonka with the inevitable, that is, with his need to dissolve their relationship. Thus he merely prolongs the agony until the relationship is destroyed by the hand of fate.

The young scientist cannot help but admire the decisive way in which Tonka's employer fired her when he discovered that she was pregnant. This tradesman had only one absolute standard, i.e., that which would best serve his business interests, and so he dismissed Tonka without a second thought. The protagonist, however, is simply unable to take such a decisive step, and so ends by torturing Tonka over a long period of time by slowly withdrawing himself emotionally from her. He chooses his invention, which is to say, himself. This mutual opposition between Tonka and the self is also revealed in an episode that occurs not long before Tonka's death. The protagonist grows a beard which, while very much disfiguring his face, reminds him of Tonka. The day Tonka leaves for the hospital never to return, he has his beard shaved off and feels as if he has now become his old self again, a free and unencumbered self who can once again continue "through life burdened

with his ideas" (203). Tonka's death coincides, significantly enough, with the completion of his invention. Although Kierkegaard chose the world of mysticism and the young scientist that of reason, both thereby escaped from having to enter into a sustained emotional relationship with a woman which might have exercised a moderating effect upon their one-sided need to dedicate themselves to an idea that transcended the concerns of everyday life. In the cases of both men, the impulse initially directed toward a woman became inhibited and desexualized and, as Freud wrote in his paper "Instincts and their Vicissitudes," transformed into its opposite, eventually to emerge in the creation of intellectual constructs.

It may be added parenthetically that Kafka's interest in Kierkegaard's life and work also centered upon what Kafka perceived as a conflict of loyalties generated by Kierkegaard's engagement to Regina. Kafka, who in 1913 described Kierkegaard as "a friend,"[57] saw a direct parallel to Kierkegaard's life in his own agonies of conscience created by his engagement to Felice Bauer. However, Kafka's conflict between his desire to marry and his need to dedicate all his energies to his writing was even more complex and generated even greater ambivalence and suffering than was the case in Kierkegaard's life. For Kafka regarded the relationship to a woman in a far more positive light than did either Kierkegaard or the young scientist of Musil's story. He once wrote: "Woman, or more precisely put, perhaps, marriage, is the representative of life with which you are meant to come to terms."[58] Kafka believed that marriage might restore him to a healthy and productive life by rescuing him from his feelings of isolation, narcissism, and self-contempt. When he broke his engagement to Felice Bauer, therefore, he was concomitantly disengaging himself from life. Kafka compared his attempt at marriage to the situation of a businessman who must suddenly draw the balance in his books. The result is "one single great liability. And now marry without going mad![59] To pass the test of marriage, Kafka believed that a man needed to possess certain negative traits that Kafka had observed in his father. He considered these negative traits as a manifestation of the animal within man, of all that is life-affirming and spontaneous,

vital as well as disorderly and obscene. But Kafka also felt that marriage was barred to him precisely because it was his father's most intimate domain. Marriage would mean, Kafka wrote his father, that "I would be your equal."[60] How could Kafka ever hope to equal his father in anything, particularly in marriage which required, he believed, a superabundance of life? Kafka eventually had to admit that his "weakness, the lack of self-confidence, the sense of guilt . . . positively drew a cordon between myself and marriage."[61] For this reason, Kafka felt that he had to renounce the possibility of marriage.

Precisely because marriage represented the realm of health and life, Kafka feared the destructive effect that marriage might have upon the most unique manifestation of his personality: his task as an artist. His art, by being as far removed as possible from everything that his father represented, became connected in his mind with life-negation, narcissism, disease, and the extinction of animal vitality. By destroying the unnatural psychological condition from which his writing arose, marriage might also destroy him as an artist. In the letter to his father, Kafka wrote that his life consisted in letting "no danger that I can avert, indeed no possibility of such a danger, approach them [his literary works]. Marriage bears the possibility of such a danger, though also the possibility of the greatest help."[62] On behalf of his art, therefore, Kafka found a second reason for breaking off his engagement.

This digression on Kafka's life in the context of Kierkegaard's conflict between woman and task has been included here for two reasons: to provide a further perspective upon the young scientist's rejection of woman and to offer a point of departure with which to evaluate his justification for sacrificing Tonka to his work. In Kierkegaard's mind, his own willingness to sacrifice Regina (Isaac) in order to be able more fully to dedicate himself to the task of confronting God alone, far from the vulgar crowd, represented an heroic resolve. But Kafka judged his own decision to sacrifice Felice Bauer to the demands of his art as a cowardly and shameful retreat from the demands of daily life. The difference between Kierkegaard and Kafka in this regard is revealed by the metaphors which they used in order to express their own evaluations of their

respective renunciations. Kierkegaard praised the "knight of faith," while Kafka described his artistic self in terms of a crippled worm which had been stepped upon and crushed by his father. Kafka's father, who often functioned in his son's life as an absolute standard of truth, actively disliked Kafka's writing or, rather, simply the fact that Kafka wrote at all. Kierkegaard, on the other hand, felt that God, the father, had called upon him to dedicate himself totally to the religious life. Kierkegaard's inner life was therefore sanctioned by God while Kafka's inner life, nourished at the expense of Hermann Kafka's condemnation, remained "unsanctified" even by the author's earthly father. Lacking this kind of justification, therefore, Kafka, for much of his life regarded his intense inner life as a form of personal pathology and its cultivation as the pastime of a self-indulgent narcissist.

The critical point of difference between Kierkegaard and Kafka on the question of the "sanctification" of the inner life is to be found in their differing perspectives on social relationships. Kafka's feelings of guilt caused by his renunciation of Felice Bauer is explicable in terms of the ethos of the Jewish community and its condemnation of the perpetual bachelor. Buber's philosophy may also be recalled in this regard: man's ethical responsibility to his fellow man is the highest mode of being and cannot be transcended by the individual's lonely encounter with God. Rather, God becomes manifest in man's daily relationships with other men. Kierkegaard, on the other hand, sets out upon the path toward God with its concomitant rejuvenation of the self only when he leaves the crowd behind. For Kafka, however, to renounce human relationships is to set out on a path that leads to sterility and despair.

The young scientist's Nietzschean justification for sacrificing Tonka may now be contrasted with the attitudes of both Kierkegaard and Kafka in this regard. The protagonist's concept of his task in Musil's story reveals the direct and quite conscious influence of Nietzsche's analysis of the "free spirit" and the priorities that must govern his life. Jaspers considered the kind of conflict experienced by the young scientist to have been a fundamental element in Nietzsche's life: "Throughout Nietzsche's life there runs an inescapable contradiction between what he desires as a *human*

being and what he wants to do as the *bearer* of his *task*."[63] Unlike Kierkegaard and Kafka, Nietzsche's evaluation of his task is in no way dependent upon external sanction, whether by a divine or real father. The task, or rather man as the bearer of his task, is self-sanctifying. There is an unshakable belief in Nietzsche's thought that the "free spirit," as he soars above all human commitments in the pursuit of his self-imposed task, carries his own justification within himself. In the perspective of the morality of the "free spirit," which is (to quote Musil on the young scientist) "ascetically" creative, "tough and austere" (189), all relationships with women must be dissolved. Because Nietzsche's "free spirit" must "fly alone,"[64] marriage is to be eschewed, for women serve only as a drag upon and a hindrance to the fulfillment of his mission.[65] Nietzsche summarized the "immorality" of women in *Human, All-Too-Human*: "women always intrigue privately against the higher souls of their husbands; they want to cheat them out of their future for the sake of a painless and comfortable present."[66] But although Nietzsche may argue that the seeker of truth requires distance and therefore independence from the responsibilities of daily life that marriage entails[67] so that the power of his thought will remain unimpaired, the reason for Nietzsche's rejection of woman in the name of his task is to be found in a more fundamental objection.

The basis of Nietzsche's fear of woman as a force that jeopardizes man's future arises from the "free spirit's" fear of sensuality and therefore his fear of woman as a threat to the stability of his emotional life. Whether or not Nietzsche's morality of asceticism was an unconscious reaction to an oedipal conflict is a question that may be passed over here. However, his view of woman as the corrupter and antithesis of masculine reason is quite clear and unambiguous: "Women are more sensual than men, although they are less aware of their sensuality."[68] The corollary of such a belief naturally follows: "But she does not *want* truth: what is truth to woman? From the beginning, nothing has been more alien, repugnant, and hostile to woman than truth—her great art is the lie, her highest concern is mere appearance and beauty."[69] Sensuality disturbs objectivity. Törless rejects Basini's overtures to him on the grounds that any emotional involvement with Basini would inter-

fere with the objectivity of his scientific observations. And there is a further suggestion that to fall into a sensual state is to become a woman oneself. In both Nietzsche's and Musil's work, masculinity is always associated with asceticism, with the repression of sensuality.

The young scientist's relief at the severance of his connection with Tonka and his optimistic evaluation of his professional future directly reflect Nietzsche's morality of the "free spirit." There is, consequently, also a certain lack of psychological depth in his analysis of the victory of his task over his feelings for Tonka. (The reactions of Kierkegaard and Kafka are, on the other hand, fraught with "background" in this regard.) The young scientist now strikes out on his way into the world, unencumbered and filled with feelings of youthful enthusiasm and confidence. We recall that Törless eventually came to the conclusion that the sufferings generated by his relationship with Basini were beneficial: for the degradation left behind "that small admixture of a toxic substance which is needed to rid the soul of its over-confident, complacent healthiness, and to give it instead a sort of health that is more acute, and subtler, and wiser" (138). In a similar fashion, the young scientist now feels grateful to Tonka in spite of the great sufferings which she has caused him: he now feels "a little better than other people, because there was a small warm shadow that had fallen across his brilliant life. That was no help to Tonka now. But it was a help to him" (222). Like Basini, Tonka has been of use and may now be discarded. The young scientist admits at this point that "he had finished [his invention]. He stood in the light and she lay under the ground, but all in all what he felt was the cheer and comfort of the light" (222). What lies ahead for the young scientist, so intelligent, unencumbered, cruel, and naive? The present study will show that the way ahead, which Musil had already prefigured in the fate of the middle-aged scientist Homo, leads directly to the emotional breakdown and mystical experiences of Ulrich, the arch-ascetic rationalist who, ignoring social involvements as far as possible, strives to apply the standards of scientific precision to daily life.

A final comparison between the young scientist's conflict with woman and that of Homo and Ketten may now be undertaken by way of summary. In terms of Musil's dialectical vision of mysticism and reason, Homo embraced one extreme and the young scientist the other. Two conclusions may be drawn from their experience. First, while mysticism is a strongly death-oriented alternative in "Grigia," the self-assertion of the rational attitude in "Tonka" saves and renews life—although the life saved may seem to be uniquely one-sided and shallow. Second, both of Musil's dialectical extremes lead to an isolation from woman; and there exists, furthermore, an inverse relationship of life and death between the two women and the respective protagonists (as pointed out above): Homo dies and Grigia lives; the young scientist lives and Tonka dies. In "The Lady from Portugal," neither death nor isolation from woman occurs. It now becomes clear why Musil chose to place this work in the center of the collection of three stories, although he wrote it last. As suggested at the very beginning of this chapter, "The Lady from Portugal" presents a synthesis in Musil's dialectical vision and therefore provides a center about which the dialectical possibilities of his work revolve, not only the stories of Homo and the young scientist but also, further out upon the axis, Törless's rational attempts to understand his confusions and Ulrich's explorations with his sister into the mystical realm. Why was Ketten able to succeed whereas all the others failed to achieve the balanced life? Why was he alone able to resolve the duality of reason and mysticism, thereby resolving his complex personal relationship with his wife as well? In what way is "The Lady from Portugal" significantly different from all of Musil's other works?

"Tonka" offers the most illuminating point of departure for the purpose of drawing a contrast between "The Lady from Portugal" and Musil's other work, for it also represents in its own way (as mentioned above) an extreme in Musil's fiction. "The Lady from Portugal" is specifically not set in the present but rather in an exotic and legendary past. In "Tonka," on the other hand, Musil placed the story for the most part in the middle of a very drab vision of twentieth-century urban and industrial life. A feeling of

grayness and poverty dominates the atmosphere of the story. But the Portuguese lady lives as the mistress of a castle in the midst of a fairy-tale-like landscape. What was possible in her world seems no longer possible in the modern world where everything is regarded from a rational, sober, masculine perspective. (That which Kierkegaard felt was possible for Abraham in the distant past of *The Old Testament* world is likewise no longer possible for Johannes de Silentio, modern man and "shrewd pate" that he is.) Admittedly, a world outside of time also makes itself felt in "Tonka," but this ideal realm exists only in the dreams of the young scientist. After fleeting experiences of this other dimension, "the realisation that everything ought to be measured by quite different standards almost broke surface—but, like all understanding, even this was ambiguous and without certainty" (215). A second, striking difference that must be mentioned is the feeling of equality which exists between Ketten and his wife, however different their temperaments may be. A fundamental aspect of love, Buber writes in *I and Thou*, is "the equality of all lovers."[70] The absence of equality between the young scientist and Tonka is strikingly evident—except in their day-dreams and reveries:

> there is a realm where she is grand, noble, and good, where she is not a little shop-girl, but his equal, deserving of a great destiny. And this is why, in spite of all the differences between them, she always believed she had a right to him . . . . But he belonged to her because at bottom he was good; for she too was good, and somewhere, after all, there must be the palace of goodness where they could live united and never part again.(221)

But the harsh reality of twentieth-century life keeps this world of goodness from breaking through the surface of daily existence. This dream world is, however, the very stage for the action of "The Lady from Portugal." By the end of the story the Ketten castle has become the "palace of goodness" which remains merely a dream in "Tonka."

Musil did not, of course, stop writing with the completion of "The Lady from Portugal." A viable perfection of love had not yet

been achieved and thus remained a task for the future. Veronica's perfection of love may well have been perfect, but it was only perfect in its narcissism and, therefore, excludes the possibility of reciprocity. The love of Ketten and his wife was also perfect, but it did not occur or subsist in the real or contemporary world. The marriage between the Kettens represents not so much a synthesis (it might be argued) as a perfect unity of continuing opposites existing as a far-off ideal in the mind of Musil, an ideal to which he gave concrete expression by projecting it into a framework that resembled his wish-fantasies more than daily reality. Thus, if "The Lady from Portugal" forms the center of Musil's work, it is a center that exists more within the realm of Musil's utopian imagination as a psychological potential than within the realm of a realized possibility in the everyday world. Had the young scientist been able to love Tonka, this would have been a true perfection of love. Nevertheless, "The Lady from Portugal" did represent a "theoretical" portrait of perfect love. It also revealed that such a state could be achieved only as a result of profound emotional suffering. The problem now remained to carry through this struggle in the context of modern life. This task falls to Ulrich in *The Man without Qualities*. He will set out upon a pilgrimage to the "palace of goodness" in the company of his own Portuguese lady, his sister Agathe. Set against the background of contemporary life in the Vienna of 1913, their journey will be a pilgrimage of equals, for who could more be the equal of Ulrich than his "siamese twin." As their pilgrimage continues, however, the stage upon which it is acted also becomes progressively more fairy-tale-like until Ulrich and Agathe seem finally almost to disappear into paradise.

V

The Rise and Fall of a Rational Man:
The Man without Qualities (I)

ULRICH, THE 32-YEAR-OLD Viennese protagonist of *The Man without Qualities*, decides one day to take a year-long holiday from being a mathematician in order to concentrate all his energies upon a search for the meaning of life. *The Man without Qualities* describes the year of his desperate search (1913-1914), a search upon which Ulrich has staked his life; throughout the year there glimmers in the background the implicit but never articulated possibility of suicide. When Musil died in 1942 at the age of 62, he was still far from completing the novel. He had intended the work to comprise four parts. "A Sort of Introduction" (Part One) was to have been balanced by "A Sort of Conclusion" (Part Four). "The Like of It Now Happens" (Part Two), which deals withUlrich's first experiment to find a meaning in life as well as with his participation in the so-called Collateral Campaign, was to have been balanced by "Into the Millennium" (Part Three), which deals with Ulrich's second experiment involving a mystical relationship with his sister Agathe. However, the novel breaks off less than half-way through Part Three. The ultimate failure of Ulrich's search is paralleled throughout the novel by Musil's description of the decadence and final dissolution of the Austro-Hungarian Empire during the last year of its existence.

The Aesthetics of Nihilism: A World Without Plot

There is no plot in any usual sense of the term in *The Man without Qualities*. Musil considered it part of his intellectual honesty as a modern writer to avoid plot as far as possible. Musil's

attack upon the idea of plot as a form of fraud in the novel was a direct consequence of his nihilistic interpretation of daily reality. The events in the everyday life of twentieth-century man are, he believed, without inherent order or meaningful sequence. But most people are continually "rewriting" their daily lives by a process of mental editing, simplifying, and rearranging. In this way, an artificial "thread of narrative" is created that gives such people the comforting illusion that their lives are progressing in a meaningful fashion. Although unaware of the fact, they are still living intellectually in the last century in accordance with a prenihilistic and romantic world-view.

Why do people refuse to take the decisive step into the twentieth century? Why do they condemn themselves to remain forever intellectually old-fashioned? Although Musil and his protagonist Ulrich take a condescending attitude toward such people, Musil does recognize the psychological benefits arising from the practice of this form of fraud. Ulrich admits that:

> the law of this life, for which one yearns, overburdened as one is and at the same time dreaming of simplicity, was none other than that of *narrative order*. This is the simple order that consists in one's being able to say: "When that had happened, then this happened." What puts our minds at rest is the simple sequence, the overwhelming variegation of life now represented in, as a mathematician would say, a unidimensional order: the stringing upon one thread of all that has happened in space and time, in short, that notorious "narrative thread" of which it turns out the thread of life itself consists. Lucky the man who can say "when," "before" and "after"![1]

Ulrich's uniqueness as well as his curse lies in his refusal (or perhaps in his simple inability) to reinterpret the events of his life in a meaningful sequence under the guiding principle of a narrative order. In this respect Ulrich's life itself expresses the same narrative principle as that of the novel in which he is the protagonist.

Musil intended not to be one of those old-fashioned novelists

who refuses to take the decisive step into the twentieth century. Since he was unable to perceive a divinely ordained narrative order in existence, Musil believed that he could not allow himself to create a traditional novel with a plot. Musil consciously decided that his novel, *The Man without Qualities*, should not follow "the law of this life, for which one yearns," that is to say, it should not present a series of actions in a unidimensional order. In fact, his novel had to be written precisely against the psychological grain of the old-fashioned reader who yearns for a plot. *The Man without Qualities*, lacking a plot, is not a novel of action but rather the supreme example in Western literature of a novel of ideas. So, too, is Ulrich a protagonist who exists not at all through his actions but mainly through his ideas, which seem to be constantly "spreading out as an infinitely interwoven surface" (II 436). It is essentially Ulrich's thoughts that constitute the center of his life as well as that of most of the novel. And it was as the creator of an endlessly thinking and rarely acting protagonist that Musil believed he had fully accepted the difficult responsibilities of being a truly modern writer.

It is not surprising that Musil was attacked even during his own lifetime by critics who felt that *The Man without Qualities* was not a novel at all but simply an endless and unrelated series of highly intelligent, pseudophilosophical essays that served merely to impede narrative progression (such as there is). Critics also objected that the novel as a whole failed to evoke a sense of life and that every character in the book seemed shadowy and insubstantial. Musil admitted that his attempt to write of life only as it appeared reflected rather spectrally in the consciousness of an intellectual searching for meaning in life presented a particularly difficult problem for the novel form.[2] Nevertheless, Musil was determined to make the attempt.

The Dialectical Vision

Concerning man's perception of reality in the twentieth century, Musil asserted in his diary: "Rationality and mysticism, these

are the two poles of our time."[3] Elsewhere, Musil expressed this polarity variously in terms of science and love, precision and the soul, fact and metaphor, and knowledge and faith. While this dialectical vision is certainly implicit in Musil's previous works, it becomes far more explicit in his last novel and gives *The Man without Qualities* its fundamentally dialectical structure. Musil follows Ulrich's mind as it constantly generates ever new ideas; and these ideas circle endlessly about the possibility of achieving a meaningful life. Such a life is to be achieved either through the strenuous application of reason or through the submersion of consciousness in mystical states. Ulrich, who possesses a powerful dialectical mind, consciously comprehends his own inner life as being divided and growing (to use his own metaphor) into two quite separate "trees" (II 360). Within the sphere of the first tree, he places the scientific attitude in general, which is characterized by reason, precision of thought, and experimentalism. Within the sphere of the second tree, he places the mystical attitude, which is characterized by love and the nonrational impulses. Ulrich's first "rational experiment" designed to find a meaning in life constitutes Part Two of *The Man without Qualities* and is dialectically opposed to his second "mystical experiment," which constitutes Part Three of the novel.

Although Ulrich conducts first a rational and then a mystical experiment, he believes that these alternative roads to truth should ultimately be combined into a single road. In spite of the fact that these two ways of apprehending reality have always manifested themselves in the minds of men precisely in terms of their mutual exclusivity, i.e., reason versus mysticism, science versus religion, fact versus faith, Ulrich believes that their reconciliation must be recognized by modern man as constituting the most vital and pressing task facing twentieth-century Western culture. Musil's utopian vision of ultimate reconciliation rests upon the presupposition—whether considered as an historical explanation or simply as a metaphorical description—that man in the distant past experienced himself as a single unit in harmony with all of reality. At some point in time he "fell" into his present unfortunate schizophrenic state. It was because of this fall that there arose in man the

need to find meaning in life. Therefore, the meaningful life, for which Ulrich is searching and which man once possessed, is ultimately founded upon the possibility that all opposites can be reconciled. Musil's purpose in writing *The Man without Qualities* was nothing less than the achievement of such a synthesis on behalf of Western culture by means of the novel. Musil hoped that out of the conclusion of *The Man without Qualities* would arise a new and more creative way of living for all mankind.

Presuppositions for the Rational Experiment: Three Negations

An uncompromising attitude of nihilism forms the philosophical basis of Ulrich's first experiment. His belief in what does *not* exist is quite unambiguous: he regards "nothing as firmly established, neither any personality nor any order of things or ideas" (I 179), and he thus accepts "nothing, no ego, no form, no principle" (I 296). Ulrich describes his situation metaphorically as an ever-present feeling of possessing neither firm ground under his feet nor a firm skin around his body. This feeling leads him to negate three fundamental areas of human experience that most men have always taken for granted (as do all of Ulrich's friends in the novel). Ulrich's triple negation is made in the name of the scientific attitude through which he hopes that man, drawing solely upon his intellectual resources, will one day be able to discover a new and more creative "right way of living."

The first negation, which Ulrich considers necessary for a scientific investigation designed to achieve the right way of living, is the rejection of the concept of God. There exists for Ulrich no divinely revealed standard of truth and, consequently, no single code of commandments prescribing exactly how all men must behave. For if God existed, then man's chief energies would be primarily directed toward bringing his own actions into conformity with those laws of behavior handed down from above once and for all time. The belief in a God (so this reasoning runs) who guarantees the existence of a single standard of the true, the good, and the beautiful would tend to inhibit or destroy those creative possibili-

ties inherent in man's nature and would limit and even make superfluous man's need to conduct a personal search for his own right way of living. In a nihilistic world without God, however, there is no longer a single and correct interpretation of the good life. It is left to man himself to find his own solution to the problem of the right way of living. For the purpose of such a search, Ulrich advocates a dynamic and unfettered attitude of mind directed toward the future, a mind which encompasses any number of as yet undiscovered and unimaginable but possible ways of living.

One day when Ulrich is asked what he would do if he were made the lord of creation for one day, he replies that he would simply get rid of reality (I 343). Ulrich rejects reality whenever it, like the concept of God, seems to interfere with the process of creative thinking. He believes that the process of thinking is embodied in its purest form in a man's "sense-of-possibility" ("Möglichkeitssinn"). But a man's "sense-of-possibility" becomes weakened if his "sense-of-reality" ("Wirklichkeitssinn") is too tyrannical. Any single occurrence or event should be regarded as representing no more than a single possibility that has managed (usually for no particularly good reason) to break into reality, pushing other possibilities into the background and declaring itself to be the most "real," that is to say, the best, the most significant, and the most important. But man must not confer any absolute value upon any single occurrence merely because it has gained reality, thereby condemning all the other possibilities to remain forever unrealized ideas. For whenever that which has happened is absolutized and given more honor than that which did not happen, man's freedom of thinking of new possibilities or of what might have been and could yet be are thwarted. Reality, then, defined as that which has occurred, "holds down" all the as yet unborn possibilities and prevents them from realizing themselves. Under the surface of reality (to use Musil's metaphor), which pretends to be a hard and smooth skin, "things" are thrusting and jostling to get out (I 286). Ulrich believes that the world has it in its bones to change in any and all directions, and would do so were it not for the unfortunate opposition imposed upon it by all that which already exists. A corollary of Ulrich's aristocratic disdain for reality

as that which already exists is his belief that the real is inferior to the ideal. Whenever an idea does finally manage to break through the surface of reality, something essential has always been sacrificed in the process. What remains has been corrupted and so has lost the glorious power inherent in every pure idea.

Ulrich's third negation is directed toward the concept of personality (variously termed character or ego as well). He believes that a person with a strong sense of his own personality is unable to experience either external events or the life of the mind in all its complexity. Such a person is imprisoned in the single perspective provided by his own personality; his responses to life are always categorized into either an immediate "yes" or "no." For such people, thinking is superfluous. Ulrich does not have a character (in this sense of the term) and thus feels himself to be free from this particular form of psychological fixation. Believing that one should live hypothetically, he is able to consider all perspectives, saying neither yes nor no. From a psychological point of view, Ulrich's absence of personality can be regarded as the necessary correlative of his sense-of-possibility.

How does a person without a character behave in daily life? Ulrich, answering such a question in the negative, states: such a person should not "behave as a definite person in a definite world" (I 325). Since the primary way in which an individual becomes a particular person is through the choice of a specific profession, Ulrich must ultimately reject all professions. Although he does make various attempts to achieve some professional substance, first as a soldier, then as an engineer, and finally as a mathematician, something always seems to prevent him from making a final and complete commitment to any one of them. As Musil writes: "a character, a profession, a definite mode of existence—for him [Ulrich] these are notions through which the skeleton is already peering" (I 297).

An illuminating parallel may here be drawn between Dostoyevsky's exploration of the problem of the absence of character in his novel *Notes from Underground* and Musil's treatment of this theme in Ulrich's life. It should be added parenthetically that Musil read Dostoyevsky's work avidly throughout his life and consid-

ered the Russian writer to be one of the great psychologists of his age.[4] Musil found in Dostoyevsky's work brilliant confirmation of some of his own thoughts on the nature of character. The man from the underground confesses that he has no character and consequently says of himself: "I couldn't manage to make myself nasty or, for that matter, friendly, crooked or honest, a hero or an insect."[5] He wishes that he could at least be lazy, for if he were lazy, he could boast of possessing at least one definite trait. Laziness for him would then be almost like having a vocation, a calling, even a career. But he can never achieve any one state, since his life is informed by a spirit of contradiction. To every one of his beliefs, thoughts, or acts he finds it possible to oppose another belief, thought, or act. He possesses a veritable genius for thinking of all possibilities and this facility leads him into endless series of contradictions and denials. Thus he remains undefined and undefinable. He will not bow down before the "stone wall"[6] of reality anymore than Ulrich will accept the idea that a "realized possibility" is more necessary or meaningful than all the other possibilities that have as yet remained unrealized. In this radical fashion, both Ulrich and the underground man believe that they have managed to preserve their freedom through a self-created network of ever possible possibilities and dialectical reversals.

Dostoyevsky asserts, as does Ulrich, the existence of a mutual opposition between character and intelligence. The underground man makes the following statement:

> Now I'm living out my life in a corner, trying to console myself with the stupid, useless excuse that an intelligent man cannot turn himself into anything, that only a fool can make anything he wants out of himself. It's true that an intelligent man of the nineteenth century is bound to be a spineless creature, while the man of character, the man of action, is, in most cases, of limited intelligence."[7]

Like Ulrich, the underground man because of his intelligence often seems to be paralyzed between various possible ways of acting. He rationalizes his inability ever to commit himself to any one action,

to any one plan by arguing that in order to act one must be completely satisfied beforehand that one has chosen the best and the only possible action, that one has, to use Ulrich's phrase, finally discovered a sufficient cause or reason to act. Dostoyevsky's protagonist continues: "How can I ever be sure? Where will I find the primary reason for action, the justification for it? Where am I to look for it? I exercise my power of reasoning, and in my case, every time I think I have found a primary cause I see another cause that seems to be truly primary, and so on and so forth, indefinitely."[8] The underground man is eventually led to the thought that too much consciousness, too much lucidity is a disease—a conclusion at which Ulrich also arrives after the onset of his nervous breakdown.

A significant factor in Ulrich's ability to remain aloof from life is that he is independently wealthy. When Ulrich leaves his house and walks through his front gate in the morning, he does not know whether he should turn right or left. He feels no compulsion to turn one way rather than the other. But other people in the same situation are always on their way to their jobs, and so such decisions are made for them. The underground man is very poor. But twenty years earlier he had inherited a small sum of money upon which he had been able to retire from the world. Therefore, although the underground man may live in a "mousehole" and Ulrich in a small chateau, their existences with regard to daily physical survival are not that dissimilar: both men have created for themselves an inner environment in which they are able to live quite detached from the world of daily labor and daily wages.

Ulrich's aloofness, which manifests itself in total indecision, is given its most humorous formulation in the episode where he decides to renovate and redecorate his new house, a bizarre castlelike structure composed of many styles. He can afford to buy or have designed whatever he likes. But because he is able to imagine all possible styles of furniture and architectural design, no one possibility seems to him to be preferable to any other. Finally, he is forced to give the whole matter into the hands of interior decorators. Such people have no difficulty in making decisions, in saying an immediate "yes" or "no" to any idea, for their minds are

"hedged in by prejudices, traditions, difficulties, and limitations of every kind." (I 17). The style of Ulrich's house, therefore, finally expresses not the personality of its owner but that of the servants and the tradespeople he has hired.

Ulrich's decision to give his affairs over for a time into the hands of servants with characters is reminiscent of a theme elaborated in Musil's play *Vinzenz and the Girl Friend of Important Men.* It presents the case of a man who, having neither a character nor any financial means, decides by the end of the play to become the servant of some important man with a strong character as well as with a large bank account. In this way, his life will be given some structure by the duties and tasks demanded of him by his employer. The play takes place during a birthday party given by Alpha (the girl friend of the title) in her own honor, to which she has invited several of her admirers. Vinzenz, a mathematician who possesses a cold, logical, and somewhat ruthless streak, lives on the periphery of society, detached from and uncommitted to its values. From the point of view of society, he is a total failure. At this party he meets some of Alpha's suitors, all of whom are reducible to their professions: a merchant, a scholar, a musician, and a politician. All these men may be highly successful, but in the pursuit of their respective careers they have become hopelessly one-dimensional. In contrast to these suitors, Alpha and Vinzenz possess a strong sense-of-possibility. Such people as themselves, Vinzenz declares, must either create a great work or hide behind someone else's life. Alpha rejects all her suitors and considers whether she should become a servant too or else marry an extremely rich aristocrat with a character; she will probably do the latter. Vinzenz leaves the party to find an employer.

It should by now be obvious that for Musil the man most suited for living in a world without the three absolutes of God, reality, and character is called "the man-of-possibility" because he is dominated by a strong "sense-of-possibility." This type of man, whom Ulrich associates with the first tree of his life, fully recognizes the need for the experimental attitude now that the existence of any immutable and permanent truth has been denied. It is the task of the "man-of-possibility" to try various experiments upon

himself and his own life. Of course, such experiments are neither intended nor able to meet the most fundamental requirements of scientific investigation, namely, verification by empirical data and repetition by objective observers. Such experimentation as Ulrich advocates can appeal for verification only to the total life experience of each thinking individual. Musil, in fact, terms these intellectual experiments "thought-experiments" ("Gedankenversuche" [II 411]). What is the purpose of Ulrich's thought-experiments? Musil answers: "There was only one question really worth thinking about, and that was the question of right living" (I 303).

Ulrich's triple negation is designed to clear the ground of fraudulent absolutes so that a new foundation may be established on which a meaningful life and meaningful activity in general may someday be built. Musil once wrote about his critics: "People demand that Ulrich act. I am concerned, however, with the meaning of action" (N 1603). As Ulrich's triple negation arose only out of various negative thoughts, his attempt to build a new foundation now leads—not to acts, admittedly—but to several positive thoughts.

Science as the Royal Road to Utopia

For Ulrich, the rational road to meaning, which he associates with the worldly, the Western, and the Faustian (as opposed to the mystical and Asiatic [N 1148]), lies in the application of a mathematical approach to everyday life. Thus Ulrich begins to entertain thoughts "about mathematical problems that did not admit of any general solution, though they did admit of particular solutions, the combining of which brought one nearer to the general solution. He might have added that he regarded the problem set by every human life as one of these" (II 65). Those men whose activity consists in the continuous pursuit of "partial solutions" (N 1538) are the scientists for whom science is a spiritual adventure. Ulrich decides to undertake such a spiritual adventure armed with the weapon and the spirit of mathematics.

Ulrich's positive attitude toward mathematics as a way of

gradually approaching the right way of living receives particular impetus, however, because of his own aversion to an attitude of mind and to a certain kind of temperament that mathematics also seems to negate. Musil writes of Ulrich: "He loved mathematics because of the people who could not endure it" (I 41). The haters of the mathematical attitude are the romantics, sentimentalists, and the idealists, who expend such enormous amounts of emotion that they are always too exhausted to make use of their intellects in solving the problems of existence. Ulrich suggests that whenever one of these starry-eyed romantics comes along with his typically large assertions and grandiose feelings, the scientist ought to take out his slide-rule and say: "Just a moment, please—first of all let's work out the margin of error and the approximate value of the thing!" (I 38). Science demands exact measurements and precise calculations which cannot be disputed; the conclusions of science, based upon mathematics, exist beyond the distorting influence of subjective emotionalism. Because science also provides insight into the various self-delusions and errors held by man, and because science rightly suspects all high-flown romantic feelings as being infantile and pathological, Ulrich concludes that life is lived very irrationally and wastefully whenever man does not proceed with the same exactitude in his daily life as he does in science.

Ulrich believes that in the twentieth century the most powerful and creative minds feel at home in the world of science. And he asserts that thinking at its very highest level is synonymous with the scientific attitude. He describes mathematics as the newest method of thinking, as intellect in its purest form. Since Ulrich believes that "to think new" is "to live differently," he hopes that mathematics will transform life by teaching him how to think correctly and therefore to live correctly (I 41). The haters of mathematics will never be able to think correctly, and therefore their actions will remain forever without meaning.

What obviously attracts Ulrich to science is not contained within the substance of science itself but is, rather, related to the systematic manner in which scientific investigation is pursued. For Ulrich the choice is clear: "So there are in reality two outlooks . . . . The one contents itself with being precise, and sticks to the facts;

the other does not content itself with that, but always looks at the Whole and draws its knowledge from what are called the great and eternal verities" (I 295). With the aid of the scientific method, mankind will be able to progress collectively to an ultimate solution in small but steady steps. The other approach to life, however, concentrates its attention upon eternal truths. Because the idealist and romantic always bases his arguments upon grandiose and unmeasurable observations, he will forever remain unable to deal with the most essential questions of life with progressive degrees of clarity as does the scientist. By surrounding his "truth" with an aura of pretentious sentimentality, he forever protects it against further modification and testing by reality. Therefore, although anyone can write another book on such a high-flown topic as "right-mindedness," such books always seem to begin anew from the beginning; each author remains imprisoned in his own preconceptions and is thus unable, as is the scientist, to begin his studies where a predecessor has left off.

Scientists and mathematicians exercise this radical attitude of extreme precision, which totally excludes emotion, in their laboratories and offices and are thus constantly laboring at the most advanced frontiers of civilization. When they leave their jobs at five o'clock in the evening, however, and return to their wives and children, they suddenly seem to revert to antiquated modes of romantic thinking. But what would happen, Ulrich asks, if one were to consider one's whole life as an experiment in the laboratory or as a mathematical problem to be worked out? What if one were to adopt exactitude as an intellectual habit and way of living and let it exert its exemplary influence on everything that comes into contact with it? Would not the scientist, Ulrich asks, become the new Moses leading mankind out of the spiritual desolation of contemporary nihilism?

Ulrich declares one evening to an astonished audience: "I don't believe God has been among us yet, I believe He is still to come. But only if we shorten the way for Him, as we haven't shortened it yet" (III 422). Ulrich believes that it is the particular task of the scientist to shorten man's road to the utopian world of the "ultimate solution," which he describes in metaphorical terms

as the coming of God. It is with almost religious fervor that Ulrich yearns for mankind's ultimate attainment of paradise on earth, the right way of living. The exact nature of Ulrich's utopia remains vague, for he is more concerned with the manner in which the right way of living might be achieved than with elaborating the precise details of such a life. The only way in which Ulrich is even able to indicate to others the desirability of striving for this utopia is to borrow, for the sake of intelligibility, a term from Christian religious thought. Such a "heaven" on earth, however, cannot be hastened by prayer but only through man's own intellectual efforts. Man's striving for "the utopia of the exact life" will entail a centuries-long plan of rational communal effort.

Although progress toward this utopia should be the task of society in general, Ulrich believes that it is the scientist who is best able to hasten the process. Because progress toward utopia must be carefully and consciously planned and executed, a superior type of person (the scientist) must be placed in a position of total control. What civilization now needs is a senate of intellectually highly evolved men who will make history instead of allowing irrational events to shape their lives. Such men will force reality to give expression to their idea of how life should be. These men, who must possess a strong sense-of-possibility, will treat society like "a large experimental station, where the best ways of living as a human being would be tried out and new ones discovered" (I 177). And it is perhaps not too surprising that Ulrich considers himself to be at least a precursor of this type of man. Although such extraordinary men are still only a possibility for the future, Ulrich feels in himself as a scientist the beginning of the utopian man, for he is fully conscious of the fact that he possesses "fragments of a new way of thinking, and of feeling too" (I 49). In the present age, however, an isolated individual such as Ulrich can possess a utopian vision the overall outline of which is at best only vaguely sketched by the possibilities inherent in science. Thus he has at most the hope "that a day, still distant, will come when a race of intellectual conquerers will descend into the valleys of spiritual fruitfulness" (I 48).

After having considered Ulrich's negations as well as his posi-

tive ideas concering the utopian direction of the scientific attitude, the reader may well be wondering at what point Ulrich's various ideas find practical expression in the novel. Do any of Ulrich's endless abstract analyses ever achieve a concrete reality? Ulrich would himself reply that such a question is entirely wrong-headed. When Ulrich is once asked whether he does not believe that the value of all thinking should lie in its application, he answers without hesitation: "No!" Although the ultimate goal of Ulrich's utopian vision may be the influencing of life through ideas, such a possibility seems to exist for him only in the distant future. Today, as he says, "it is simply my conviction . . . that thinking is an institution all on its own, and real life is another one" (I 326). And rather than living, he prefers to continue endlessly thinking.

There is obviously something dangerously abstract about the way in which Ulrich decisively separates life from thought, urging man to direct his energy exclusively toward the latter. Though Ulrich might admit to such abstractionism, he would still insist that such an attitude is for him charged with passionate intensity. For his thought-experiments are not the result of disinterested inquiry but rather of a desperate search through the medium of a precise intellect to find a meaning for life. Should this fail, he faces the possibility of suicide. To all his friends, however, Ulrich seems like a "cold soul," one whose total energy seems to be consumed in the unflagging destructive criticism of all matters great and small.

The Cold and Malevolent Eye

Ulrich's ideas appear to have their most profound and most immediate effect not upon reality but upon his own temperament, a temperament that his friends consider to be not only cold but violent. Musil notes Ulrich's "tendency toward malevolence and hardness of heart" (II 359). Ulrich questions everything and seems to go out of his way in a spirit of pure opposition to praise that which is intolerable to others and to find something negative in that which everyone else accepts.

Ulrich possesses a profoundly suspicious nature, for he be-

lieves that when one is on the road to precise knowledge only constant suspicion will clear the way of illusions. In a word, Ulrich denies feelings, for feelings make living with exactitude impossible. But an overabundance of feeling and lack of suspicion are precisely what characterize his friends. It is specifically in the area of feeling that Musil (in Vol. I) locates the reason for man's inability to cure his spiritual illness. In Ulrich's view, it is precisely because feelings cannot be measured, weighed, or collected that life remains an emotional hothouse, all steamy with sloppy sentimentality and filled to the point of madness with contradictions, uncertainties, and half-measures.

Thus it is the duty of the powerful intellect to destroy or at least attempt to limit feeling, for intellect is something that must by nature weigh, divide, and collect like a materialistic old banker (to use Ulrich's metaphor [II 233]). Ulrich aligns himself not with the poets but with the bankers, not with the idealists and do-gooders but with the warriors and beasts of prey, i.e., with those whose nature it is to be cruel and violent. Is there not, Musil asks, a great measure of demonic cruelty and lack of compassion in the scientist's desire to force the mind to probe beyond the surface of man's romantic illusions? Musil calls modern science "the miracle of the Anti-Christ"(I 360). Thus Ulrich, as a scientist, sides with the devil against a heaven of lofty and grandiose sentiments and feelings.

By not providing Ulrich with a wife and child, Musil manages to a certain extent to avoid treating those difficulties that the man-of-possibility might experience in maintaining close interpersonal relationships because of his singular lack of sentiment and emotion. In Musil's first play, *The Visionaries (Die Schwärmer)*, the protagonist Thomas, a cool, rational, and cerebral scientist, is married to a rather sensuous and passionate woman named Maria. But Thomas regards life from too many perspectives and is aware of too many other possibilities to be able to take any single perspective very seriously, even when this possibility has become a reality—as for instance, his marriage. Even in his marriage he is as uncommitted as if such a relationship were merely one possibility, one that is in no way any more important than any other as yet unrealized possibility. By the end of the play, Maria, who can by

this time no longer tolerate her husband's emotional detachment, runs off with Anselm, a rival of her husband's from their boyhood days. Anselm may be both an immature man and a fraud, but he is filled with intense emotions. In his company, Maria feels needed. When she tells Thomas that she is leaving him, Thomas reacts hardly at all. For with the departure of his wife, he can become even more completely a man-of-possibility and thus even freer to experiment and speculate intellectually about life.

False Ways of Living

Ulrich's manner of thinking finds its most concrete expression not so much in what he creates as in what he opposes and whom he disdains. What dramatic tension there may be in *The Man without Qualities* consists to a great extent in the contrasts that Musil consciously erects between Ulrich, who is desperately searching for the right way of living, and his acquaintances, who function as grotesque illustrations of decadent ways of living. It is in Ulrich's uncompromising opposition and superior disdain that Musil's skill as as a satirist emerges. Ulrich casts a cool and analytical eye upon his friends and the various forms of self-deception they practice in order to give their lives a semblance of coherence and meaning. All these people, who have become victims of some particular obsession, lack Ulrich's sense-of-possibility; they have attached themselves to some pretentious "ism," "ology," or slogan and have thereby achieved a false sense of direction and significance, i.e., have given a plot to their lives. Ulrich, who stands aloof, alone, and uncommitted, pitilessly observes with his cold and malevolent eye a panorama of various representatives of Austrian culture, its socialites, artists, intellectuals, aristocrats, and civil servants, each of whom advocates some pseudomystical solution such as "back to the land," "back to God and country," "back to the whole and integrated personality," or "back to the joys of the simple life." Each of these concepts is offered as a means of achieving a "new totality" in the face of the ever-increasing fragmentation of modern man's intellectual, moral, and cultural life.

Ulrich's disdain is based upon two fundamental objections: his friends lack any semblance of intelligence and they live their lives by reaction and resentment. Not only do they not know how to use their minds and thus not know how to arrive at a solution in a proper manner (i.e., rationally) but they are also afraid of thinking *per se*. Consequently, they fail to bring intelligence to bear upon reality. While Ulrich's mental energies are directed toward some future utopian solution, his friends tend to advocate a return to the past, that is to say, their lives express a reaction against science, reason, and the intellect. While they are blindly submerged in their personal fantasies designed to save mankind, they are totally unaware of the imminent destruction of the Empire. To understand their resentment and fear of the modern world is, Musil indicates, to understand some of the reasons for the collapse of European culture in 1914.

At the center of Musil's ironic vision of Austrian culture is the so-called Collateral Campaign ("Parallelaktion"), the moving spirit behind which is Ulrich's cousin Diotima. When it is learned that the Prussians plan to celebrate the thirteenth jubilee of Wilhelm I in 1918, the Austrians decide to set up a parallel celebration for their Emperor, Franz Joseph, upon his seventieth jubilee in the same year. (The irony is made the more intense by the reader's knowledge that in 1918 the Austrians had only the defeat of their Empire to contemplate.) Many of the meetings of the Campaign are concerned with the problem of finding some unifying and guiding idea for this celebration. Diotima finally decides that the Campaign must direct itself toward rediscovering that "human unity" in man's life which has been lost because of the advent of modern materialism and scientific reasoning: Prussia may well have expanded its political power and industrial might in recent years to fearful proportions, but Austria still has "soul." Because Austria alone still has so much "soul," the nations of Europe will someday be forced to look to it for that redeeming power which is needed to heal the modern world of its emotional and intellectual schizophrenia. By some grotesque quirk of fate, Ulrich is asked to become the General Secretary of the Campaign. He is so passive a character that he does not even bother to object to this chairmanship. Thus

he finds himself in the absurd position of heading a campaign whose aims he regards as utterly ludicrous, of chairing a committee inspired by a woman whose fiery idealism and self-election as a priestess of "the spheres of greatness" he considers totally ridiculous.

Ulrich and Diotima possess diametrically opposed attitudes and temperaments, and it is in the description of this opposition that Musil's concept of the scientific and healthy, on the one hand, and the romantic and decadent, on the other, becomes clear. As a fervent champion of the emotions and the mysteries of the heart, Diotima finds herself in a state of constant antagonism toward Ulrich, who champions the power of the destructive intellect and the relativity of truth. Whenever she talks of physical beauty, Ulrich talks of fat tisssue supporting the skin; whenever she speaks of love, he immediately speaks about the annual curve revealing the automatic rise and fall in the birth rate; whenever she talks of great artists, he stresses the chain of borrowing that links these men to each other. Musil summarizes this fundamental opposition in the following metaphor: while Diotima considers man to have been placed by God on the seventh day like a pearl in the shell of the world, Ulrich thinks of mankind as a little heap of dots on the outermost crust of a dwarf globe (I 333). Diotima, however, rejects all of Ulrich's criticisms as being merely symptoms of disease arising from the emotional desert caused by twentieth-century scientific materialism.

The activities of the Campaign present a distorted image of Ulrich's own attempts to find a meaning in life. But the Campaign is dedicated to the resurrection out of the past of the true, the good, and the beautiful, three concepts that Ulrich considers to be both boring and nonsensical. How can anyone still be interested in such outmoded chatter about good and evil, when it is today generally accepted by intelligent people that good and evil are not constants but are dependent upon historical circumstance? What could anyone still want with the Apollo Belvedere, Ulrich asks, when we are able today to contemplate the sleek lines of a turbo dynamo and the smoothly gliding movements of a steam engine's pistons? (I 37). Nevertheless, and in spite of such a great difference

in their means toward a similar goal, Ulrich wonders whether it might not be possible to redirect the activities of the Campaign and utilize all its resources in furthering his own private experiment. Thus he makes the following suggestion to a rather startled audience: "There is only one task for the Collateral Campaign—that it should constitute the beginning of a general spiritual stock-taking . . . . What you should do is found, in His Majesty's name, a terrestrial secretariat for Precision and the Spirit. Until that is done, all other objectives remain unattainable, or at best they are sham objectives" (II 366). Ulrich's suggestion that the Campaign might provide the context for the ultimate synthesis of reason and the soul is one that no one seriously entertains, not even Ulrich himself.

Another important, although unofficial member of the Campaign is Paul Arnheim, the Prussian industrialist and man of culture. He believes that he has managed to achieve "a whole personality" in which the conflicting demands of money and culture have been reconciled. At once a multimillionaire and the author of numerous books on a wide variety of intellectual topics, he considers himself to be at home in any and all subjects. He is able to talk with ease on molecular physics, mysticism, and pigeon-shooting, on love and economics, chemistry and canoe trips. Ulrich finds him to be a particularly fascinating form of modern intellectual fraud. He remains totally suspicious, therefore, of the synthesis that this "great personality" says his life embodies. It eventually becomes evident that this "great personality," who has been expressing such profound admiration for the Austrian "soul," has been manipulating the Campaign for his own interests all along. What he really wants is to gain control of the Austrian Empire's oil fields in Galicia. Arnheim's deception is carried out on such a grand scale and with so much panache that Arnheim himself remains his own most convinced and devoted admirer.

Aside from the members of the Campaign, the people Ulrich most pities are the married couple Walter and Clarisse. The opposition between the Wagnerian fanatic Walter, who is termed by Musil "the man with character" (I 65), and the rational Ulrich, who is termed "the man without character," expresses an antago-

nism as irreconcilable as that between two warring brothers in mythology. In fact, Walter loathes Ulrich to such an extent that Clarisse finally suggests that Walter murder him. But their mutual hatred transcends the personal level. While Walter's life is centered upon music, Ulrich hates all music, particularly Wagner's music, with an almost violent and irrational passion. For although music can invoke the most subtle emotional states, it is unable to give expression to logical thought. In fact, music has the effect of robbing the mind of its incisiveness, thus providing a fertile ground for sensuality and vague yearning. During a scene in which Ulrich is listening to Walter playing Wagner's music on the piano, Musil writes: "Something immeasurable was happening. A dimly outlined balloon filled with hot emotion was being blown up to the bursting-point" (I 50). It may be partially because of the existence of Wagner's music, thinks Ulrich, that the worship of immeasurable feeling has taken the place of precise thought and reason in modern life; only the immeasurable is now in fashion and Ulrich considers this new change to be a "disease," as reflecting nothing else than "downright ordinary stupidity" (I 63). Thus he declares "music to be a failure of the will and a confusion of the mind" (I 51). In the midst of all this music, he feels like a stern and silent owl sitting on a branch surrounded by singing birds (N 1456).

Walter possesses an ability (or disability, as Ulrich would say) for experiencing everything in life with extreme emotional violence. As opposed to Ulrich, he finds opportunities for expressing his vivid feelings everywhere and at the drop of a hat. Of such a peculiarity, Ulrich merely asserts: "But this capacity to experience more is one of the earliest and subtlest signs by which mediocrity can be recognized" (II 61). Walter rejects exactitude in the name of feeling because it is only in the absence of exactitude that his life seems to acquire depth. When he is drawn down into the immeasurable depths of the emotions, he feels able to reach into the very "pit" of the soul. He suffers deeply and thereby assumes that his life has become correspondingly profound.

Walter considers himself to be the kind of romantic genius who experiences divine inspiration when submerged in states of intoxication induced by music. Even when he was an adolescent

everyone thought that Walter was destined to become a great and inspired genius. But Ulrich regards Walter's inspired moments as nothing more than instances of pathological self-inflation; in such states, the artist deludes himself into believing that through his God-given sensibility, he has managed to gain direct intuitive insight into a higher realm that is forever closed to the cruder sensibilities of the scientist. Musil in fact distinguishes between two concepts of genius: the outdated and the modern. The modern concept of the boxer or of the race horse as genius possesses, Musil believes, a distinct advantage over the now antiquated concept of the romantic genius. For the achievement of a race horse can be unambiguously measured and the best race horse can be ascertained without difficulty. But just try to reach an agreement as to which of several poets is the deepest!

The most crushing attack that Musil launches upon Wagnerianism consists in his diagnosis of Walter as a man whose playing of Wagner reflects both his own sexual pathology as well as a fundamental fear of reality. Walter plays the piano with the kind of bad conscience produced by the practice of a boyhood vice. And of the piano itself, Musil writes: "The base intoxication of sluggishly sensual music lured him [Walter] back. The piano behind his back lay open like a bed that had been rumpled by a sleeper who did not want to waken because he did not want to face reality" (I 65). Musil sees, further, an opposition existing between the feminine and the masculine, between the romantic, artistic, and decadent, on the one hand, and the rational, scientific, and healthy, on the other. Thus Musil with fair frequency points out both Walter's rather feminine features and Ulrich's athleticism and powerful masculine physique.

Walter's attitude toward Ulrich can be summarized as the resentment and envy of the inferior brother towards the superior. He resents Ulrich's condescending attitude toward Wagner as well as Ulrich's incessant destructive irony directed against Walter's concept of himself as the possessor of an "unbroken soul." But he also envies Ulrich's health and physical superiority. Walter bears a fundamental grudge against the moden world as a whole and therefore against Ulrich, whose thinking represents for him a par-

ticular instance of the destructive intellect of the twentieth century. Ulrich's life and thought symbolize for Walter the disease that is destroying life, that is making reality unbearable. For Ulrich represents specialization, skepticism, analysis, machine-building, and soulless technology. In direct reaction to Ulrich's form of existence, therefore, Walter attempts to persuade himself that his own concept of the good life is far superior to that of Ulrich. Walter believes that what people desperately need today is to return to the land and to the simple life. Happiness means coming home from one's work in the evening, drinking a cup of coffee with one's wife, listening to the birds singing, exchanging a few words with one's neighbor, and taking a stroll through the woods at sunset.

Walter deems it necessary in today's soulless age of science to consider everything after Bach, Stifter, and Ingres as being decadent—a somewhat paradoxical opinion for a fervent Wagnerian. In a time in which spiritual roots are so poisoned by rationality, he comes to the decision that an artist who is honest must finally refrain from all creativity. If Europe has become totally decadent, then he is the healthy one. Suddenly his life is provided with a glorious justification: his apparent sterility now reflects the sacrifice that a great artist must make in these degenerate scientific times. Thus he interprets his resentment against Ulrich and the modern age as an example of his own moral integrity.

Clarisse, like Ulrich, is also attempting to discover the right way of living. To this end she declares herself a disciple of Nietzsche and begins to call for the immediate transformation of European society. She is not at all certain how this is to be accomplished—perhaps by proclaiming a Nietzsche-Year? Clarisse is not clear, however, about the ways in which Nietzsche thought society ought to be changed. Nevertheless, she demands that Ulrich (who had once given her Nietzsche's works as a wedding present) act, that he finally do something, anything! Ulrich's response to her command is to point out the difference between Walter's "passive passivism" and his own "active passivism," which he compares to the waiting of a prisoner who will someday break out of his prison (II 63). If Walter seems to say "no" to reality, Ulrich merely says "not yet." Clarisse is not impressed by such talk. In fact, she wants

a child from Ulrich as soon as possible, a child who will then become the savior of Europe. As her mental disturbance increases throughout the course of the novel, she becomes ever more fascinated by a certain Christian Moosbrugger, a psychotic murderer of prostitutes who is awaiting trial. She finally identifies him with Nietzsche and Christ and attempts to convince Ulrich that if they forcibly released Moosbrugger from prison, the redemption of society would be at hand.

Ulrich's disdain is also directed toward the so-called "do-gooder," who out of cowardice limits his acting and thinking to the sterile and oppressive morality of the herd. Ulrich thinks that morality ought to be like "the great ocean" in which one can swim in any direction. Instead, Ulrich finds that moral codes function like the all too rigid and solid "limestone of life" (III 33). The morality of the day is nothing but a form of strait-jacket that forces everyone to act in the same way. It enforces a single universally condoned possibility for action and thereby excludes all latent possibilities for living. People are good and honest only out of habit; they "do" good without having any real goodness within them. Ulrich in fact wonders whether being good is really a good thing. Hagauer, Ulrich's self-righteous and complacent brother-in-law, and Lindner, nicknamed "the do-gooder," confirm Ulrich in his opinion concerning the destructive effects of morality upon the individual, for such people strike Ulrich as being lifeless, as suffering from exhausted emotions. He wonders how such a form of life could have come into being. Nietzsche had argued that it is the community itself that creates the "good man." Since habitual and expected ways of acting give the members of the community a feeling of security, such rather lifeless behavior is termed by them "the good." Therefore, the reinforcement that society gives to the "good man" really represents its fear of possible actions that are new, different, and hence psychologically disturbing. In other words, the "good man" is born out of a reactionary spirit. The result of centuries of Christianity is that man, like the two academics Hagauer and Lindner, has become small, weak, gloomy, and tame.

The Scientific Morality

Because conventional morality has stifled man's creative potential, Ulrich finally asserts: "Morality itself is not [moral]" (III 426). In opposition to the traditionally venerated and now bankrupt codes of behavior, Ulrich undertakes to establish for himself a new and constructive morality through science so that his every action will be endowed with meaning. The difference between an uncreative morality, generated from Christianity, and a new morality, to be generated from the scientific attitude, is quite clear to Ulrich: the scientific morality arises from natural laws and is based solely upon the observation of empirical data; the morality of inherited law is based upon the "eternal verities," that is to say, upon Christian concepts of the true, the good, and the beautiful.

Ulrich feels that no morality in his sense of the term has as yet existed in the modern world. Because he believes that "there is no morality if there is no solid basis for it" (III 439), he conjectures that perhaps science alone of all the products of the human mind can serve as the foundation for the new morality; for this new morality must be ever-changing and ever-evolving as is the body of facts in scientific research from day to day. The scientific attitude seems to Ulrich to offer the perfect instrument, since it is as sharp-eyed for the factual as it is blind to the eternal verities. In place of the solidified, the final, and the absolute, it substitutes the movement of endless new facts.

How, precisely, does one act in accordance with such a "mathematical morality," as Musil terms it? Musil is at any rate quite clear as to how one should *not* act. Because the eternal verities no longer exist, because the Christian metaphor that ordered and structured life in the Middle Ages has lost its vitality, heroic and romantic moral gestures have also lost their vitality. In an age without inherent order, man must proceed soberly from step to step as one does in a mathematical problem without the assurance that his progress is always meaningful. After all, the ultimate solution, which can only in retrospect give meaning to all the small steps, may yet lie hundreds of years in the future. Ulrich explains that in the meanwhile one must act like a soldier who does his

duty, a soldier who for some unknown reason receives no orders "from above" and thus must act without any overall comprehension of the battleplan.

Ulrich also recognizes the existence of a problem in his concept of a mathematical morality. He explains: "What I said was: not the wrong step is what matters, but the next step after it. But what matters after the next step? Obviously the one that follows after that. And after the nth or the nth-plus-one step?" (III 81). The "scientific moralist" would have to be able "to live without ends or decisions, in fact without any reality at all" (III 81). But since in practice Ulrich is psychologically unable to deal with this endlessly moving series, he concludes his explanation of a scientific morality on one occasion with the admission: "sometimes I feel remorse for my whole life" (III 81).

The Collapse of the Scientific Experiment

Ulrich's despair finally deepens to the point of a nervous breakdown. At the end of Part Two of the novel ("The Like of It Now Happens"), and after 123 chapters devoted to Ulrich's thoughts on a variety of philosophical topics as well as to his ironic and satirical observations concerning the foibles of his friends, half of Ulrich's year has passed, that year at the end of which he might commit suicide if he has not succeeded in finding a meaning for his life. His search so far has proved to be a complete failure.

The first significant sign of a breakdown occurs when Ulrich experiences a strange hallucination which he observes with an air of detached curiosity, as is his way. Ulrich is standing at a window watching a crowd in the street below. He feels as if he is standing in an opening between the curtains on a stage, with the stage of the world in front of him and a second stage, that of the room, behind him. Suddenly the room behind his back "contracted and turned inside out, passing through him or flowing past him" (II 412). During this hallucination of spatial inversion, he seems plunged into an atmosphere at once glassy, empty, and totally tranquil. This experience is immediately followed by the thought that he,

who passes his life thinking rather than acting, must commit some decisive act. For Ulrich, the curtain on the stage of his life has yet to rise, the play yet to begin. Musil indicates that Ulrich at this moment "felt utterly oppressed by a profound repugnance for the unnaturalness of the solitary man and for his intellectual experiments" (II 411). Shortly thereafter, Ulrich has a conversation with Arnheim in which he is offered a high position in Arnheim's vast business empire. Ulrich, of course, refuses to commit himself and experiences thereupon a sudden irrational urge to murder Arnheim. Walking up behind Arnheim, he reaches for his pocket knife in order to stab him in the back. But he refrains, and on his way home feels himself to be nothing more than "some phantom wandering through the gallery of life, aghast at being unable to find the frame it should slip into" (II 433). When Ulrich reaches home, he has an hallucination of staring into the barrel of a gun. This existence of endless possibilities has apparently led to only one impossibility, the impossibility of living this kind of life for even another day.

From a philosophical point of view, the experimental attitude of the man-of-possibility may well represent a courageous and masculine attitude. But from the psychological point of view, Musil admits: "This development is at present still in flux, and in the individual human being it indicates a weakness as well as a strength" (I 14). Because Ulrich represents for Musil a higher type of man, one of incomparably greater complexity than the average man, he also exists continually upon the threshold of disintegration.

Ulrich's friends may be significantly less intelligent than he but they are united in their conclusion that his way of life is unnatural and can only come to a bad end. Walter, for instance, characterizes Ulrich as a man who would like to abolish the stomach for the sake of pure ideas (II 75). He declares that everything that Ulrich says is inhuman because Ulrich is himself no longer a human being. Ulrich can't take life as it comes, he has to strain everything through the sieve of his intellect. "You are the kind of person," Walter tells Ulrich, "who declares that the meaning of fresh vegetables is tinned vegetables" (II 75). To this accusation

Ulrich replies that it is also true to say that he is the sort of person who will only cook with salt. Ulrich must add the spice of critical intellect to that which is merely natural. At the end of his experiment in scientific living, however, he admits to Agathe: "Food without salt is unbearable, but salt without food in great quantities is a poison" (N 1421). But if Ulrich is poisoning himself, where is the antidote that could make him more of a human being? He does admit that under the influence of his scientific experiment he really has been changing into "a monster" (I 344). But since he sees around himself only such people as Walter, Clarisse, Arnheim, and Diotima, he declares that he has no other alternative but to refuse to be a human being until further notice.

Dostoyevsky's underground man, that other major protagonist in world literature who also suffers from an absence of character, offers both an analysis and a prediction of the psychological consequences of a life of extreme reason such as that pursued by Ulrich. For Ulrich in his first experiment embodies that ideal of civilized man which Dostoyevsky's protagonist never ceases to attack.   Civilization, the underground man believes, has set out "to cure man of his bad old habits and reshape his will according to the requirements of science and common sense."[9]   Such an attempt presupposes that "the corrections" which reason and science exercise upon the irrational life of man will be to his advantage. The underground man regards the Crystal Palace at the International Exposition in London as a central symbol of the times: it stands as a monument to the exercise of man's powers of organization put to the creation of a society based totally upon a careful rational evaluation of those conditions advantageous to man's existence. But man possesses an instinctive fear of achieving the purely rational life; in the underground man's view, man should at best contemplate such a utopian existence, but he should not attempt (as does Ulrich) to live it.

What would happen if man did manage to find "a real mathematical equation" upon which to base his daily existence, the underground man asks?   If man functions according to a timetable, he will soon cease to feel any joy and eventually any desire whatsoever. Thus he will change "from a man into an organ stop or

something like that, for what is a man without will, wishes, and desires, if not an organ stop?"[10]   Dostoyevsky's protagonist summarizes for the reader his psychological objection to the ideal of the rational life: "And twice two, ladies and gentlemen, is no longer life but the beginning of death."[11] If such an existence is achieved, there will be nothing left for a man to do but "to block off our five senses and plunge into contemplation."[12]   It is precisely such an ascetic plunge into pure thinking which characterizes Ulrich's experiment in scientific living.

The underground man places his subjective world of feeling in opposition to all the laws of reason and, therefore, to civilization's systematic accumulation of knowledge throughout the centuries which has culminated, specifically, in the construction of the Crystal Palace. He does not deny that reason may be "a good thing," but life is still life and "not a series of extractions of square roots."[13] Desire, feeling, emotions are the manifestations of life itself. Man would generate his own nervous breakdown in order to pry himself loose from the rules of reason, he asserts. Ulrich's breakdown has precisely this effect. But whereas Dostoyevsky's protagonist gives expression to the irrational dimension in his life through whims and capricious desires, Ulrich, in a rather more systematic and Germanic fashion, undertakes an experiment in mysticism. Ulrich's collapse into mysticism is, as the underground man's analysis suggests, already implicit and inevitable at the very beginning of the novel in Ulrich's overvaluation of reason.

Ulrich first drafted his scientific concept of the man-of-possibility at the age of 26. Now, at the age of 32, and six months into his experiment in the systematic application of the mathematical attitude to his life, he is beginning to feel that something has gone radically wrong. He begins to wonder what it is that is missing from his life and has caused his relationship to the world to become so "pale, shadowy, and negative" (I 314). He admits eventually: "I can't go on with this life, and I can't go on rebelling against it!" (II 412). This conclusion is presented to him most vividly one evening in a dream. He is climbing a mountain. The incline becomes ever steeper and the air ever thinner. Feeling suddenly sick and dizzy, he wonders if he should not simply abandon his long

and weary attempt and take the commonly used and comfortable road running through the valley. Although the perspectives upon life as lived below may increase as one ascends the mountain, life itself becomes ever more difficult and finally comes to a stand-still here. The very body revolts (II 346).

Towards the end of Part Two, Ulrich increasingly regards his present life with feelings of panic and no longer in terms of courageous manliness. He appears to himself as a man imprisoned, as one being held back from life by intellectual preparations that will never cease. Although in theory the scientific attitude of recognizing endless possibilities may be designed to permit the individual to choose the one possibility that is most creative and meaningful for him, it seems (in terms of its immediate effect) to function only to destroy life. For the ultimate choice of turning one possibility into a reality is always postponed in the name of discovering yet more possibilities. In fact, Ulrich is accused quite rightly of always living as if the world were about to begin tomorrow. Ulrich merely observes. Kierkegaard's analysis of the inevitable psychological collapse of the detached spectator of life provides an illuminating parallel with regard to Ulrich's nervous breakdown.

Ulrich's feeling of despair and meaninglessness may be made more comprehensible when diagnosed and evaluated in a perspective taken from Kierkegaard's comparison of Don Juan and Faust. Kierkegaard regarded Faust as a rebirth of the Don Juan figure,[14] as representing the second phase of the aesthetic dialectic. Faust, who entered the Middle Ages later than did Don Juan, arrived upon the scene at that point in European history when intellectual speculation was beginning to replace the pursuit of sensual pleasure as an ideal. The transition from Don Juan to Faust indicated a transition from healthy self-confidence and romantic hedonism to skepticism and abstract intellectualism. But just as Don Juan became lost in countless erotic possibilities, so Faust loses himself in the speculation of numerous intellectual possibilities. Such a man as Faust is the eternal spectator, one who continually attempts to reduce the complexities of existence to the rational structures of thought and thus to substitute reflection upon general truths for the responsibilities of concrete and personal commit-

ment. Because he is obsessed with possibilities, he, like Don Juan before him, never makes the move into the realm of ethical choice, but wishes to remain forever in the lowest mode of being, the aesthetic. Aestheticism, however, never leads to decisive action; for by living a life of theory and observation, he will be able to continue to shuffle the chips of possibility endlessly and thus endlessly avoid committing himself either to any mode of ethical behavior or to another human being. Kierkegaard's evaluation of the Faustian mode of life is unsparingly negative. The aesthetic life of pure thought as well as of pure sensuality must inevitably lead to total boredom and despair, to a feeling of profound inner emptiness. Thought, as a pure intellectual possibility, is not life, for life can only be lived through a process of decision-making in which all but one possibility is negated and that one then transformed into a reality. There always exists the danger that the abstract intellectual will arrive at a point in his life where, because he has suspended judgment so frequently, he will have become incapable of ever making any decision again. The resulting detachment from life produces a form of psychopathology which Musil describes very powerfully in Ulrich's nervous breakdown. The aesthete (however intellectual) is concerned only with himself. If he is to overcome his feeling of boredom and desperation, he must begin with a conscious decision to ally his life with that of another human being.

A second cause of Ulrich's nervous breakdown lies in his asceticism, i.e., in his fanatic, even masochistic dedication to his "mission" and in the psychological imbalance that results from his application of scientific objectivity to all aspects of his life. The renunciation of all the common joys of life that is implicit in Ulrich's way of living strikes even him as being similar to that undertaken by ascetics, saints, and pilgrims of old. So, too, is his unworldly dedication. He hasn't the least desire for the possessions and honors of life. From Arnheim's point of view—a man who is very much concerned with fame and money—Ulrich seems like someone who is fighting for a cause in voluntary poverty. Musil called such people as Ulrich "Trappists of the modern world."[15] Ulrich's life as a scientist can be compared to the ascetic's never-ending struggle against the needs of the instincts on behalf of the

demands of the intellect and the spirit. Ulrich has had to withstand and constantly fight against every natural inclination within himself. Musil clearly states: "In all those years of pure exactitude he had merely been living against himself." (I 304).

The nature and meaning of Ulrich's breakdown reveals the unmistakable influence of Nietzsche's critique of asceticism particularly as elaborated in *The Genealogy of Morals*. Nietzsche believed that it is instinct (and not intellect) which is the precondition for life and that suppression of the intincts by the scientific and intellectual man represents a form of decadence. In fact, Ulrich's life could serve as an illustration of Nietzsche's analysis of and attack upon the phenomenon of asceticism. The following examination of the decadence of ascetism is based upon the connections made by Nietzsche between nihilism, asceticism, and science. Nietzsche's definition of the ascetic ideal, which also suggests the connection between "the void" and Ulrich's search for meaning, is based upon his conception of a nihilistic world: "*This* is precisely what the ascetic ideal means: that something was *lacking*, that man was surrounded by a fearful void—he did not know how to justify, to account for, to affirm himself; he *suffered* from the problem of his meaning."[16] Asceticism provided existence with a meaning so that "the tremendous void seemed to have been filled"; but such a solution ultimately created only more suffering, a suffering that was more inward, more poisonous and more life-destructive. Science, Nietzsche asserted, is the very latest form of the ascetic ideal,[17] for science also causes an impoverishment of life by substituting intellectual perspectives and dialectics for instinctual reactions. The very gathering of objective knowledge is in itself a form of asceticism,[18] since the ability to renounce all general interpretations and "halt before the facts" expresses as much the will to asceticism as does the denial of sensuality. Nietzsche asserted that any attitude which wishes merely to ascertain or to describe "is to a high degree ascetic; but at the same time it is to an even higher degree *nihilistic*, let us not deceive ourselves about that!"[19]

It is against this background of Nietzsche's analysis of asceticism that Ulrich's life becomes comprehensible as a particular form of decadence in which the protective agency of the instincts

has been destroyed, thus leaving man with consciousness as his only guide. Nietzsche asserts that at the present stage of human development, consciousness is only very insufficiently developed. Because life cannot rely upon it, man still needs "the conserving bond of the instincts."[20] For this reason, Nietzsche regards consciousness as a danger, even as a disease.[21] Because Nietzsche believed (at one point in his philosopical career) that the perfect life is one which is least conscious, he assumed that a decline, a decadence in the history of man must have set in with Socrates' denigration of the instincts and his postulation of consciousness as the more valuable state. The Greeks thereby reduced themselves to thinking, calculating, inferring, which is to say, they reduced themselves to their most fallible organ, consciousness. The important point here is that in the early phase of Nietzsche's thinking, the phenomenon of Socrates represents the disintegration of natural, instinctual responses. Thus, from a Nietzschean perspective, the extreme consciousness of Ulrich reflects severe maladjustment because it questions the instincts and thus destroys the unconscious balance of life forces. To question any instinctive action is to create the possibility of various alternatives; action is thereby inhibited. Ulrich describes the moment when an action occurs as representing a spontaneous unity between the body and the instincts; and he adds: "Whenever it was not like that, whenever anything went wrong and let even the smallest ray of conscious thought fall into this darkness [of the unconscious mind], then the whole operation was bound to fail" (I 27). It is for this reason, Nietzsche writes, that we must "close the inner eye while performing an action (even if only while writing letters or eating or drinking).[22]

In several ways, Ulrich's manner of existence follows the Socratic ideal of the philosophic life as described by Plato, an ideal founded upon reason as a guide to meaningful behavior. The basis for the following comparison between Ulrich and the Socrates of Plato's dialogues is to be found in Socrates' concept of the soul, a concept which has dominated European thought for over two thousand years. The soul as redefined by Socrates provides a justification for and an explanation of the phenomenon of the modern thinker's ascetic life-style. Before Socrates, the soul, termed "psy-

che," was present in man during his life and departed at his death. Metaphorically speaking, this soul was no more an essential part of the human being's existence than was a man's reflection in a pool of water. It had no consciousness, remained uninfluenced by the mental life of the individual, and did not function as the unique bearer of personality. For Socrates, however, it is only by virtue of what he called the soul that an individual may be described as wise or foolish, good or bad. Because the soul in Socrates' thought is very much influenced by the intelligence and behavior of the individual, he urged a life dedicated to its cultivation. Such dedication is not characterized by the observance of religious rituals and rites of purification, but only by the cultivation of rational thinking and rational conduct. It is man's duty to be able to give a rational justification for his every action. Therefore, the question of how the individual may attain the good life, a life based upon right conduct, forms the center of the philosophical mode of existence. Socrates believed that it was only through the use of reason as an analytical and critical instrument that man could achieve an ethical and meaningful life.

Socrates' high evaluation of reason is based upon a radical division in his philosophical thought between the real and the ideal, the everyday world of the senses and the higher world of ideal and pure forms. Knowledge of the higher world can be gained only by means of the soul, as Socrates argues in *Phaedo*: "the soul is most like that which is divine, immortal, intelligible, uniform, indissoluble, and ever self-consistent and invariable, whereas body is most like that which is human, mortal, multiform, unintelligible, dissoluble, and never self-consistent."[23] While the body can perceive only the sensible, visible world, and thus all that is impermanent and corruptible, "what the soul itself sees is intelligible and invisible."[24] A philosopher's life, therefore, is nothing but a long rehearsal for dying, for the "soul secures immunity from its desires by following Reason and abiding always in her company, and by contemplating the true and divine and unconjecturable, and drawing inspiration from it."[25] The soul achieves its ultimate independence from the desires of the flesh upon the death of the body, for the pursuit of wisdom is hindered throughout life by the

grossness of the physical body which serves only to diminish man's ability through reason to perceive the absolute forms. Because the philosopher rejects the gratification of the body as well as all worldly rewards and honors, and strives to lead a highly ascetic life, he is viewed by the ordinary person as being already half dead, a partial corpse even during his lifetime. But it is the death of the body for which the philosopher has been striving his whole life.

In spite of the fact that Socrates, as opposed to Ulrich, conceived of the soul as a metaphysical entity, the similarity between Socrates' ideal of the rational life and Ulrich's first scientific experiment is striking. Moreover, Nietzsche's reinterpretation of the Socratic ideal in *The Birth of Tragedy* points not only toward a positive similarity in the theoretical presuppositions of Socrates' and Ulrich's respective life-styles, it also contains a further negative evaluation concerning the practical psychological impossibility of their modes of living. Thus Nietzsche's identification of Socrates as the father of science and his condemnation of the psychological pathology inherent in the life of pure thought as an ideal foreshadows the inevitable collapse of Ulrich's life based on the Socratic ideal. Ulrich's breakdown first manifests itself in the form of an "attack of mysticism." That mystical area of his inner life, which he had been attempting to suppress for years by assuming the mask of the scientist, reasserts itself. Ulrich, the man of reason, topples before its stronger presence. This breakdown need not, however, be regarded as representing only the failure of the scientific ideal. It may also be seen as an inevitable dialectical reversal and a necessary step in Ulrich's pilgrimage toward utopia. As Nietzsche argued in *The Birth of Tragedy*, only when reason has reached the extremest point of its development (which he termed the Socratic life) does it collapse and thus open the door into the mystical realm beyond.

To what extent is Ulrich's change from a life of reason to one of mysticism really a complete dialectical reversal? The development of Socrates' concept of the soul in Western religious thought furnishes a perspective through which it becomes clear that Ulrich's reversal is at most only a partial one. Socrates' life of reason as an attribute of the soul was, as A. E. Taylor has written, "the

Hellenic counterpart of the 'mystical way' of Christianity."[26] For the Christian mystic as for the Socratic philosopher, the highest form of life was a "dying life," a life spent in contemplation rather than in action. Thus, the Socratic soul guided by reason and the Christian soul guided by the mystical impulse are closely related to the extent that both denigrate the reality of the physical body and the need for sensual gratification. Both the life of reason and that of mysticism are dedicated to a truth that transcends the body and it is in this sense that Ulrich's existence as a scientist is comparable to that of Christian Trappists, with whom Ulrich is at one point compared. A dialectical reversal is possible and meaningful only when the opposites revolve about a single fixed point which is, in this case, a profound abhorrence of sensuality and a desire to discover a world beyond the impermanence and corruptibility of everyday life. From this point of view, the rational Socrates also generated a mystical Socrates. Eduard Zeller has summarized Socrates the man and Socrates the philosopher in a way which applies equally well to the life and work of Musil and to his major protagonist, Ulrich:

> [Socrates'] character shows a remarkable combination of critical shrewdness and a deep religious sense, of sober rationalism and mystical belief. Both these sides, however diametrically opposed they might have been, had their roots in one and the same thing—in the passionate longing which drove him in search of something absolute and unconditioned, which could be apprehended by the intellect and serve as a norm for moral conduct . . . . [27]

VI ✤

A World of Lost Feelings:
The Man without Qualities (II)

NOW THAT ULRICH'S scientific experiment has come to a sudden end, he turns in desperation toward "a kind of second reality" (II 338). Ulrich's experiment in mysticism, which comprises the second half of the novel, represents his commitment to a possibility that he had already been aware of even at the height of his scientific experiment, a possibility that he had associated with the second tree of his life. He now consciously initiates a mystical experiment designed to realize his once expressed wish that everyday reality be totally abolished. In such circumstances, Ulrich says, his life would no longer be a " 'life of research' or a life 'by the light of science' "; instead he would dedicate his energies to a " 'quest for feeling,' similar to the quest for truth, only with the difference that in this case truth did not matter" (III 443).

Mysticism Reborn

From a biographical point of view, Ulrich's second experiment represents the revitalization of a mystical state that he had experienced twelve years before at the age of 20 when he was a cadet, an experience that he has been attempting to suppress ever since. On the day of his hallucinatory "mystical attack" at the age of 32, which occurs in a chapter entitled "The Turning Point," Ulrich all at once recalls his long-forgotten affair with the Major's Wife and realizes that this episode represents the only significant experience of mysticism in his life to date. But, as Musil wrote while correcting proofs, "In reaction to this experience, Ulrich took the cold scientific road."[1]

Why did Ulrich flee from the Major's Wife and his first experience of mysticism? At the time, Ulrich had attempted to convince

the Major's Wife that true love has nothing whatsoever to do with physical possession, which arises out of the vulgar world of appropriation and gluttony. True love means renunciation, for only through renunciation will the intense feeling of love be able to grow and to expand in all directions. It is in this manner that man's soul "grows." Otherwise, the emotions will be discharged into mere sexual activity. Ulrich's interpretation of his affair with the Major's Wife reflects once again Musil's belief in the necessary opposition of dionysian and contemplative mysticism, which has already been discussed in connection with "The Temptation of Quiet Veronica." As Ulrich admits much later, he loved not the Major's Wife, who was a mere pretext, but the mystical state within himself that love created. Ulrich finally left the Major's Wife in order (he says) to protect this state which, in the absence of the woman herself, he hoped to convert into "the impersonal centre of energy, the subterranean dynamo that supplied his illumination" (I 145). (Ulrich believed that such illumination could then be utilized not only in the creation of further mystical states throughout his life but also in the creation of "soul.") But for reasons never fully explained, Ulrich was so overcome by fear of his relationship with this considerably older woman that he not only rejected her in the name of preserving his newly discovered mystical soul but also finally repressed his soul by taking refuge in the world of science. Because of these fears, Ulrich's relationship to all women since the time of the affair with the Major's Wife have totally lacked "soul." Although Ulrich has had affairs with women since the Major's Wife, these relationships (for example with Bonadea and Leona) have existed on an entirely physical level. He has always been careful not to involve those deeper levels of his being of which he first became briefly aware during his affair with the Major's Wife. Distance and an ironic attitude toward women characterize Ulrich's behavior until he meets his sister Agathe once again.

In now returning to his first mystical period, Ulrich returns to a more fundamental level of his being. The scientific and skeptical phase of his life was merely a mask, an eccentric pose. He now rediscovers what he once lost. For on the day when Ulrich rejected the Major's Wife and took flight into science, he lost his soul and

became the devil, as he is referred to on several occasions in the novel. Or, to be more precise, his soul was not lost but merely became temporarily (i.e., for twelve years) inactive. Its influence upon Ulrich's daily life even during his most scientific period was so strong, however, that he never considered his active rational self to be more than "provisionally useful" (II 361). Even at the height of his scientific experiment, he could not help but feel guilty that he had for so many years been keeping himself back from those more genuine soul-experiences, which spoke to him "in tones of closest kinship, with a soft, dark inwardness that was the opposite of the hectoring tones of the mathematical and scientific language" (I 141). The strain of living hidden behind his false scientific self finally becomes too great. (The analogy with Veronica's thirteen-year repression of her first sexual experience with a dog is striking.)

All at once Ulrich feels himself moving (or being moved) "into a softer and larger condition" (II 453), as did Claudine in "The Perfecting of a Love" when she seemed to be moving backwards into her earlier life. He describes this state as a "loosening, as though a tightly knotted ribbon were coming undone" (II 453). Something seems to be drawing him, as it did Törless, through a secret door into another world. He is beginning to feel "great longing for that filmy, slippery state, for abandonment and oblivion" (II 347). Ulrich seems to be growing "soft" and his habitual posture of the aggressive and cynical intellectual appears to be turning into a desire for tenderness and dream. Regarding these feelings with a critical eye, Ulrich ironically terms them in a somewhat clinical fashion as "an attack of the major's wife" (II 454).

As a young cadet, he had felt that such a mystical state represented a great danger to him. He now begins to wonder, however, whether his salvation might not lie precisely in that area where he once believed that the danger was the greatest. But, he believes, there exists no woman in his present life with whom he could revive and continue his early and abruptly terminated mystical experience with the Major's Wife. In the chapter "The Turning Point," something finally does happen, an event that shakes him out of his little Viennese castle as well as out of his world of endless thinking. Learning that his father has died, Ulrich sets off by train

for his father's house in the provinces in order to arrange for the funeral and settle the estate. In his childhood home, Ulrich again meets his sister Agathe after a separation of many years. Through her he eventually manages to renew contact with his lost soul. With this meeting begins Part Three of *The Man without Qualities*, entitled "Into the Millennium" (or "The Criminals"), of which Musil published only thirty-eight chapters.

The Sister as the Awakener of the Soul

After meeting Ulrich, Agathe decides to leave her husband, Professor Hagauer, a self-righteous and complacent pedant, whom she has grown to despise, and to return with Ulrich to Vienna. Together they plan to retire from the world totally, in order to carry on what Musil terms "Holy Conversations." They decide that it might be best to tell everyone that they are about to leave Vienna for a vacation. In this way, their communion and their conversations will be protected from disturbances arising from the outer world, for they both believe that nothing must be allowed to jeopardize this new opportunity. Through their life together, they hope to find entrance into the mysterious utopia of the so-called "Millennium." In this realm the question of the right way of living will be solved not by aggressive application of reason but by the surrender and submersion of two selves in a state of heightened love.

The intense spiritual relationship ("contemplatio") formed between brother and sister in *The Man without Qualities* was foreshadowed not only by the relationship between Veronica and Johannes but also by that between Thomas and his sister-in-law Regine in *The Visionaries*. (Musil's women-of-possibility always seem at once attracted to scientific men-of-possibility, such as Ulrich, Thomas, and Vinzenz, and repulsed by their academic husbands; in *The Man without Qualities*, Agathe leaves Professor Hagauer; in *The Visionaries*, Regine leaves Josef, a high official in the Ministry of Education; and in *Vinzenz and the Girl Friend of Important Men*, Alpha leaves Dr. Apulejus-Hahn.) With the depar-

ture of his wife with Anselm, Thomas and Regine are left alone in the house. Calling himself and Regine brother and sister, Thomas declares that a profound spiritual union has come to exist between them. But it proves to be only of temporary duration. Apparently, a profound relationship between Musil's man and woman-of-possibility is not possible over any extended period of time. At the end of the play, Regine returns to her husband, leaving Thomas completely alone, an episode that points forward to the resolution of Ulrich's second experiment.

Ulrich believes that mankind has been attempting to return to an original primal state throughout history. The second tree of Ulrich's life, the Tree of Love, is the metaphor by which Musil expresses this primal state of harmony, a tree out of which all mankind fell in the mythical past when man fell out of love. Speaking metaphorically, therefore, Ulrich believes in the Fall of Man and in the concept of Original Sin, which resulted in a fundamental change in man's basic attitude toward himself and the world similar to that which occurs when an individual falls out of love. The fall out of the Tree of Love was caused by "the apple of 'knowledge' " (III 246). Those in a state of love do not need science. Those out of love are merely using science in the hope that it will lead them back to love. But scientific knowledge leads only to truth and never to love, which is a state of grace. Agathe and Ulrich prepare themselves for this state of grace.

Until this point in the novel, Ulrich seems to have been a person singularly lacking in love. How is it possible, then, for Ulrich, this ironic and detached spectator of life, to fall in love with someone at his late date? Since Agathe is his shadowy double, a complementary nature, and is thus himself all over again but transformed as in a dream (III 325), the way lies open for Ulrich to accept a person for the first time without a defensive attitude of irony. For she is at once himself but also not himself, at once within him while also existing in the external world. Therefore, Agathe represents the only possibility for Ulrich to overcome his feeling of being divided from the outer world. Concerning his feeling of being divided *within* himself, Ulrich believes that this unfortunate condition has arisen because: "I'm not fond of myself"

(I 178). With Agathe, however, he is able to say: "Now I know what you are: you're my self-love!" (III 274). Ulrich's love extends no further than to his twin sister, which is to say, hardly further than to himself. But even such a state represents for Ulrich an almost miraculous extension of feeling.

Three Presuppositions for the Mystical Experiment

As we learn from his conversations, Ulrich's mystical experience involves three vital assumptions concerning the relationship of mysticism to God. First, Ulrich observes that during his mystical experience no God ever seems to arrive upon the scene. As was also the case in the scientific experiment in search of the paradise of "exact living," Musil states that Ulrich and Agathe begin their "pilgrimage" without believing in God or in the existence of a world beyond. They are, as it were, searching for the kingdom of God while denying God's existence.

Second, because no God appears, Ulrich decides that an attitude of unquestioning irrational acceptance is irrelevant. Man need not renounce the use of his critical and intellectual faculties in his attempts to describe and comprehend mystical states. In one of his "Holy Conversations" with Agathe, he wonders whether, in fact, technology might not be able to bring him to his mystical goal more quickly. He suggests that perhaps one might travel to "the world of lost feeling" by car or "on metal wings" rather than, for example, by donkey with staff in hand as did the pilgrims of old in their search for God (III 99, 116). With the aid of reason, Ulrich wants to create a "daylight mysticism" (N 1089), in which man will be able to have "exact visions" (III 111). It is unfortunate, he feels, that this area of human experience has so often been abandoned to the poets, clerics, and other weak-minded people. Musil once asserted in an essay: "We do not have too much reason and too little soul, rather we have too little reason in matters of the soul."[2] Since man has managed to achieve a "strict attitude" in matters of the intellect, why should he not be able to do something similar for the feelings?

During his retreat from the world with Agathe, Ulrich begins to study the lives of saints with great interest. Unlike the saints who immediately expressed their mystical experiences in terms of particular theological constructions and thus distorted and obscured their original feelings, Ulrich believes that the mystical experience is deeper than any and all religious interpretations that describe mystical states or communion with a particular God. (Jung also believed that profound mystical experience precedes and is thus more fundamental than Church dogma. In fact, as occurred in the case of brother Nicholas von der Flüe, which is discussed by Jung in his book *The Archetypes and the Collective Unconscious*, "primal" mystical experience in the West always tends to be immediately assimilated into the "secondary" dogmas of the Catholic Church.) Ulrich, therefore, feels that the pure core of mystical experience ought to be able to withstand investigation according to the strict empirical principles of science. He explains to Agathe how they should proceed along the mystical way: "Now let's look at this as soberly as possible, to see what's going on here" (III 101).

A third presupposition concerning Ulrich's attitude toward mystical states involved the necessary absence of what Musil calls "motorische Ekstase," that is to say, dionysian frenzy. Ulrich's experiment with Agathe not only excludes but lives precisely upon the exclusion of sexuality. We recall that Musil noted the existence of two kinds of mysticism, dionysian mysticism and nondionysian "contemplatio"—often termed the Other Condition ("der andre Zustand") in *The Man without Qualities*. In both forms of mysticism, man's rational relationship to the world is destroyed on behalf of a state of absolute feeling. In dionysian mysticism, the individual feels himself being dissolved into sheer muscular activity; in "the Other Condition"—a state in which man first makes contact with the soul—the individual feels overwhelmed by a sense of complete stasis and silence, a sense of undisturbed harmony with all things. Thus from the viewpoint of the mutual exclusivity of these two forms of mysticism, Ulrich's flight from the Major's Wife reflects Musil's belief that the growth of the soul is directly related to the inhibition and renunciation of sexuality. If Ulrich's relation-

ship to the Major's Wife was in danger of becoming a dionysian affair charged with the fear of mother-son incest at least on a psychological level (since there was no blood relationship between this couple), Ulrich's relationship with his sister is threatened by actual incest. Should his experiment, conducted within the nondionysian sphere of the second tree of his life, ever tip over into dionysian mysticism, then Ulrich knows that his second experiment will also have failed.

Ulrich's striving to maintain a state of "contemplatio" while holding the dangers of sexuality at a distance (his second experiment) parallels his championship of reason and intellectual discipline against the dangers of emotionalism (his first experiment). Both experiments are based upon a strong rejection of the same area of human experience: man as an animal. It may be that a strong unconscious connection between sexuality in general, and his own fears of incest in particular, play some part in Ulrich's constant revulsion against any form of dionysian activity. (Eithne Wilkins's publication of some earlier versions of the novel as well as her discussion of Musil's relationship to his mother give some weight to such an hypothesis.)[3] From this point of view, Ulrich's disgust with Walter's submersion in Wagner's music, his feelings of repugnance toward Clarisse's increasing mental deterioration, and his rejection of Moosbrugger seem more comprehensible. For all three of these characters experience moments when, like Ulrich, they feel themselves pressing through some "hole" or "tear" in daily reality and penetrating into a nonrational mystical realm. But unlike Ulrich's experience of "contemplatio" in the mystical realm, these characters wish either for temporary or permanent residence in a realm of dionysian mysticism. As a state of pure activity untouched by reason, Ulrich considers such an existence tantamount to temporary or permanent madness. Musil therefore intended to stress, in the part of the novel that he did not live to complete, the difference between the dionysian mystical attraction of Clarisse to Moosbrugger (which is analogous to that of Törless to Basini) and the nondionysian mystical relationship of Ulrich and Agathe.

A World of Love

How can the mystical state for which Ulrich and Agathe strive be described? It cannot be described directly but only by means of various metaphors. In connection with the two trees of his life, Ulrich notes that there are two fundamental attitudes toward life: the unequivocal one of the first tree of reason and the metaphorical one of the second tree of mysticism. Musil, continuing his analysis, comments: "Unequivocality is the law of waking thought and action . . . . Metaphor, on the other hand, is a combining of concepts such as takes place in dream; it is the sliding logic of the soul, and what corresponds to it is the kinship of things that exist in the twilight imaginings of art and religion" (II 361-62). The literal and unequivocal word, language in general and scientific thinking in particular, which are tools intended to manipulate the world of waking thought and action, are unable to comprehend and express the most fundamental aspects of Ulrich's dreamlike mystical experiences. (Törless found for similar reasons that language could not give expression to his sexual experiences.) Ulrich says of Christ, for example, that he lived continually in a mystical state that could not be described in discursive language, a state in which one loves metaphors. When Christ spoke of "paradise" and "the kingdom of God," he was not making metaphysical statements of a geographical nature. He was simply using metaphors to express the mystical realm in which he lived and moved.

Ulrich and Agathe have, nevertheless, a clear conception of this realm. Ulrich provides a concise definition for the nondionysian form of mysticism when, citing the Bible, he writes in his diary: "Everything in the world is love!" (N 1239); "Everything that happens in love happens in God. For God is love" (N 1240). It is a state in which there exists only pure acceptance, only the great "yes." It should be noted here that even the atheist Ulrich feels the need to use the word God in order to communicate mystical experience, although the term God is employed here only as a linguistic device. Agathe also recalls how Christ said to his followers: don't defend yourself, don't fight, exclude, hate, or resist. For Christ,

negation was not possible. In such a state of love, man can no longer tolerate anything that divides and detaches. In mystical love all boundaries and distinctions are absent, and all phenomena in the world appear interwoven and unified. To experience such love one must again become as a child in relationship to all that exists.

The mystical state of "contemplatio" is one of total stasis. The highest form of feeling to which man can aspire is created not through an enlarged, egoistic, possessive relationship to the world but rather "a static condition in which nothing ever changed, like still waters" (II 316). There can be nothing of cause, desire, or purpose in this state because it allows no concentration. It only sends out wave after wave rippling away in circles which are never able to gain sufficient concentration to initiate a current of action. In this state, Ulrich asks whether it is not true that love and asceticism stand together like brother and sister "without any aim or target, in contrast with life, which is all aims and targets?" (II 318). He characterizes metaphorically the total passivity of the mystical state by admitting that it has "something feminine about it" (N 1314). Ulrich, once an intellectually aggressive, masculine man of reason, now says: "I have indeed become its wife. . . . We are three sisters, Agathe, I, and this state" (N 1369).

Ulrich, in spite of being an atheist, is sufficiently attracted to Christ as mystic to feel the need to understand Christ's life and example (N 1169-70). Christ's exhortation that man should live permanently in a state of mysticism has, Ulrich believes, degenerated through the centuries into the rigid commandments of a particular faith. But Christ's fiery mysticism, as opposed to its impoverishment by the church into an unequivocal dogma, was not a faith. It represented a new way of living, not a new way of believing, an idea which Nietzsche also argued in his *The Antichrist*. It was a state of pure inwardness oblivious to outer reality. Christ did not say that man must strive to be "good" in order to gain access to paradise in the afterlife; for to live daily in a state of mystical love is to be already in paradise. Christ's way of life, therefore, is as possible today as it was two thousand years ago. Taking such terms as "paradise" and "the kingdom of God" as metaphors for a state of feeling, Ulrich says that he too is looking for "the Gate of

Paradise" (N 1426) and thus his relationship to Agathe represents a "journey into paradise" (N 1407).

A Mystical Morality

Ulrich's interest in mysticism is directed particularly toward the question of whether it can form the basis for a new and creative morality now that science has failed in this regard. Projecting into a future society his own attempts to find a new morality that would supersede the present one, Ulrich says during one of his "Holy Conversations":

> But I believe perhaps that some day, before very long human beings will be—on the one hand, very intelligent [scientists], on the other, mystics. Perhaps our morality is even today splitting into these two components. I might also call it: mathematics and mysticism—practical amelioration and adventuring into the unknown. (III 122)

With Agathe at his side, Ulrich will attempt to establish this second form of morality based upon nondionysian mysticism.

What, we may well ask, is a mystical morality? A mystical morality is based not upon society's unimpassioned codes and laws but only upon the feelings of the individual. Ulrich believes that morality should be based solely upon the individual's acting in harmony with his emotions. Thus Musil wrote in his diaries that Ulrich should not attempt to act in such a way that his action could become a moral prescription for the way in which all men ought to act. He should only behave in such a way that his actions have "worth."[4] And whether or not an action is worthwhile can be determined only by reference to the mystical state within him from which the impulse arises and not to the needs of society that the impulse may satisfy. For Musil, mystical morality is like a "fire," whereas the morality of society is nothing but a system of police regulations designed to dampen that fire (III 430).

But what does it mean to assert that in essence each individual

must himself determine what is moral in terms of whether the particular action is in harmony with his emotions? Musil admits that this kind of morality is "undefinable"; he notes that for actions arising out of the mystical realm, "there is no other criterion than whether a thing will lift one up or let one down" (III 155). It is obvious that two such moralities, one based upon mysticism and the other upon the needs of society, must exist in a state of constant mutual conflict.

Ulrich believes that those actions which society condemns as being criminal and evil are often the cause of a "rising feeling" in an individual, while the good, which is based upon external regulations, usually results in a "sinking feeling," in a deathlike condition. Evil actions often arise from passionate feelings, and good ones from the lack of such feelings. Because Ulrich uses the word morality in the sense of passion, he concludes with the Nietzschean assertion that "all Evil is enacted with more or less imagination and passion, whereas the Good is characterized by unmistakable pitifulness and poverty of emotion" (III 183). Traditional moral attitudes are merely a list of restrictions upon the emotions. But the mystical state, which represents a realm of the pure "yes" and a source of creativity, functions beyond good and evil. Thus Ulrich's final justification for living beyond good and evil is based upon an advocacy of those conditions that he believes to be necessary for achieving a creative life.

How does Ulrich evaluate the behavior of those great criminals of human history who, although they may have committed brutal murders, acted out of a passionate need? In that their actions arose from a mystical inner realm beyond traditional morality, Ulrich suggests that they cannot be condemned. To support this idea he cites Martin Luther. He reminds Agathe that Luther— while no doubt under the influence of the mystics—distinguished between a man's actions and his soul. While society may condemn the crimes of the outer man, the criminal's soul remains forever innocent—an idea also advanced by Claudine in her evaluation of the murderer G. Ulrich asserts early in the novel that Luther, as well as mystics and saints, might well have acquitted Moosbrugger (I 140). The case of Moosbrugger becomes a source of general

fascination throughout the Empire. Quite aside from the "crazy Clarisse," even the superrationalist Ulrich feels held as if in a spell by Moosbrugger and his case. The Moosbrugger phenomenon seems to Ulrich to arise out of an area of experience totally different from that which he connects with the first tree of his own life. The murderer's behavior seems to be generated in a mystical realm in which everything an individual does is justified and in which everyone is forever innocent, a dreamlike realm that cannot be comprehended or controlled by reason. (Ulrich says that if mankind could dream collectively, it would dream Moosbrugger. In other words, he regards the irrational crimes of Moosbrugger as an external correlative of all mankind's unconscious urges toward violence.) Nevertheless, psychiatrists, jurists, clerics, and various other learned men attempt to understand rationally and thereby dispose of this uncomfortable phenomenon, a murderer and a carpenter with the first name of Christian. However varied the many interpretations may be that attempt to account for Moosbrugger's criminality, all the experts agree that his behavior is "bad." But Moosbrugger considers his criminal actions to have been "good," because they always made him feel "good." European morality is unable to deal with such a concept of goodness, Ulrich believes, because its rigid codes are based upon purely social and hence external standards. And these standards in practice function only to inhibit or destroy those feelings of goodness that arise solely from within man himself. It should be added that however innocent Ulrich may consider Moosbrugger's soul to be, he nevertheless rejects Moosbrugger's life as an example of a dangerous morality that is pathological precisely because it arises out of dionysian rather than nondionysian mysticism.

Agathe listens at times with great impatience to Ulrich's endless abstract theorizing on the question of morality. She complains that whenever she attempts to get an answer out of him, he seems to dissolve into thin air. One day, however, she decides to give Ulrich's theory a reality, to put it to the test. Ulrich appears shocked by the fact that a definite action based upon his theories is about to occur. Nevertheless, it is an action that seems to meet his own Nietzschean criterion for a moral act whose value arises out of

the mystical realm, as he once stated it: "I shall take my bearings solely from whether its presence makes me feel a rising or a sinking. Whether it arouses me to life or not" (III 122). Almost in a state of paralysis, Ulrich watches Agathe forge her father's will so that her much-hated husband, Professor Hagauer, will be denied his rightful share of her inheritance. At first Ulrich feels that her actions have, as it were, descended out of another world from that concerned with mere everyday decisions. He finds in her actions an indistinguishable blend of innocence and criminality. And so he decides to wait and see whether in this particular instance his mystical morality will prove superior to the simple morality of everyday honesty.

Ulrich soon begins expressing doubts. What he approves of is the courageous and openly defiant morality of the highway robber, not that of the mean sneak-thief, and the forgery of the will seems to him more like an example of the latter. If one were acting out of a heightened mystical state, it should be theoretically impossible to commit any mean act. Their one effort to test this morality thus leads to a decided "sinking" rather than a "rising feeling," for the forgery finally appears to Ulrich to have occurred out of an all too human weakness and not out of an impulse of creative morality.

While Ulrich and Agathe have been conducting their very private experiment, Musil has not totally neglected the lives of the other characters introduced earlier in the novel. Diotima has called several meetings of the Collateral Campaign, into which Ulrich and Agathe have been drawn against their will. Clarisse has been becoming ever more obsessed with Moosbrugger, and Agathe's husband has started considering various maneuvers to force her to return to him. But all these events, external to the private world of Ulrich and Agathe, remain very much on the periphery of Musil's interest in the published portion of Part Three. Musil had intended to have Ulrich return to the world of the Collateral Campaign after the failure of his experiment with his sister and her departure from his life. However, Part Three breaks off at Chapter 38. (It is probable that Musil planned to include a further eighty-five chapters in order to balance the hundred and twenty-three chapters of Part Two.)

The Failure of the Mystical Experiment

Ulrich's experiment to find a creative morality through mysticism does not succeed. Even before the experiment of the forgery, Ulrich had stated his belief to Agathe that anyone who attempts to achieve this most perfect of all existences, in which acting is in complete harmony with feeling, necessarily lives in the greatest danger. For failure would then inevitably mean that "he ends up in twilight. In mist and mush. In unarticulated ennui" (III 122).

Ulrich claims that with Agathe he has managed for moments at a time to return to those "islands of right living" originally abandoned when he left the Major's Wife. Ulrich declares: "the state of excitement in which we live is that of rightness." He continues in his diary: "There is also not the slightest difference of opinion between Agathe and me, that the question: 'How shall I live,' a question we had both asked ourselves, has been answered: 'I shall live like this' " (N 1213). Nevertheless, Ulrich concludes that his second experiment is also a failure. He considers that the success of his mystical experiment depends upon whether the illumination can be extended into a "permanent state," whether mysticism can finally be combined with the social framework of daily living. The influence of mysticism upon Ulrich's life would in this case have to represent more than merely the occasional descent of a few flakes of fire that serve to make life interesting, more than a temporary and exotic holiday from sober reason. Mysticism as a successful way of life would mean going permanently on holiday. But when Agathe asks Ulrich whether the mystical state can be "practiced as real life," she receives a negative reply. Ulrich explains to Agathe: "We have followed an impulse contrary to order . . . . A love can grow out of defiance, but it cannot consist of defiance. Rather, it can only exist within a society. It cannot be the content of a life . . . One cannot live from negation alone" (N 1426). Ulrich's two experiments were designed to bring forth possible possibilities not yet "in" reality rather than possibilities that would remain forever impossible; but the "journey to the furthest limits of the possible" (III 111), which the relationship between

Agathe and Ulrich was to have signified, reveals itself finally to have been a trip to the edge of the impossible.

Ulrich ultimately condemns the self-sufficient absoluteness of the mystical state with the assertion: "everything absolute, one hundred percent perfect, true [is] completely contrary to nature" (N 1421), and declares that with too much spirit, life becomes impossible. Elsewhere, he describes mysticism as a "blessed state of doing nothing and thinking nothing" (N 801), as a sheer negation of life, a *natura morte* emanating the "breath of a still life that touches and paralyzes to the bone" (N 1141). Ulrich eventually admits the necessity of what he terms "the appetitive desires." By this term he means all that which "urges one to action, to movement, to pleasure" (N 1147). Ulrich comes to the conclusion that it is the instincts that the world must thank for all its beauty and progress. Pure mysticism, he writes in his diary, simply puts one eventually to sleep.

Such states of contemplative mysticism can never be long sustained except in pathological instances; they always seem to "collapse back into the normal state."[5] In a sketch for a chapter entitled "Journey into Paradise," a decisive occurrence takes place. Ulrich and Agathe have actually left Vienna and traveled to an unnamed island in the Mediterranean. It is there that Ulrich's experiment with Agathe eventually collapses. They are unable to prevent their mystical experience from tipping over into dionysian ecstasy. The spiritual incest becomes physical incest. They decide that their special relationship is at an end and that they must part.

Musil's final comment upon Ulrich's two utopian experiments is that they have both yielded no practical results (N 1579). Ulrich does not achieve the ultimate synthesis of reason and mysticism, science and love, precision and the soul. Musil summarizes Ulrich's final situation with the simple statement: "The synthesis of soul-reason has failed" (N 1592). Ulrich's life remains fragmented and paralyzed and therefore sterile. For it is only through the discovery of a middle ground, of an area between the two worlds, that a new foundation might have appeared upon which a creative and unified life could have arisen. In the Appendix to the novel, Musil

presented his own analysis: "One has only the following choice: to participate in these degenerate times (to howl with the wolves), or to become a neurotic. Ulrich pursues the latter course" (N 1594).

When regarded in the light of *Young Törless*, Ulrich's inability to combine the two perspectives of reason and mysticism appears inevitable and but a further stage in the failure of all attempts to synthesize opposites. Although Musil did not complete *The Man without Qualities*, thus making it difficult to arrive at any definite conclusion concerning Ulrich's achievement of a synthesis, he did finish *Young Törless*. In the earlier novel the problem of synthesis is articulated and analyzed by Törless himself. We recall Törless's desperate "urge to search unceasingly for some bridge, some connection, some means of comparison" (79) between the two perspectives of reason and dionysian mysticism. He finally realized that he would never be able to find a middle term because there is no middle area. Sometimes he will see life from the perspective of reason and sometimes from that of mysticism. As Törless could not manage to unite reason with dionysian mysticism, so Ulrich is unable to unite daily life with nondionysian mysticism as a permanent state ("Dauerzustand" [N 1216]). Törless seems to have realized, as Nietzsche wrote in *On Truth and Lie in an Extra-Moral Sense*, that the most that can exist between two totally different perspectives is an aesthetic relationship. Thus, in the novels *Young Törless* and *The Man without Qualities* Musil is able to present both perspectives only in terms of their aesthetic relationship rather than in terms of their ultimate synthsis.

Ulrich's Failure and the Collapse of Europe

Since Musil asserts that Ulrich must be regarded as a representative of the problems of his times and that as an Austrian citizen he is also a representative of the modern world as a whole (N 1595), his fate is of more than personal interest. The attempts and failures of the Collateral Campaign to achieve a meaningful way of living is but a distorted image of Ulrich's own experiments.

Musil believed that there was a profound connection between the failure of all these experiments (both personal and collective) to achieve "the right way of living" and the catastrophic historical event of World War I: "The synthesis of soul-reason has failed. That leads in a direct line to the war" (N 1592). "The Collateral Campaign leads to the war!" (N 1575). "All lines empty into the war" (N 1575). While everyone has been searching to find that factor that would sum up and unify all aspects of life, a unifying factor in the form of war finds and swallows them all. It now seems totally irrelevant whether the experiments have been carried out honestly and painstakingly, as in Ulrich's case, or stupidly and carelessly, as in the case of the members of the Collateral Campaign. Disaster is the fate of all.

If Ulrich is a representative of his age, then the tipping over in his own life of nondionysian mysticism into the dionysian mysticism of sexuality is but a personal parallel to the dialectical reversal that also occured in Austrian society. The pseudomysticism and irrationality existing at every level of Austrian society, particularly as revealed in the antics of the Collateral Campaign, finally tipped over into the dionysian mysticism of war-fever. It is in the general popular support given to the idea of having a great war that the Empire's moral and cultural bankruptcy—a reflection of cultural nihilism—is most clearly revealed. In an age in which man feels himself fragmented and paralyzed, condemned to live without direction and a sense of purpose, he is unable to resist final surrender to the all-engulfing self-destructive nature of dionysian mysticism. As Musil wrote in the Appendix to *The Man without Qualities*: In such a nihilistic world nothing seems left for the individual and for the nation but a "final flight into sexuality and war" (N 1593).

In a sketch intended for Part Three, Agathe says to Ulrich that they should continue living together as if nothing had changed. In Musil's rather telegraphic style, which is evident in some of the unfinished chapters found in the *Nachlass*, Ulrich answers: "No. Suicide. I am going to war" (N 1573). Agathe replies that should he be killed, she will poison herself. Although Musil left behind numerous partial sketches and plans, it will not be possible to arrive at any certain conclusions concerning Ulrich's

future until a definitive edition which includes the *Nachlass* is published. Thus for the reader Ulrich may well remain (in a sense not planned by his creator) a man of endless possible life-styles, for even the publication of the *Nachlass* may leave essential questions unanswered. Indeed, Musil seems to have changed his mind several times with regard to the end of the novel.

Musil presented in a planned preface to the novel his own interpretation of Ulrich's fate, and it is an interpretation which will remain valid regardless of later additions to the critical text: "Ulrich not to be presented as the 'truthful and strong' human being, but as a significant example of a man who has gone astray. Mood. It is the tragedy of the more intelligent form of human being . . . , who is always alone, in contradiction with everything, and unable to change anything. Everything else is merely a logical consequence" (N 1597-98).

VII ⚬

The Open Horizon

INSTEAD OF ATTEMPTING to present a perhaps expected restatement or direct summary of the nature and scope of Musil's work, this concluding chapter sets itself a quite different task, although one which may also serve secondarily and indirectly as a summary of Musil's intellectual preoccupations and literary achievement. Although some parallels to Musil's work will be drawn from the fiction of Franz Kafka and Thomas Mann in order to set Musil's treatment of the hovering life in a broader literary context, the following analyses will not be primarily literary. This final chapter will, rather, undertake a somewhat far-ranging examination of some of Musil's major themes by way of comparing them with their analogous treatment or evaluation by a limited number of thinkers working in nonliterary disciplines. Musil, after all, himself recognized that his work dealt with a number of fundamental and perennial problems in German intellectual and cultural history; he specifically wanted his fiction to be regarded in its widest context as representing a contribution to the continuing reformulation and debate of the most urgent questions concerning twentieth-century man in Western society. Thus, one profitable and efficient way of comprehending the cultural and intellectual dimension of his work is to regard it through perspectives provided by psychology and philosophy.

The analogies to be drawn in this concluding chapter will seek to indicate not only similarities of theme but also basic differences in the evaluation of particular problems. The following areas will be examined with reference to the various positions taken by Musil in his fiction. First, Musil's evaluation of the world of lost feeling will be compared with Freud's and Jung's analysis of the irrational element in the human psyche and the question of its proper function in the healthy balanced life. Second, Ulrich's ideal of life as a scientific experiment will be placed in the context of the Existentialist's negative critique of life based upon the scientific ideal of

total objectivity. Third, Musil's concept of synthesis as well as his inability to achieve it in his fiction will be compared with the same concept and problem in the thought of Kierkegaard, Nietzsche, and Jung. The purpose of this third comparison is to demonstrate how Musil's desired success in his particular life-long quest for synthesis could only have signalized his intellectual and artistic failure. Thus it will be argued that the final vision in Musil's work remains that of a utopian writer: his hopes for the ideal of the unified life look ever forward into the future while his artistic imagination and intellectual energies are always directed toward treating the insoluble conflicts and complexities of life in the present.

It is obvious that such broad issues viewed within the context of such major thinkers as Kierkegaard, Nietzsche, Freud, and Jung cannot be systematically pursued to any conclusion here. These particular writers have been selected, however, because their exploration of the balanced, creative life provide varying representative and extreme positions in theology, philosophy, and psychology. The result of such a highly selective presentation may, admittedly, result in an oversimplified view. But such a reduction also facilitates a more rigorous concentration of attention which is particularly illuminating. The purpose of this overview is to suggest the appropriateness of Musil's work to a few critical questions treated by psychoanalysis and existentialism and thus to offer perspectives upon his fiction previously absent in Musil criticism.

Perspectives on the Irrational Realm

The adult protagonist in all of Musil's major works initially finds himself in the same unhappy situation: for some reason life has lost its meaning and become incomprehensible. Though the characters may be as different as Veronica and Ulrich—to cite two extreme cases in Musil's work which will serve as examples for analysis throughout this section—they all seem to be suffering from a decline in vitality due primarily to an atrophied emotional life. The protagonist feels that he has "gotten stuck" and that a

private search for some form of rebirth must be undertaken, regardless of the cost. The key to the revitalization of life in the works of Musil, Freud, and Jung lies in the recapture and integration of the irrational or mystical element of man's psyche into his mental life as a whole.

In Musil's fiction, rediscovery of the irrational life and the consequent problems of its relationship to the individual's conscious activity finds two quite different expressions depending upon whether the protagonist is a woman or a man. Musil's differing treatment and evaluation of the irrational world in these two cases reveals a difference in approach and attitude toward the unconscious that finds an analogy in the fundamental conflict between Freud's and Jung's theories on the function of the unconscious in the healthy mental life. Before turning to an analysis of Musil's differing evaluation of the unconscious (specifically in "The Temptation of Quiet Veronica" and *The Man without Qualities*) in the context of psychoanalytic theory, Freud's and Jung's respective positions on this question will be summarized.

A thinker's attitude toward the place and function of mystical and irrational forces in man's daily life obviously depends upon the point of view from which he evaluates the worth of nonrational phenomena in mental life. Following in the tradition of enlightenment thought, Freud judges the processes of the whole psyche from the single perspective of the ego, which is (metaphorically) the seat of reason and the window upon external and social reality. Jung, however, assumes the equal validity of reason and mysticism and does not attempt to devalue one in terms of the other—although given the imbalance in favor of reason in the modern psyche, he may seem in practice to place greater emphasis upon the importance of the mystical impulses. Thus Jung considered Freud's tendency to judge the operations of the whole psyche from the single standard of the ego to be a form of intellectual arrogance, for Jung believed that the ego was too weak and fragile to serve as the center of the whole psychic system. In fact, Jung felt that it might even be sometimes advisable for the ego to declare defeat in certain intrapsychic battles and turn for help to the greater powers lying in the (collective) unconscious.

Freud's and Jung's differing evaluation of the psychological phenomenon of introversion (a term coined by Jung) will serve to clarify further their basic opposition. A fundamental presupposition in Jung's thought is that psychic energy (the libido) constantly flows back and forth between opposite poles. This opposition possesses a regulatory function so that when one extreme is reached the libido passes over into its opposite. Such an unceasing dialectical flow of energy is an inherent feature of the psychic system. Thus introversion, in which psychic energies are withdrawn from the outer world, directed inward, and reinvested in unconscious processes, should be regarded not only as a positive occurrence but at certain times even as a necessary one for the maintenance of psychological equilibrium. In addition, introversion is positive in that it constitutes a prerequisite step in the individual's discovery of the religious impulse within himself; and, for Jung, man's confrontation with the mystical dimension is a necessary step in the individuation process. No man can become complete, then, unless he has experienced recurring periods of introversion. Jung's positive evaluation of introversion directly contradicts Freud's moral and psychological imperative: where id was there shall ego be. In Freud's mind, introversion strongly suggest retrogression, narcissism, and the ego's surrender to the irrational forces of the id.

A comparison of the presuppositions of Freudian and Jungian therapy will yet further clarify the fundamental differences in their thought and will also serve as a point of departure for an analysis of Musil's treatment and evaluation of the unconscious in the mental lives of Veronica and Ulrich.   Freudian therapy concerns itself primarily with the traumatic origin of sexual repression. But Jung asserted that many of his patients were suffering from a sense of the emptiness and meaninglessness of their lives rather than from problems involving disturbances in psychosexual development. Thus, the emphasis in Jung's theory and therapy is not directed primarily toward tracing neurotic conflict back to a single repressed instinctual factor in the past—although Jung does on occasion admit the need for such a causal or reductive approach to the psyche in young patients. Rather, since Jung attributes mental disorders to a general disturbance or imbalance in the psyche as a

whole, Jungian therapy concentrates upon the meaning of a conflict in the present and within the context of the individual's whole
psyche. With regard to this difference in therapy, Jolande Jacobi
writes: "Jung's great step forward, and the justification of the term
'synthesis' as he uses it, lies in his break with this linear causal
thinking of the old psychology . . . . "[1] Jung considered his method
(as opposed to that of Freud) to be constructive and prospective;
from a condition of neurotic imbalance in the present, it attempts
to build synthetically toward the future in the hope of achieving
resolution of conflict in a higher state of psychic balance which
would issue from a unification of the rational and nonrational aspects of the psyche. Although many of Jung's patients may have
been initially prompted to undergo psychoanalytic therapy because of some pathological condition in their sexual lives, these
patients eventually directed their attention toward the future
achievement of general psychic harmony. For Jung, conflicts are
purposive. Therefore, Jung asks to what end, while Freud asks why
and from where. It may be added parenthetically that Freud was
only too aware of Jung's radical reinterpretation of the irrational
realm, and he deplored the fact that Jung had ceased to be a
physician and felt the need to become a prophet of the spirit instead. While Freud strove in his therapy merely to relieve the patient of various symptoms which incapacitated his daily life, Jung
appeared to be offering nothing less than a road to salvation.
Freud considered it sufficient to resolve certain neurotic inhibitions
and conflicts, and he assumed that life—rather than a secularized
theology in the guise of psychology—could then be relied upon to
take its own course.

The conflict, then, may be reduced to the following impasse:
For Jung, Freudian therapy was inadequate because it did not
fully recognize that man could and must be more than a sexually
well-adjusted animal; it did not acknowledge the fact that man
constantly feels within himself an impulse to give his life greater
meaning. From the Freudian perspective, however, Jungian salvation by means of radical introversion tends to ignore the absolute
and fundamental reality of sexuality as well as the need for man to
adjust to society in spite of his aggressive impulses. Jung evades

these distressing and irremediable facts of psychological reality; from the Freudian perspective, therefore, the ultimate Jungian synthesis of all psychic opposites, an ideal which will at any rate always remain unrealized, can be approached (unfortunately) only by ever greater degrees of abstraction from daily life. In other words, salvation is approached only by ever greater degrees of depersonalization.[2] Jung's yearning for depersonalization is confirmed in his therapy. Although Jung claimed to accept the validity of the personal unconscious as set forth in Freudian theory, Freud felt that Jungian therapy tended in practice to ignore its fundamental importance. Thus, analysis of the symbolic abstractions of the archetypes of the collective unconscious in Jungian therapy replaces a close examination of a particular sexual trauma in a particular human life. Man as an animal—and thus the primal reality of the physical body—is soon left behind in the more noble and elevating Jungian quest for the "higher man." It is, therefore, totally consistent for Jung to reject as reductive the Freudian idea of sublimation, that the inhibition of man's sexual and aggressive impulses is responsible for the creation of higher forms of culture. Jacobi, in Jung's defense, emphasizes the uniqueness in psychological thought of Jung's insight "that the *spirit* must be viewed not as a mere epiphenomenon or 'sublimation' but as a principle *sui generis*, a formative and hence supreme principle which is the indispensible condition of all psychic and perhaps even physical form.[3]

We shall pursue the Freudian analogy first. In "The Temptation of Quiet Veronica" the protagonist's psychological energies are directed, at first surreptitiously and then ever more obviously, backward to an earlier period in her psychic development. The Freudian approach to the unconscious is also essentially reductive, as has been observed, in that it too strives to lead the patient's attention backward in time to some very definite trauma in the past. Its purpose is to recapture an earlier lost fragment of the psychic life and thereby facilitate its reintegration into the individual's mental life as a whole. In treating psychic material analytically, Freudian therapy strives toward "normalizing" the psychic processes by removing emotional blocks to psychosexual development caused by early psychic trauma. Therefore, the cornerstone

of Freud's theory as well as the fulcrum of Musil's *Unions* is the existence of repression. Both Freudian therapy and the internal narrative line of *Unions* are directed toward the overcoming of repression so that the past can "catch up" with the present and the unification of a divided psyche can be effected. But the forces of the unconscious in Musil's story of Veronica finally prove to be destructive. Rather than providing a means for a rebirth of the self, the rediscovered id (to use Freud's terminology) swallows the ego and thus reverses the direction of Freud's moral and psychological imperative.

In *The Man without Qualities*, the unconscious life in the form of the mystical impulse is regarded as a positive and creative source of meaning—although with the ultimate proviso that Ulrich will eventually be able to reintegrate it into the structure of daily life. Thus Ulrich's mystical experiment with Agathe presupposes (at least initially) the same kind of positive evaluation of introversion found in the thought of Jung as elaborated above. Jung's and Ulrich's presupposition is that man requires for the healthy and well-balanced life more than instinctual satisfaction as argued in Freudian therapy. There exists a higher need, one that can be fulfilled only by means of a synthesis of his own complex and fragmented nature. Musil metaphorically describes such a uniquely human need for synthesis in terms of Ulrich's desire to connect the two trees of his life, that is to say, to unify the two roads of reason and mysticism. Ulrich is not concerned with the sexual problems that may be glimmering in the background of all his relationships to women. He wants only to overcome the feeling of aimlessness and emptiness in his life. But the final synthesis was not achieved and this failure cannot be ascribed merely to the fact that Musil did not live to complete the novel. If Veronica's ego seemed to sink down into the id, Ulrich comes to the insight that the mystical state can never be raised and satisfactorily integrated into the structures of daily living.

A noticeable feature of Ulrich's search for synthesis is the abstract quality of his life, a kind of depersonalization which Jung incorporated into his concept of synthesis but which Freud condemned. As Ulrich moves from the one extreme of reason to the

other extreme of mysticism he seems to pass over his own personal life. Therefore, Ulrich's life as a perspectivist can be regarded from the Freudian point of view as a form of defense against his having to take seriously any particular and possibly unbearable episode or aspect in his emotional history. It may be recalled that Ulrich constantly tries to persuade himself that whatever happens is no more important than what does not happen, indeed, that whatever happens is *less* important than what might yet occur. In neutralizing reality in general, such an idea necessarily neutralizes any traumatic event in the individual's past as well. Ulrich as a mystic may recover "the childhood of the race" but he does not recover—and apparently does not want to recover—his own childhood. Considering the enormous length of *The Man without Qualities*, the novel is remarkably lacking in the kind of personal psychological observation that a Freudian critic would find illuminating. Of course, such a critic could no doubt find material for analysis in Ulrich's defective relationship with women which, in turn, could be traced back to oedipal problems arising in the nuclear family. But Musil's vision and interest in his last novel is directed elsewhere, always toward the future and the realization of man's highest ideal in the fully creative human life. In spite of such noble Jungian sentiments, however, the Freudian critic would point out that the whole direction of *The Man without Qualities* toward some future synthesis always seems to be pointing away from something intentionally not revealed. In this regard Musil, like Veronica, always seems to be circumventing a dark center, a center which (as is clear from his other fiction) consists of a highly morbid strain of sexual pathology. Musil treated the theme of sexual pathology in a male protagonist with directness only in his first work, *Young Törless*. He apparently felt the need thereafter to keep at an ever greater distance from this problem. Dionysian mysticism, which is almost always pathological in his fiction, was henceforth treated more or less exclusively in the characters of women or in madmen such as the murderers G. and Moosbrugger. From the Freudian perspective, therefore, the mere idea of synthesis suggests evasion, and Ulrich's noble quest is but poorly hidden pathology. It was Freud's

belief that the healthy person, i.e., the one not suffering from intro-version, does not ask questions about the higher meaning of life.

The Hovering Life: An Existential Critique

To be a master of the hovering life—as is Musil's typical mas-culine protagonist—means precisely not to be a master of life itself. Musil criticism, however, has largely avoided any negative explo-ration of the masculine protagonist's lack of relationship to life as lived experience. From a negative and psychoanalytic point of view, we have already described the abstractness of Ulrich's emo-tional life as a form of "Freudian evasion." And from the positive and scientific point of view of Nietzsche's "free spirit," we have also argued Musil's justification of the hovering life in terms of the man-of-possibility who is able to entertain all perspectives simulta-neously. The hovering life in Musil's fiction will now be examined from a third (and once again negative) perspective, that of existen-tialism. For in spite of the internal differences among the existen-tialists on various issues, this philosophical movement has, in gen-eral, attempted to bring the human mind to bear upon the very banal but most fundamental problems of daily existence. An exis-tentialist exploration of the absence of the banal and everyday in Musil's work at once yields illuminating critical insights into the nature of the hovering life and also furnishes a basis for a negative moral evaluation of such an existence. Because Ulrich's life pro-vides the most extreme and detailed example in Musil's fiction of the hovering life, his experiment in rational living will now be analyzed in terms of the negative existentialist critique of science and the scientific temperament. The following analysis of the scien-tific attitude and its relationship to daily life is particularly justified and necessary, since Musil devoted the major portion of his fiction to a treatment of this theme; the nearly seven hundred pages that Musil expended upon Ulrich's first experiment exceed in sheer length all the rest of his published fictional works combined. Fi-nally, this critique of Ulrich's life as a scientist will be set within

the related context of the existentialist demand for a way of life based upon ethical commitment.

It should first be recalled that Ulrich's relationship to science is not to be found in his dedication to the ideal of the pursuit of truth. Nor can his interest in science be reduced to an idle and abstract curiosity in the workings of the natural world. Rather, his attitude toward science seems at first, in fact, to be existential in that it arises out of a desperate need to inform his daily life, even his most banal decisions, with meaning. The implicit possibility of Ulrich's committing suicide if his quest for meaning proves unsuccessful reveals how complete his commitment is. In its practical effect, however, the influence of the scientific attitude upon Ulrich's life is the reverse of existential. This becomes clear when two issues are viewed in the perspective of existential thought: the necessary impersonality of science and the absence (indeed irrelevance) of ethical decision in the scientific attitude.

All existential philosophers from Kierkegaard to Marcel agree that life cannot be reduced to the perspectives inherent in the scientific attitude. Such an assertion is based upon the assumption that there exist two kinds of truths. There are truths which can be appropriated into the individual's inner life and affect in a positive fashion the way in which he lives and there are truths which cannot and should not be so appropriated. To attempt to live one's life according to the scientific ideal is to confuse these truths and this confusion serves only to impoverish rather than enrich existence. This is precisely the mistake that Ulrich makes, an error that brings him to the verge of a nervous breakdown. The existentialists not only exhort man not to confuse these truths, but take issue with the scientific ideal whenever it threatens to arise as the sole criterion for the good life. What, then, is this scientific ideal, what kind of special truths does it espouse, who attempts to live according to its precepts, and what dangers does it pose for the individual? The scientific ideal (to generalize) challenges the individual to rise above the world of change and chance, above the flux of life and time so that man in a state of pure cognition may perceive phenomena objectively. The truths it seeks, best exemplified by the propositions of mathematics and the natural sciences, are thus de-

tachable from all merely personal considerations. In fact, the scientific ideal holds it as desirable to reduce the human-all-too-human aspects of the scientist's life to a minimum. The truths of science, once arrived at, remain true regardless of the individual who may be working with them. The existentialist objection to Ulrich's way of life as a scientist may be summarized in one sentence: to ignore or cancel the truth of the individual's own unique and complex experience in order to take refuge in the abstract simplicities of a scientific truth perceived and expressed in the limiting perspective of impersonality is to reduce man to an objective recording consciousness, in short, to a machine.

The impersonality of science, which tends to diminish the vitality and complexity of the individual life, is not unconnected to the irrelevance of ethical decision in the operation of the scientific method. The ethical is opposed to the experimental, at least on the level of daily living: the situation of human choice is not at all the situation of the scientific experiment. The ethical life is constituted of a series of individual choices that have been made and thus has a content which is not only certain but quite specifically not hypothetical. A situation is experimental when scientific controls have been established in such a way that the experiment can be endlessly repeated and its conclusions measured and fully expressed in scientific language. But the individual's life does not permit such a degree of control nor can that which is meaningful to the individual's life be expressed in scientific terminology. Life does not allow the degree of detachment attainable in scientific observation because it demands that continual and quite irreversible ethical choices be made. Thus, the ethical is an urge to the particular, the unique, and the individual. It involves the kind of risk and courage of which Ulrich in his hovering state as a man-of-possibility is quite ignorant.

These two existential objections to science and the scientific temperament were specifically raised by Kierkegaard in regard to Hegel's philosophy. Kierkegaard not only condemned Hegel for having lost the existing individual in the magnificent abstractions of his philosophical system; he also asserted that Hegel completely omitted the ethical from his thought. If we accept Kierkegaard's

analysis of the absence of the ethical dimension in science and the resulting psychological consequences for the scientist's life, we shall come full circle, returning to the problem of Musil's world without plot and a human life without character. Kierkegaard argues (most particularly in *Concluding Unscientific Postscript*) that the difficult problem facing each individual is how to give life continuity, a sense of direction and purpose amid the fragments and ruins of the inner and outer worlds. A sense of unity and coherence can only be achieved by the individual's making ethical decisions and by continually renewing them in his daily activities. Only by constantly forming and reforming his life through decision, which is the reverse of the experimental attitude, does he gain a sense of reality, for such decisions represent an inward commitment to a particular vocation, marriage, friendship, etc. From such a Kierkegaardian perspective, Ulrich's rejection of narrative line in his personal life does not arise first of all out of a will to truth at all costs. Nor does it primarily reveal the extent of his courage in comparison with the solutions found by those more cowardly and less intelligent among his acquaintances who are unable to face the void which has now become so apparent in the twentieth century. An absence of character and a lack of plot in one's daily life arises, rather, from a continual denial of ethical responsibility. Ulrich's intellectual rationalizations for the perspectivism of the hovering life but poorly disguise a fear of any and all forms of personal and social commitment. As Nietzsche, who along with Kierkegaard was the greatest hoverer in modern philosophy, understood so well, there is a void glimmering behind the experimental life—and it is a void that can never be overcome—except, as Kierkegaard urged, through a life of ethical decision.

The Hovering Life: Two Literary Parallels

The most brilliant metaphoric expression of the hovering life in modern literature is to be found in Kafka's late novella "Investigations of a Dog." The most discursive elaboration of this theme—with the exception of *The Man without Qualities*—is pro-

vided by Mann's *Magic Mountain*. The similarities between the lives of Kafka's dog, Mann's Hans Castorp, and Musil's Ulrich are striking. Equally striking, however, are Kafka's and Mann's differing evaluations of this form of life.

Kafka's narrator, a dog who is investigating various aspects of life and behavior in the world of dogs, notes at one point the highly peculiar phenomenon of the floating or hovering dog (*der Luft-hund*). These creatures are invariably seen sailing along the horizon, floating quite alone and high up in the air. The earth-bound narrator is especially troubled by two questions. First, how do the hovering dogs manage in their splendid isolation to reproduce? Second, since they are never seen either to contribute to the community or to take anything from it, how do they manage to survive? The narrator is amazed by the sheer incomprehensibility of such a freakish existence. What justification can possibly be found for such a sterile, parasitic, lonely, and ascetic form of existence? Since life does go on with its uniquely banal but urgent daily problems, however, who can afford to give more than a passing glance to such an oddity as a hovering dog? Consequently, the narrator's attention soon turns with greater interest toward an investigation of the more concrete questions of life, problems that concern dogs with their feet on the ground, such as the source of food. Kafka's moral condemnation of the hovering life in this late story is clear and partially reflects his own feelings of guilt concerning his bachelorhood, a theme which is present even in his earliest work. Being an independently wealthy bachelor, Ulrich, like the *Lufthund*, is also quite unconcerned about the necessities of life such as food or shelter. He directs his energies primarily toward the enrichment of his inner life rather than toward serious investigations of interpersonal and communal relationships. Ulrich's existence is in this sense no less sterile, parasitic, lonely, and ascetic than that of Kafka's hovering dog.

In *The Magic Mountain*, Mann, like Musil, also writes of a young man who has decided to take a holiday from life in order to devote himself completely to a highly personal search for new experiences in the realm of the mind and the emotions, for new values to replace those which have lost their validity for him. His

quest is, like that of Ulrich, set against a background of the spiritual and social decay of Europe on the edge of moral and economic collapse. And like Ulrich, Castorp is not chained to "life below" by family obligations, professional responsibilities, or the financial need to support himself. Hans Castorp's mountain-top "stock-taking," the material for which is provided by his intensive investigations into the most diverse fields of human intellectual activity as well as by his encounters and experiences with representative figures of European society, is enacted in a state of metaphorical and literal hovering above the world.[4] He too passes from experiences and experiments in reason (Settembrini) to those of the irrational (Clavdia Chauchat). In the world as it is evoked in both novels, the hovering life of the protagonist is seen as a necessary prerequisite to the discovery of a creative and meaningful inner life. At one point in *The Magic Mountain*, Clavdia Chauchat accuses Hans Castorp of a vice which she considers to be typically German: he is not interested in experience for the sake of experience but only as it may contribute to the enrichment of his inner life. The results of Hans's and Ulrich's hovering life are indefinable and intangible. No substantial and unambiguous conclusions concerning a socially viable creative life are forthcoming either from Mann or Musil. The *Bildungsroman* as a guide to the perplexed has come to a bitter end in *The Magic Mountain* and in *The Man without Qualities*.

The objections—particularly forthcoming from Anglo-Saxon readers—which have been leveled against Thomas Mann's novel are equally relevant, if not more so, to the fiction of Robert Musil. These objections will be detailed here, not because of their persuasive validity but because in every objection, if only by virtue of its unjust exaggeration, a grain of truth is present that may serve to illuminate a general tendency or characteristic of the author's fiction. Mann's style is faulted for being too highly intricate and subtle. Too great (it is charged) are the demands made upon the endurance and intelligence of the reader. But Mann's inclusion in his novels of large blocks of weighty intellectual material finds an even more extreme successor in the often highly abstruse essays which constitute an important part of *The Man without Qualities*.

The result of so great a direct display of the powers of the mind (it is further asserted) are novels that "hover," that seem to lack a kind of vital energy and a feeling of passion, in works lacking spontaneity and liveliness of plot. Not much seems to happen in German novels in general, and what does happen usually concerns only subtle changes in the inner development of the protagonist. The events of the outer world rarely seem to make any great impact upon the protagonist's consciousness. The protagonists seem only capable of very limited and dampened responses to the outer world. The gaiety and joy so evident in the great English and Russian social novels is buried under a very solemn pall of heavy symbolism. An atmosphere of high seriousness pervades everything, for questions no less important than the meaning of life and the feasibility of continued existence are under consideration.

A final observation may serve to summarize the unique relationship (or lack of relationship) existing between the modern hovering protagonists and social reality in these *Bildungsromane*, a state of affairs which receives its most extreme presentation in *The Man without Qualities*. Ulrich and Hans Castorp are engaged in endless intellectual and spiritual preparations for the journey of life, preparations that never cease because life for them never begins. The hovering protagonist refuses to land, so to speak, until all the major problems of life have been answered to his satisfaction. In this sense, Ulrich has not denied the ethical life; rather, the ethical life remains always in the future because he has not yet been able to accept or create a standard of values which is the precondition for ethical activity. *The Man without Qualities* is preoccupied with prototypical adolescent problems and when the time comes for Ulrich's graduation from the hermetic sphere of emotional and intellectual self-absorption, when he must therefore face the spectre of actual social reality looming ahead, the novel falters and stops. The typical protagonist of the German *Bildungsroman* is left standing upon the threshold of life.[5] All his best energies seem to have already been spent in the exploration of theoretical possibilities which seem in any case much more fascinating than any particular reality. Ulrich and Hans are the two modern German protagonists who have come closer to the realization of the philo-

sophical life in fiction than have any other characters in world literature. *The Man without Qualities* represents—for good or ill— a culmination of the German *Bildungsroman*. But the *Bildungsroman* may itself be regarded as reflecting and expressing certain perennial problems in German intellectual thought centering upon the quest for a creative balance in man's intellectual and emotional nature, a quest for individual psychological health and moral integrity in the context of societal pressures. The exploration of these problems achieved their philosophical culmination in the thought of Kierkegaard and Nietzsche, those two philosophers who, precisely because they were the most skilled masters of the hovering life, never ceased urging man to choose, to act, to live—although apparently without ever being able to take their own advice.

The Experiment that Failed

Since Musil was unable to achieve an ultimate resolution to Ulrich's dialectical experiment, the question must be asked: does not the fact that *The Man without Qualities* remains a gigantic fragment severely limit Musil's achievement both in this novel as well as in his work as a whole? For if Musil's fiction (with the exception of *Unions*) was directed toward some ultimate synthesis that was never achieved, does not such a situation thereby condemn even those works he did complete to remain at most merely tentative statements lacking the ultimate sanction that only a conclusion could have provided. Or, to rephrase this question in positive terms: what did Musil achieve in his life's work in spite of the fragmentary nature of his longest novel, a work which was intended to present the ultimate synthesis of that dialectic of reason and mysticism that underlies the striving of all his male protagonists from Törless to Ulrich?

The criticism directed toward Musil's undeniable fragmentariness can most succinctly be countered by a brief consideration of the nature and completeness of Musil's achievement in *The Man without Qualities*. Such a task involves two questions: first, how fully was Musil able to explore the problems of reason and mysti-

cism posed in this novel? Second, since it was not his sudden death that hindered the final presentation of a synthesis, why was Musil unable in the end to provide any positive conclusion whatever?

The reader is able to follow to its conclusion the problem posed by Ulrich's scientific experiment, that is to say, what happens when, in the service of man's search for meaning, the masculine attitude of mind (as defined in the West) is pushed to its most extreme point. The literary depiction of the resulting form of life is without parallel in the modern novel. The unalloyed masculine temperament, as Musil conceives of it, is reflected in a protagonist who functions primarily as an objective recording consciousness. Musil forcefully describes what happens when a totally scientific attitude toward life is maintained. He powerfully evokes for the reader the despair of the individual who has existed for far too long in a state entirely removed from all sources of feeling. As a result of Ulrich's inability to accommodate the exercise of his critical reason to the psychological necessities of daily life, he condemns himself to a state of paralysis and eventual mental collapse.

A second central idea, which Musil fully elaborates for the reader, concerns his belief that salvation lies in the recovery of pure feeling, that the key to "the right way of living" is to be found in the mystical realm. It will be recalled that Musil had analyzed the realm of lost feeling in all his major fiction from *Young Törless* to *The Man without Qualities*. Like Kierkegaard, Nietzsche, Jung, and Freud, Musil was preoccupied with defining the nature and function of the irrational: how feeling is discovered and in what way it is corrupted; to what extent it is (or should be) related to the faculty of reason as well as to the external world and to what extent it is not; how its "blessings" are experienced and where its dangers lie.

In *The Man without Qualities*, Musil explores in Ulrich's second experiment the feasibility of adopting a more or less exclusively feminine attitude toward life. The ultimate significance of Ulrich's scientific experiment only becomes clear in the light of his experiment in mysticism. So, too, does his obsessive and often intolerant behavior toward others. Because of the particular nature of Musil's dialectical vision, Ulrich first needed to travel away

from all feeling on his journey to the world of lost feeling. And it was because he could not hope to achieve a state of pure feeling until some point in the future that he first felt required to assume a daily existence based upon pure reason. Therefore, Ulrich had first to become an extreme rationalist, antisentimentalist, and anti-idealist in order to protect the purity of his feeling from contamination by adulterated forms of feeling indulged in by various decadent types of people, that is to say, by sentimentalists, idealists, romantics, and other egomaniacs and infantile personalities exemplified by his friends and acquaintances. Ulrich's reason was meant to function like a cutting tool designed to clear away the emotional and intellectual rubble of modern life so that pure feeling would be able to come to the surface on some distant utopian day.

Ulrich's hope of achieving pure feeling is fulfilled and Musil does evoke this highest state of being for the reader in *The Man without Qualities*. In Ulrich's love for his sister, he achieves a sense of wholeness, harmony, and unity. Thus, Musil implies that it is only through nonpossessiveness, i.e., love drained of its dionysian impulses, that man is able to overcome the nihilistic despair generated by his analytic reason. Love alone imbues all life with meaning and significance. However, Musil also presents the various problems that arise from living in such a state. If escape from nihilism into a state of love brings salvation, he shows that living permanently in a state of "contemplatio" is also a sheer impossibility. For no form of life can long survive which attempts to exist completely outside of all social structures.

Musil's various experiments in extreme possibilities, designed ultimately to achieve a synthesis, may seem to some readers to have resulted in a series of excellently described failures. Thus, Musil's readers may well experience a sense of never arriving. But surely the heroic and complex literary spectacle of Musil's ever-continuing, albeit ever-failing quest for the balanced life carries its own justification. Musil's achievement as a whole cannot be negated merely because his work ends with a negative conclusion, or because he was unable to provide a viable answer, an ultimate synthesis, to the problem of living in a meaningless world. In fact, the opposite will be argued here.

If the concept of synthesis yet to be achieved functions as a positive feature in the work of Kierkegaard, Nietzsche, and Jung, why should the unattained synthesis in Musil's work be used to underscore Musil's failure? To say that Musil is writing fiction while the others are not is to skirt the real issue. In order to pursue this question with regard to Musil's work, however, it is first necessary to make a distinction between the concept of synthesis as it is employed in Hegel's philosophy and the same concept as embodied in the work of Kierkegaard, Nietzsche, and Jung. Hegel's logic posits a dialectic in which two conflicting opposites, thesis and antithesis, are eventually resolved in the form of a higher synthesis. But such reconciliation of opposites is achievable only in the pure thought of Hegel's mind where the two conflicting alternatives can be embraced by a more inclusive abstract idea, the synthesis. The history of the world, as regarded by Hegel, is a record of numberless achieved syntheses. In the thought of Kierkegaard, Nietzsche, and Jung, however, the concept of synthesis is removed from that of the World-Spirit realizing itself in history and is appropriated into the context of the personal inner life. Synthesis then becomes transformed into a goal to be realized at some future stage of the individual's psychological and religious development.

Modern man's quest to overcome through a process of synthesis the fragmentation inherent in his inner life lies at the center of Kierkegaard's, Nietzsche's, and Jung's utopian vision. In Kierkegaard's thought, Christ presents the single example in history of the perfect synthesis, of the man-god, whose perfection the Christian must attempt to imitate in his daily life. The synthesis to be effected in the individual's own life is predicated upon a dialectical leap from the ethical and rational mode of life into that of the religious; in such a leap, however, the individual does not leave the world behind but receives it all back again at a higher mode of being. As Christ became man, man attempts to become like Christ. Nietzsche, operating within the dialectic of the apollonian and dionysian modes of being, posited the Superman as the synthesis yet to be achieved. Apparently Nietzsche was no longer able to tolerate the tensions of his own unresolved dialectic and thus eventually posited this single poetic symbol of fulfillment to be realized at

some point in a future stage of the human race's psychic development. Looking beyond the failure of even the most superior man of
the present day, Nietzsche asks the reader to gaze upon the heights
at this generalized synthetic abstraction. Nietzsche's philosophy
thus betrays an almost religious yearning for a form of redemption
existing beyond the particular and the present. As Kierkegaard
regards perfection as having already been achieved in history in
the figure of Christ, Nietzsche seeks a savior from nihilism in a
higher form of man to come. Jung's method, as Jacobi summarizes
it, "is also intrinsically dialectical, because it is a process which, by
confronting the contents of consciousness with those of the unconscious, the ego with the nonego, provokes an interaction aimed at,
and culminating in, a third term, a synthesis which combines and
transcends them both."[6] The archetypal image of synthesis is expressed by the so-called "uniting symbol" in Jung's theory. In fact,
all the symbols and archetypal figures in Jung's psychology are
"uniting symbols" and thus vehicles of what he terms "the transcendent function," that process by which all opposites existing
within the psychic system are unified in a synthesis transcending
all of them.

As Nietzsche in effect replaced Kierkegaard's image of Christ
with that of the Superman, so Jung in turn employed his own
eclectic symbols for synthesis drawn from the religions, myths, and
fairy tales of all cultures. In his long essay *Answer to Job*, Jung uses
as metaphor for the individuation process the same symbol that
Kierkegaard used in order to make certain absolute metaphysical
statements, specifically, about the nature of Christ. Thus Jung argues that the symbol of Christ cannot be dismissed merely as a
theological concept in religious dogma; rather, it possesses a profound psychological reality in the individual Christian life which is
striving toward psychic synthesis. Jung argues in *Answer to Job*
that Jahweh's desire to become man in Christ is a metaphoric
representation of the desire of the unconscious to enter into consciousness and there to effect an equilibrium or synthesis between
consciousness and unconsciousness. The resulting synthesis can be
symbolized psychologically by the archetype of psychic wholeness,
the Self. Man's achievement of the archetype of the Self or his

imitation of the life of the man-God, Christ, results in the complete unification of his fragmented inner life.

The above analysis reveals two ways in which the concept of synthesis may function at the center of a system of thought—and neither is Musil's way. Hegel's method of abstraction was never a possibility seriously entertained by Musil. Although some of the presuppositions underlying Ulrich's experiment in reason reveal certain affinities with Hegel's Logic, reason itself was regarded by Musil as providing only one aspect of the ultimate synthesis. The second possibility involves the expression of a synthesis by means of a poetic symbol taken from an old religion (Kierkegaard's Christ), a rhapsodic philosophy (Nietzsche's Superman) or a new psychology (Jung's Self). If Hegel took flight into abstract thought, Kierkegaard, Nietzsche, and Jung might be accused of having escaped into aestheticism. Musil may well have shared Kierkegaard's and Jung's high evaluation of the mystical impulse but at the same time he completely rejected the Christian Church and the collective unconscious as symbols for the synthesis of the mystical and rational aspects of life. He also understood Nietzsche's noble vision of the potentials latent in man's nature which might gain expression through the Superman in some future age; but he found Nietzsche's concept of the Superman to be absolutely alien to his own temperament.

If final evaluation rests mainly upon the question of whether or not the ultimate synthesis was achieved, then Kierkegaard, Nietzsche, and Jung failed no less than did Musil. Yet their failure is not regarded as a resounding negation that undermines the significance and value of their quest for human wholeness. When the reasons for the final inability of these writers to unify all aspects of the self are examined, it becomes clear that Musil's quest too had to fail and for similar reasons. Moreover, his failure will then be seen as a proof of his unflagging honesty. For Kierkegaard, the wholeness of the individual exists in a timeless realm within the hearts of men and can be achieved by anyone who is able to take the leap of faith. Yet Kierkegaard's great works largely owe their very existence to his own inability to make such a leap. Kierkegaard struggled throughout his life for that unification of the inner

self which he felt could be achieved only through the religious mode of being. But even had he been able to make the leap, struggle would not have ceased. Kierkegaard believed that the religious man must continue to wrestle with the claims of everyday life and reason, on the one hand, and those of faith, on the other. The very acceptance of this continuing struggle constitutes the test of a man's faith. Nietzsche's asserted synthesis, the Superman, has remained for Western culture no more than a poetic symbol for a life in which all conflicting drives have been synthesized into a higher creative potential. Contemporary man can at most struggle to achieve this ideal, although without any hope of ever being able to realize it in his own life. Nietzsche regarded even himself merely as a path marker, as a lone voice pointing out the direction man should take as he journeys toward the Superman. It should be noted, too, that Nietzsche's definition of the Superman specifically affirms that struggle must continue even in this highest possible form of human life. The test of the Superman is whether or not he can endure the most diverse conflicts at the highest pitch of intensity. Finally, Jung also admitted that his utopian goal of ultimate self-realization, the synthesis of all opposites, would always remain an unattainable ideal, although one for which men should nevertheless continue to strive. Nowhere does Jung ever assert that psychic development, even under the direction of the best of therapists, leads ultimately to a condition in which there is no more suffering and conflict. For Jung, struggle is a natural, necessary, and ever-present attribute of all human existence. Complete self-realization will always remain no more than a utopian hope.

Musil's failure can now be reassessed as a victory of moral reserve. His work, no less than that of Kierkegaard, Nietzsche, and Jung, seems but courageously to reconfirm man's natural condition of struggle and failure. Because Musil believes that man is most fully human not in his successes but, rather, when he is engaged in an endless struggle to overcome his fragmented self, his work specifically deemphasizes any real possibility of finding some permanent ultimate solution which would resolve life's problems.

It may be added parenthetically that Musil in many of his works does identify one area of human existence in which all prob-

lems and conflicts are resolved: the dionysian states in their various forms such as madness, sexuality, and war. But such states represent dissolution rather than solution or synthesis, a pathological retrogression by an individual or a society that lacks the courage and intellectual energy to affirm life as an endless struggle. It is not accidental that none of Musil's male protagonists after the adolescent Törless strive for or fall victim to dionysian mysticism. Only the five women in the two collections *Unions* and *Three Women* live in or yearn for this other world, and then only for brief periods. The male protagonists in *Three Women*, as well as Törless and Ulrich, regard the world of sexuality with varying degrees of incomprehension and suspicion. The very existence of Ulrich's experiment with Agathe is based upon the continued absence of dionysian mysticism in their relationship. The dionysian state could not possibly represent a utopian solution to the problem of "the right way of living," for in such states, the individual becomes sheer activity, sheer living — and nothing else. Therefore, dionysian mysticism represents only a transformation of the self into "total living" and not into "right living." In such states, questions of right and wrong have no meaning. The way out of Western man's present schizophrenia lies not backward in the unselfconscious bliss of the lower animals, but rather painfully forward in a higher form of human existence.

Musil presents a series of often extreme and grotesque possibilities for living rather than a well-balanced synthesis. He consequently makes it easy for the reader to take a condescending attitude toward these various forms of existence which are often so outlandishly one-dimensional and so obviously wrong-headed from the very beginning. But this very one-sidedness is consciously experimental and both presupposes and reveals the heroic dimension of Musil's writing. In this regard, no greater thinker or more courageous human being can be called in Musil's defense than Kierkegaard. In *Concluding Unscientific Postscript*, Kierkegaard asserts that one-sidedness should be considered as representing "a vigorous resolution of the will. . . . Every distinguished individual always has something one-sided about him, and this one-sidedness may be an indirect indication of his real greatness . . . . "[7] In spite

of his praise for such an individual, however, Kierkegaard does feel the need to make one qualification: "so far are we human beings from realizing the ideal, that the second rank, the powerful one-sidedness, is pretty much the highest ever attained; but it must not be forgotten that it is only the second rank."[8]

Musil could find no "middle term" between extremes and thus he came to the same conclusion at the end of his life which he had already reached in *Young Törless*, albeit on a lower spiral. In this failure, Musil's work approaches the pessimistic conclusions of Albert Camus, for whom any synthesis represented a form of intellectual and emotional fraud. Life can never pass beyond struggle. If Musil's utopian hopes are a direct development of ideas in the nineteenth century, the failure of these hopes reflects the pessimism of the twentieth century. Musil's inability to reach the final synthesis does not damage his success as a writer. Rather, the reverse is true: a life in which the struggle for change has been eliminated would no longer be a life that is comprehensible to us. Buber fully understood this fact: "Whoever tries to think a synthesis destroys the sense of the situation . . . . It is to be lived in all its antinomies."[9] And further: "I may not try to escape from the paradox I have to live by relegating the irreconcilable propositions to two separate realms; neither may I seek the aid of some theological artifice to attain some conceptual reconciliation."[10] In this sentiment, Buber reflects a central tenet of existential thought: there is no solution to the disharmonies of life. The very use of the word "solution" in the context of man's existential situation is wrong; the word "solution," which belongs in the vocabulary of science and engineering, erroneously seems to suggest the possibility of some kind of blueprint that would in a systematic fashion deliver man from the suffering and confusions of life. But man's most profound and personal problems do not in the least resemble problems in mathematics and engineering.

The key to an understanding of Musil's fiction remains the concept of the unachieved utopian vision. This is not because of the specifics of the ideal that it projects into the future, which is extremely vague as is the case in most utopian visions, but rather because of its implications for Musil's view of life in the present.

Life is apprehended as being in some fundamental way inadequate. The only meaning and purpose in man's life is to be found in the task which he assumes in order to close the perceived lacuna in his existence. From Musil's perspective, this task may involve a search through the past of one's inner life for some "lost" traumatic event in order to effect a unification of the inner self, or it may consist of striving forward toward some ultimate synthesis between reason and mysticism in the future. In practice, man's life becomes defined by the manner in which he struggles to overcome the defects in his existence. Thus if Musil had presented some ultimate synthesis, it could have represented no more than an artificial and unconvincing solution tacked on to the end of his life's work out of a sense of exhaustion and desperation. In spite of the fact that the purity of his utopian vision served finally not to bring him any closer to the perfect synthesis but only to exacerbate the intensity of the struggle in the present, he remained a dedicated and uncompromising utopian writer. His integrity never faltered.

The Final Vision

Life is struggle. Perfection cannot be achieved. Too much reason incapacitates human activity. The dionysian escape from human conflict represents a retrogressive solution. Mysticism is alien to the structures of social behavior. What a series of resounding clichés seem finally to evolve out of Musil's work! Yet the rediscovery of certain banalities may represent for the writer a triumph over profound despair and confusion. There is, in fact, a tendency in many German novels for the protagonist to have to fight through the most obscure and esoteric problems in order to discover what everyone else knew from the very beginning. In this regard, the German protagonist typically lacks common sense and so must experiment with all those possibilities long before rejected by more sensible people as being quite impractical and silly. Thus the protagonist wins back the ordinary, a situation which, surely, must be quite different from that of having accepted and begun with the ordinary in the first place. Perhaps the most striking ex-

ample of such an occurrence in the German novel is to be found in the case of Musil's own Törless who, after having pursued the answers to his personal problems through higher mathematics, Kant's critique of reason, and nonsensical mystical discussions, comes to the anticlimactic conclusion that everything is quite simple, things merely happen, one after another.

If we may be willing to perceive Musil's success precisely in his failure, Musil himself was not. Such a comforting interpretation of his labors would probably have seemed to him to be too bourgeois, too readily prepared to pick up all the pieces in the end and to declare his effort noble, courageous, and (certainly in aesthetic terms) brilliantly achieved and executed. But Musil was an absolutist and he wanted nothing less than to offer modern man a new morality that would lead him out of the morass of nihilism. In his last years of life in Geneva, he seemed to be slowly becoming aware that perhaps he had aimed too high and that the answers for which he had been seeking his whole life would remain forever beyond him. With the knowledge that the end of life was approaching—indeed, death came much sooner than he had ever expected—painful questions must have arisen in his mind. Was he now, in fact, any nearer to the solution of life's great problems than he had been half a century before? Had his work consisted of nothing more than the demonstration of various impossibilities? Could all his sacrifices and sufferings have been made on behalf of a great adventure of the spirit that had gone hopelessly astray? In one of the last notations made by Kierkegaard before his death, he reaffirmed in his own eyes—in the very eyes of God Himself—the justification for his sufferings. Alluding to the loneliness of his youth and the unhappiness of his young manhood, Kierkegaard stated his certain belief that God had called upon him to suffer for the faith and to be reborn in the love of Christ.[11] Thus he embraced anew every moment of pain experienced throughout his life as a blessing. Nietzsche was saved from a final evaluation of his life's work by the twilight of madness. Nevertheless, although he may often have felt that no one was listening to him, he did believe throughout his philosophical career that he had discovered the way beyond present despair to a rebirth of higher man. He knew him-

self to be a prophet and never doubted the significance of his task. But Musil felt no divine sanction, had no audience, and knew that he had not yet found the way. His last years were years of great depression. At the same time, however, he seemed to mellow, to take an interest in nature for the first time in his life, and to gain a new humility. He began to wonder whether quite simple and active men, such as his friends Robert Lejeune and Fritz Wortruba, might not possess unconsciously in their daily lives that which he had consciously been seeking in vain through the medium of his work.

Musil will remain for us, however, like his great protagonist Ulrich, a hero of cognition, an intrepid explorer who, in the furthest reaches of the intellectual and emotional realm, dared to take a lonely road that led "between religion and knowledge, between example and doctrine, between *amor intellectualis* and poetry." His life and work suggest that man cannot of himself and in solitude give rebirth to himself. But if Musil failed in his own terms, men may nevertheless recognize in him a more courageous brother who went on ahead, chartered an inhospitable landscape, and served to warn less adventurous spirits away.

Notes

I. The Writer in Search of Utopia

1. Robert Musil, *Tagebücher, Aphorismen, Essays und Reden*, ed. Adolf Frisé (Hamburg: Rowohlt Verlag, 1955), p. 313.
2. Ibid., p. 361.
3. Robert Musil, *Prosa, Dramen, Späte Briefe*, ed. Adolf Frisé (Hamburg: Rowohlt Verlag, 1957), p.788.
4. Ibid., p. 787.
5. Musil, *Tagebücher*, p.300.
6. Ibid., pp. 527-28.
7. Musil, *Prosa*, p. 738.
8. Musil, *Tagebücher*, p. 569.
9. Ibid., p. 386.
10. Robert Musil, *The Man without Qualities*, trans. Ernst Kaiser and Eithne Wilkins, Vol. I (London: Secker and Warburg, 1961), p. 302.
11. Ibid., p. 301.
12. Musil, *Tagebücher*, p. 92.
13. Quoted by Eithne Wilkins, *"Der Mann ohne Eigenschaften* and Musil's 'Steinbaukastenzeit,' " *Oxford German Studies*, 3 (1968), p. 196.
14. Musil, *Prosa*, p. 810.
15. Musil, *The Man without Qualities*, I, p. 301.
16. Ulrich Karthaus, "Musil-Forschung und Musil-Deutung," *Deutsche Vierteljahrsschrift*, 39 (1965), p. 459.
17. Musil, *Prosa*, p. 696.
18. Musil, *Tagebücher*, p. 475.
19. Harry Goldgar, "The Square Root of Minus One: Freud and Robert Musil's Törless," *Comparative Literature*, 17 (1965), pp. 117-32.
20. Annie Reniers, "Törless: Freudsche Verwirrungen," *Robert Musil: Studien zu seinem Werk*, ed. K. Dinklage (Hamburg: Rowohlt Verlag, 1970), pp. 26-39.
21. Musil, *Tagebücher*, p. 398.
22. Ibid., p. 494.
23. Lida Kirchberger, "Musil's Trilogy. An Approach to *Drei Frauen," Monatshefte*, 55 (1963), pp. 167-82. Karthaus, "Musil-Forschung," p. 459; Elizabeth J. Boa, "Austrian Ironies in Musil's *Drei Frauen," The Modern Language Review*, 63 (1968), p. 120.
24. C.G. Jung, "Psychology and Literature" in *The Spirit in Man, Art, and Literature*, Vol. XV, *The Collected Works of C.G. Jung*, trans. R.F.C. Hull (New York: Bollingen, 1953-), p. 86.
25. Ibid., p. 88.
26. Ibid.
27. Ibid., p. 91.
28. Ibid., p. 90.

II. Trapdoor into Chaos: *Young Törless*

1. The terms "character," "personality," and "ego" used by Musil in his fiction and nonfiction are regarded as interchangeable terms in this study except where specifically indicated.

2. Robert Musil, *Young Törless*, trans. Ernst Kaiser and Eithne Wilkins (New York: Signet Classics, 1964), p. 15. Further page references to quotations from this work will be cited directly in the text.

3. Musil, *Tagebücher*, p. 284.

4. Except where specifically indicated, the terms Other Realm, Other World, and Other Dimension will be used interchangeably in this study to designate both types of mystical state, dionysian and contemplative. The term Other Condition ("der andre Zustand") refers only to the one form of mysticism, "contemplatio."

5. Friedrich Nietzsche, *The Joyful Wisdom*, trans. Thomas Common (New York: Ungar, 1964), Aphorism 125, pp. 167-68.

6. Robert Musil, "Ein Mensch ohne Charakter," *Prosa*, pp. 507-13.

7. Robert Musil, *Der Mann ohne Eigenschaften* (Hamburg: Rowohlt Verlag, 1965), p. 1150. The passage has not yet been translated into English: "Man mochte den einen [einen Mann ohne Eigenschaften] auch einen Nihilisten nennen...."

8. Musil, *The Man without Qualities*, I, p. 175.

9. Nietzsche, *The Joyful Wisdom*, Aphorism 354, pp. 296-300.

10. Friedrich Nietzsche, *The Will to Power*, trans. Walter Kaufmann and R.J. Hollingdale (New York: Random House, 1967), Aphorism 477, pp. 263-64.

11. Blaise Pascal, *Pensées*, trans. A.J. Krailsheimer (Harmondsworth, England: Penguin Books, 1975), p. 92.

12. Ibid., p. 95.

13. In Nietzsche's so-called second period, in which he reverses many of the fundamental ideas argued in the first period, he developed the concept of "the free spirit." This is the period of brilliant aphorisms, from *Human, All-Too-Human* to *The Joyful Wisdom*.

III. The Return of the Repressed: "The Perfecting of a Love" and "The Temptation of Quiet Veronica"

1. Musil, *Tagebücher*, p. 809.

2. Ibid.

3. Ibid., p. 811.

4. Ibid., p. 188.

5. For Musil's definition of "contemplatio," see Musil, *Tagebücher*, p. 284.

6. Robert Musil, "The Perfecting of a Love" in *Tonka and Other Stories*, trans. Ernst Kaiser and Eithne Wilkins (London: Secker and Warburg, 1965), p. 14. Further page references to quotations from this work will be cited directly in the text.

7. See J.B. Leishman and Stephen Spender, "The Great Lovers," Appendix I, *Rainer Maria Rilke: Duino Elegies*, trans. with a commentary by Leishman and Spender (London: The Hogarth Press, 1963), pp. 148-50.

8. See Rainer Maria Rilke, *Briefe* 1907-1914 (Leipzig: Insel Verlag, 1933), pp. 175-78.

9. Robert Musil, "The Temptation of Quiet Veronica" in *Tonka and Other Stories*, p. 81. Further page references to quotations from this work will be cited directly in the text.

10. Sigmund Freud, *Moses and Monotheism*, Vol. XXIII, *The Standard Edition of the Complete Psychological Works of Sigmund Freud*, ed. and trans. James Strachey (London: The Hogarth Press, 1953-1964), pp. 94, 95.

11. Otto Fenichel, *The Psychoanalytic Theory of Neurosis* (New York: W.W. Norton, 1972), p. 440. In connection with the majority of cases of schizophrenia, Fenichel wrote that the regression from reality is undertaken not in order to gain instinctual pleasure but to combat instinctual drives: "reality is repudiated less because of its frustrating effects than because it holds temptations....The break with reality in schizophrenics may be not so much a break with the prohibiting and punishing but rather with the tempting aspects of reality."

12. Sigmund Freud, *Civilization and Its Discontents*, Vol. XXI, *The Standard Edition*, p. 64.

13. Ibid.

14. Ibid., p. 65.

15. See Sigmund Freud, *The Future of an Illusion*, Chapter 3, Vol. XXI, *The Standard Edition*, pp. 15-20.

16. Fenichel, *The Psychoanalytic Theory of Neurosis*, p. 439.

IV. Three Mysterious Women:
"Grigia," "The Lady from Portugal," and "Tonka"

1. Robert Musil, "Grigia" in *Tonka and Other Stories*, p. 115. Further page references to quotations from this work will be cited directly in the text.

2. Friedrich Nietzsche, *The Birth of Tragedy*, trans. Walter Kaufmann (New York: Vintage Books, 1967), p. 98.

3. C.G. Jung, "Psychological Commentaries on 'The Tibetan Book of the Great Liberation' and 'The Tibetan Book of the Dead' " in *Psychology and Religion: West and East*, Vol. XI, *The Collected Works*, pp. 475-526.

4. Musil, *Prosa*, p. 706. Here Musil admits that he sometimes feels as if there is nothing he can write that Nietzsche did not already say and in a better fashion: "ich muss annehmen, dass ein tatsächlicher Einfluss im Spiel ist."

5. C.G. Jung, "The Syzygy: Anima and Animus" in *Aion*, Vol. IX, Part II, *The Collected Works*, pp. 11-22.

6. C.G. Jung, *Psychological Types*, Vol. VI, *The Collected Works*, p. 468.

7. Jolande Jacobi, *The Psychology of C. G. Jung* (New Haven: Yale University Press, 1968), p 121.

8. C.G. Jung, *The Archetypes and The Collective Unconscious*, Vol. IX, Part I, *The Collected Works*, p. 30.

9. M.-L. von Franz, "The Process of Individuation," *Man and His Symbols*, ed. Carl G. Jung (Garden City, New York: Doubleday, 1971), p. 178.

10. Ibid., p. 195,

11. Jacobi, *The Psychology of C.G. Jung*, p. 105.

12. Musil, "The Lady from Portugal" in *Tonka and Other Stories*, p. 146. Further page references to quotations from this work will be cited directly in the text.

13. von Franz, "The Process of Individuation," p. 185.

14. C.G. Jung, "Aims of Psychotherapy" in *The Practice of Psychotherapy*, Vol. XVI, *The Collected Works*, p. 41.

15. Jacobi, *The Psychology of C.G. Jung*, p. 108.

16. von Franz, "The Process of Individuation," p. 166.

17. Ibid., pp. 166-67.

18. "The little cat from the world beyond" was one of Musil's early "working titles" for this short story.

19. Novalis, *Novalis Schriften*, ed. Paul Kluckhohn, Vol. III (Leipzig: Bibliographisches Institut, n.d.), p. 232 (translation mine).

20. Ibid., p. 339.

21. Franz Grillparzer, "Der Genesene," *Sämtliche Werke*, ed. Peter Frank and Karl Pörnbacher, Vol. I (München: Carl Hanser Verlag, 1960), p. 123 (translation mine).

22. Heinrich Heine, *Heines sämtliche Werke*, ed. Ernst Elster, Vol. III (Leipzig: Bibliographisches Institut, n.d.), p. 404 (translation mine).

23. See Friedrich Nietzsche, *The Case of Wagner*, Section 5, trans. Walter Kaufmann (New York: Vintage Books, 1967); Friedrich Nietzsche, *Ecce Homo*, "Why I am so Clever," Section 2, trans. Walter Kaufmann (New York: Vintage Books, 1967).

24. Sigmund Freud, *Outline of Psychoanalysis*, Vol. XXIII, *The Standard Edition*, p. 185.

25. Sigmund Freud, *Moses and Monotheism*, p. 75.

26. Heine, Vol. III, p. 235 (translation mine).

27. Frieda Fordham, *An Introduction to Jung's Psychology* (Harmondsworth, England: Penguin Books, 1961), p. 70.

28. Jung, *Psychology and Religion: West and East*, p. 46.

29. Ibid., p. 82.

30. Musil, *Prosa*, p. 707.

31. Fordham, p. 59.

32. Musil, "Tonka" in *Tonka and Other Stories*, p. 189. Further page references to quotations from this work will be cited directly in the text.

33. C.G. Jung, "Commentary on 'The Secret of the Golden Flower' " in *Alchemical Studies*, Vol. XIII, *The Collected Works*, p. 15.

34. Walter H. Sokel, "Kleist's Marquise von O., Kierkegaard's Abraham, and Musil's Tonka: Three Stages of the Absurd as the Touchstone of Faith," *Wisconsin Studies in Contemporary Literature*, 8 (1967), pp. 505-16.

35. Soren Kierkegaard, *Fear and Trembling*, trans. Walter Lowrie (Princeton: Princeton University Press, 1974), p. 31.

36. Louis Mackey, "The View from Pisgah: A Reading of *Fear and Trembling*" in *Kierkegaard: A Collection of Critical Essays*, ed. Josiah Thompson (Garden City, New York: Doubleday, Anchor, 1972), p. 421.

37. Kierkegaard, *Fear and Trembling*, p. 43.

38. Ibid., p. 44.

39. Albert Camus, *The Myth of Sisyphus and Other Essays*, trans. Justin O'Brien (New York: Alfred Knopf, 1955), p. 28.

40. Ibid., p. 22.

41. Ibid., pp. 41-42.

42. Ibid., p. 40.

43. Kierkegaard, *Fear and Trembling*, p. 48.

44. Ibid., p. 49.

45. Camus, *The Myth of Sisyphus*, p. 28.

46. Martin Buber, *I and Thou*, trans. Walter Kaufmann (New York: Charles Scribner's, 1970), p. 66.

47. Ibid., p. 88.

48. Ibid., p. 85.

49. See Frederick G. Peters, "Kafka and Kleist: A Literary Relationship," *Oxford German Studies*, I (London: Oxford University Press, 1966), pp. 114-62.

50. Musil, *Tagebücher*, pp. 73-74.

51. Patrick Mullahy, *Oedipus: Myth and Complex* (New York: Grove Press, 1955), pp. 26-27.

52 Fenichel, *The Psychoanalytic Theory of Neurosis*, pp. 486-87.

53. Ibid., p. 96.

54. Ibid., p. 92.

55. Ibid., p. 477.

56. Walter Lowrie, *Kierkegaard*, Part III, Chapter 1, "Regina" (New York: Harper, 1962), pp. 191-231.

57. Franz Kafka, *The Diaries of Franz Kafka: 1910-1923*, ed. Max Brod, trans. Joseph Kresh (Harmondsworth, England: Penguin Books, 1949), p. 230.

58. Franz Kafka, "The Eight Octavo Notebooks," *Dearest Father*, trans. Ernst Kaiser and Eithne Wilkins (New York: Schocken Books, 1954), p. 98.

59. Franz Kafka, *Letter to His Father*, trans. Ernst Kaiser and Eithne Wilkins (New York: Schocken Books, 1966), p. 121.

60. Ibid., p. 113.

61. Ibid., p. 97.

62. Ibid., p. 117.

63. Karl Jaspers, *Nietzsche: An Introduction to the Understanding of His Philosophical Activity*, trans. Charles F. Wallroff and Frederick J. Schmitz (Tucson: The University of Arizona Press, 1965), p. 84.

64. Friedrich Nietzsche, *Human, All-Too-Human*, ed. Oscar Levy, trans. Helen Zimmern (Edinburgh and London: T.N. Foulis, 1909), Part I, Aphorism 426, p. 311.

65. Ibid., Aphorism 435, p. 315.

66. Ibid., Aphorism 434, p. 315.

67. Friedrich Nietzsche, *On the Genealogy of Morals*, trans. Walter Kaufmann and R.J. Hollingdale (New York: Vintage Books, 1967), Third Essay, Section 7, 8, pp. 106-12.

68. Friedrich Nietzsche, *Die Unschuld des Werdens* I (Stuttgart: Alfred Kröner Verlag, 1965), Aphorism 917, p. 301.

69. Friedrich Nietzsche, *Beyond Good and Evil*, trans. Walter Kaufmann (New York: Vintage Books, 1966), "Our Virtues," Aphorism 232, p. 163.

70. Buber, *I and Thou*, p. 66.

V. The Rise and Fall of a Rational Man:
The Man without Qualities (I)

1. Robert Musil, *The Man without Qualities*, trans. Ernst Kaiser and Eithne Wilkins, Vol. II (London: Secker and Warburg, 1961), pp. 435-36. (Vol. I, 1961; Vol. III, 1960). Further page references to quotations from this three-volume translation will be cited directly in the text, preceded by the volume number I, II, or III. The English translation stops with Chapter 38 in Volume III. Page references beyond this chapter are taken from the German edition: *Der Mann ohne Eigenschaften*, ed. Adolf Frisé (Hamburg: Rowohlt Verlag, 1965). They will be cited directly in the text and prefaced by the letter N (*Nachlass*). The translations are mine.

2. See "Letter to G," *Prosa*, pp. 724-27; "Gedanken zu einem 'Vorwort,' " *Der Mann ohne Eigenschaften*, pp. 1597-98; "Aus einem Notizbuch (1932)," *Der Mann ohne Eigenschaften*, p. 1598.

3. Musil, *Tagebücher*, p. 237.

4. Musil, *Tagebücher*, p. 207. Musil read Dostoyevsky's work avidly in his youth (see *Tagebücher*, p. 805) as well as in his later life (see *Tagebücher*, p. 861). In 1942, he wrote: "When I am unable to work, I now often read Dostoyevsky" (*Prosa*, p. 826).

5. Fyodor Dostoyevsky, *Notes from Underground*, trans. Andrew R. MacAndrew (New York: New American Library, 1961), p. 92.

6. Ibid., p. 98.

7. Ibid., p. 92.

8. Ibid., p. 103.

9. Ibid., p. 115.

10. Ibid., p. 111.

11. Ibid., p. 117.

12. Ibid., p. 118.

13. Ibid., p. 112.

14. Soren Kierkegaard, *Either/Or: A Fragment of Life*, trans. David Swenson and Lillian Swenson (Princeton: Princeton University Press, 1949), Vol. I, "Margaret," pp. 168-76; and Soren Kierkegaard, *Soren Kierkegaard's Journals and Papers*, trans. Howard Hong and Edna Hong (Bloomington: Indiana University Press, 1970), Vol. II, "Faust," pp. 34-37.

15. Quoted by Kaiser and Wilkins, *Robert Musil: Eine Einführung in das Werk* (Stuttgart: Kohlhammer Verlag, 1962), p. 40, taken from one of Musil's unpublished notebooks (Number 22) entitled "Der Spion."

16. Nietzsche, *On the Genealogy of Morals*, p. 162.

17. Ibid., p. 147.

18. Friedrich Nietzsche, *The Antichrist* in *The Portable Nietzsche*, trans. Walter Kaufmann (New York: The Viking Press, 1954), p. 645.

19. Nietzsche, *On the Genealogy of Morals*, p. 157.

20. Nietzsche, *The Joyful Wisdom*, p. 47.

21. Ibid., p. 299.

22. Friedrich Nietzsche, *The Wanderer and His Shadow* in *Human, All-Too-Human*, Part II, trans. Paul V. Cohn, ed. Oscar Levy (London: George Allen and Unwin, 1911), p. 316.

23. Plato, *Phaedo* in *The Last Days of Socrates*, trans. Hugh Tredenick (Harmondsworth, England: Penguin Books, 1969), p. 132.

24. Ibid., p. 136.

25. Ibid., p. 137.

26. A.E. Taylor, *Plato: The Man and His Work* (New York: Meridian Press, 1956), p. 181.

27. Edward Zeller, *Outlines of the History of Greek Philosophy*, trans. L.R. Palmer (New York: Meridian Press, 1955), p. 116.

VI. A World of Lost Feeling:
The Man without Qualities (II)

1. Eithne Wilkins, "Musil's 'Affair of the Major's Wife': with an Unpublished Text," *The Modern Language Review*, 63 (1968), p. 77.

2. Musil, *Tagebücher*, p. 638.
3. Wilkins, "Musil's 'Affair of the Major's Wife,' " p. 86.
4. Musil, *Prosa*, p. 704.
5. Musil, *Tagebücher*, p. 683.

VIII. The Open Horizon

1. Jacobi, *The Psychology of C.G. Jung*, p. 63.
2. An excellent example of the idea of salvation through depersonalization can be seen in Hermann Hesse's novel *Steppenwolf*. The ideal for which Harry Haller is striving is represented by the Immortals who, in their transcendent wisdom, are strongly reminiscent of the Jungian archetypes. (Hesse underwent a brief period of psychotherapy with a Jungian analyst.)
3. Jacobi, *The Psychology of C.G. Jung*, p. 63.
4. In his powerful intellect, cutting irony, and cool wit, Adrian Leverkühn in Mann's *Dr. Faustus* is a protagonist who seems more closely related to Ulrich than is Hans Castorp.
5. For a detailed argument on this point see Pascal's study of the *Bildungsroman*. Roy Pascal, *The German Novel* (Manchester: Manchester University Press, 1956).
6. Jacobi, *The Psychology of C. G. Jung*, p. 67.
7. Soren Kierkegaard, *Concluding Unscientific Postscript*, trans. Daniel F. Swenson and Walter Lowrie (Princeton: Princeton University Press, 1941), p. 312.
8. Ibid.
9. Buber, *I and Thou*, p. 143.
10. Ibid., p. 144.
11. See Kierkegaard's article "My Task" quoted in *Kierkegaard*, Walter Lowrie (New York: Harper and Row, 1962), Vol. I, pp. 230-31.

Selected Bibliography

Editions

Gesammelte Werke in Einzelausgaben. Ed. Adolf Frisé. 3 Vols. Hamburg: Rowohlt Verlag. *Der Mann ohne Eigenschaften,* 1965; *Tagebücher, Aphorismen, Essays und Reden,* 1955; *Prosa, Dramen, Späte Briefe,* 1957.
Sämtliche Erzählungen. Ed. Adolf Frisé. Hamburg: Rowohlt Verlag, 1968.
Robert Musil, Three Short Stories. Ed. Hugh Sacker. London: Oxford University Press, 1970.

English Translations

(All are translated by Ernst Kaiser and Eithne Wilkins)
The Man without Qualities. 3 Vols. London: Secker and Warburg, 1953-1960. Also, New York: Putnam Capricorn Paperback, 1965.
Young Törless. London: Secker and Warburg, 1955. Also, New York: New American Library, Signet Classic, 1964.
Tonka and Other Stories. London: Secker and Warburg, 1965. Also, *Five Women.* New York: Delacorte Press, Delta Paperback, 1966.

Bibliographies

Dinklage, Karl. *Robert Musil Exhibition-Catalogue.* Klagenfurt, 1963.
Karthaus, Ulrich. "Musil-Forschung und Musil-Deutung (Ein Literaturbericht)." *Deutsche Vierteljahrsschrift,* 39 (1965), 441-83.
Thöming, Jürgen. *Robert-Musil-Bibliographie.* Bad Homburg: Verlag Dr. Max Gehlen, 1968.
——"Kommentierte Auswahlbibliographie zu Robert Musil." *Text und Kritik,* 21/22 (1968), 61-67.

Secondary Literature (German)

Albertsen, Elizabeth. *Ratio und "Mystik" im Werk Robert Musils.* München: Nymphenburger Verlag, 1968.
Allemann, Beda. *Ironie und Dichtung.* 2nd edition. Pfullingen: Neske, 1969.
Arnold, Heinz-Ludwig, ed. *Robert Musil. Text und Kritik,* 21/22 (1968). (A Collection of essays.)
Arntzen, Helmut. *Satirischer Stil bei Robert Musil.* Bonn: Bouvier, 1960.
Bauer, Sibylle. *Ethik und Bewusstheit* in *Studien zu Robert Musil.* Köln: Böhlau, 1966.
Baumann, Gerhart. *Robert Musil: Zur Erkenntnis der Dichtung.* Berne: Franke, 1965.

Bausinger, Wilhelm. *Studien zu einer historischen-kritischen Ausgabe von Robert Musils Roman "Der Mann ohne Eigenschaften."* Hamburg: Rowohlt, 1964.

Berghahn, Wilfried. *Robert Musil in Selbstzeugnissen und Bilddokumenten.* Hamburg: Rowohlt Monographien 81, 1963.

Braun, Wilhelm. "Musil's 'Erdensekretariat der Genauigkeit und der Seele.' " *Monatshefte,* 46 (1954), 305-16.

Brinkmann, Richard, et al. *Deutsche Vierteljahrsschrift, 39 (1965). (A collection of essays devoted to Musil.)*

Burckhardt, Judith. *Der Mann ohne Eigenschaften von Musil*; oder, *Das Wagnis der Selbstverwirklichung.* Berne: Franke, 1973.

Dinklage, Karl, ed. *Robert Musil: Leben, Werk, Wirkung.* Hamburg: Rowohlt, 1960. (A collection of articles on Musil.)

Dinklage, Karl; Elizabeth Albertsen; and Karl Corino, eds. *Robert Musil: Studien zu seinem Werk.* Hamburg: Rowohlt, 1970.

Drevermann, Ingrid. *Wirklichkeit und Mystik* in *Studien zu Robert Musil.* Köln: Böhlau, 1966.

Grenzmann, Wilhelm. *"Der Mann ohne Eigenschaften*: Zur Problematik der Romangestalt" in *Robert Musil: Leben, Werk, Wirkung,* ed. Karl Dinklage. Hamburg: Rowohlt, 1960.

Heydebrand, Renate von. *Die Reflexionen Ulrichs in Robert Musils Roman "Der Mann ohne Eigenschaften."* Münster: Aschendorff, 1966.

Hochstätter, Dietrich. *Sprache des Möglichen: stilistischer Perspektivismus in Robert Musils "Mann ohne Eigenschaften."* Frankfurt: Athenäum, 1972.

Hoffmeister, Werner. *Studien zur Erlebten Rede bei Thomas Mann und Robert Musil.* The Hague: Mouton, 1965.

Hüppauf, Bernd. *Von sozialer Utopie zur Mystik.* München: Fink, 1971.

Jens, Walter. *Statt einer Literaturgeschichte.* 5th edition. Pfullingen: Neske, 1962.

Kaiser, E., and Wilkins, E. *Robert Musil: Eine Einführung in das Werk.* Stuttgart: Kohlhammer, 1962.

Kalow, Gert. "Robert Musil" in *Deutsche Literatur im zwanzigsten Jahrhundert,* ed. Hermann Friedmann und Otto Mann. Heidelberg: Rothe, 1954.

Kühn, Dieter. *Analogie und Variation: Zur Analyse von Robert Musils Roman "Der Mann ohne Eigenschaften."* Bonn: Bouvier, 1965.

Kühne, Jörg. *Das Gleichnis: Studien zur inneren Form von Robert Musils Roman "Der Mann ohne Eigenschaften."* Tübingen: Niemeyer, 1968.

Laermann, Klaus. *Eigenschaftslosigkeit.* Stuttgart: Metzler, 1970.

Loebenstein, Johannes. "Das Problem der Erkenntnis in Musils künstlerischem Werk" in *Robert Musil: Leben, Werk, Wirkung,* ed. Karl Dinklage. Hamburg: Rowohlt, 1960.

Rasch, Wolfdietrich. *Über Robert Musils Roman "Der Mann ohne Eigenschaften."* Göttingen: Vandenhoeck and Ruprecht, 1967.

Reinhardt, Stephen. *Studien zur Antinomie von Intellekt und Gefühl* in *Musils Roman "Der Mann ohne Eigenschaften".* Bonn: Bouvier, 1969.

Renniers, Annie. " 'Törless': Freudsche Verwirrungen?" in *Robert Musil: Studien zu seinem Werk,* ed. Karl Dinklage et al. Hamburg: Rowohlt, 1970.

——*Robert Musil*. Bonn: Bouvier, 1972.
Seidler, Ingo. "Das Nietzschebild Robert Musils." *Deutsche Vierteljahrsschrift*, 39 (1965), 329-49.
Sokel, Walter H. "Robert Musils Narrenspiegel." *Neue Deutsche Hefte*, 7 (1960/ 61), 199-214.
Strelka, Joseph. *Kalfka, Musil, Broch.* Vienna: Forum Verlag, 1959.

Secondary Literature (English)

Boa, Elizabeth J. "Austrian Ironies in Musil's *Drei Frauen*." *The Modern Language Review*, 63 (1968), 119-31.
Braun, Wilhelm. "Musil and the Pendulum of the Intellect." *Monatshefte*, 49 (1957), 109-19.
——"Musil's Siamese Twins." *The Germanic Review*, 33 (1958), 41-52.
——"Moosbrugger Dances." *The Germanic Review*, 35 (1960), 214-30.
——"An Interpretation of Musil's Novelle *Tonka*." *Monatshefte*, 53 (1961), 73-85.
——"The Confusions of Törless." *The Germanic Review*, 40 (1965), 116-31.
Cohn, D. "Psyche and Space in Musil's 'Die Vollendung der Liebe.' " *Germanic Review*, 49 (1974), 154-68.
Goldgar, Harry. "The Square Root of Minus One: Freud and Robert Musil's *Törless*." *Comparative Literature*, 17 (1965), 117-32.
Kirchberger, Lida. "Musil's Trilogy. An Approach to *Drei Frauen*." *Monatshefte*, 55 (1963), 167-82.
McCormick, E. Allen, "Ambivalence in Musil's *Drei Frauen*. Notes on Meaning and Interpretation." *Monatshefte*, 54 (1962), 183-96.
Pike, Burton. *Robert Musil: An Introduction to His Work*. Ithaca: Cornell University Press, 1961.
Prawer, S.S. "Robert Musil and the 'Uncanny.' " *Oxford German Studies*, 3 (1968), 161-82.
Reichert, Herbert W. "Nietzschean Influence in Musil's *Der Mann ohne Eigenschaften*." *The German Quarterly*, 39 (1966), 12-28.
Sokel, Walter H. "Kleist's Marquise of O., Kierkegaard's Abraham, and Musil's Tonka: Three Stages of the Absurd as the Touchstone of Faith." *Wisconsin Studies in Contemporary Literature*, 8 (1967), 505-16.
Stern, J.P. "Viennese Kaleidoscope." *The Listener* (1 November 1962).
Stopp, Elisabeth. "Musil's Törless: Content and Form." *The Modern Language Review*, 63 (1968), 94-118.
Wilkins, Eithne. "Musil's 'Affair of the Major's Wife' with an Unpublished Manuscript."*The Modern Language Review*, 63 (1968), 74-93.

Index of Works by Musil

General Index